I0803529

Famine, Sword, and Fire:
The Liberation of Southwest China in World War II

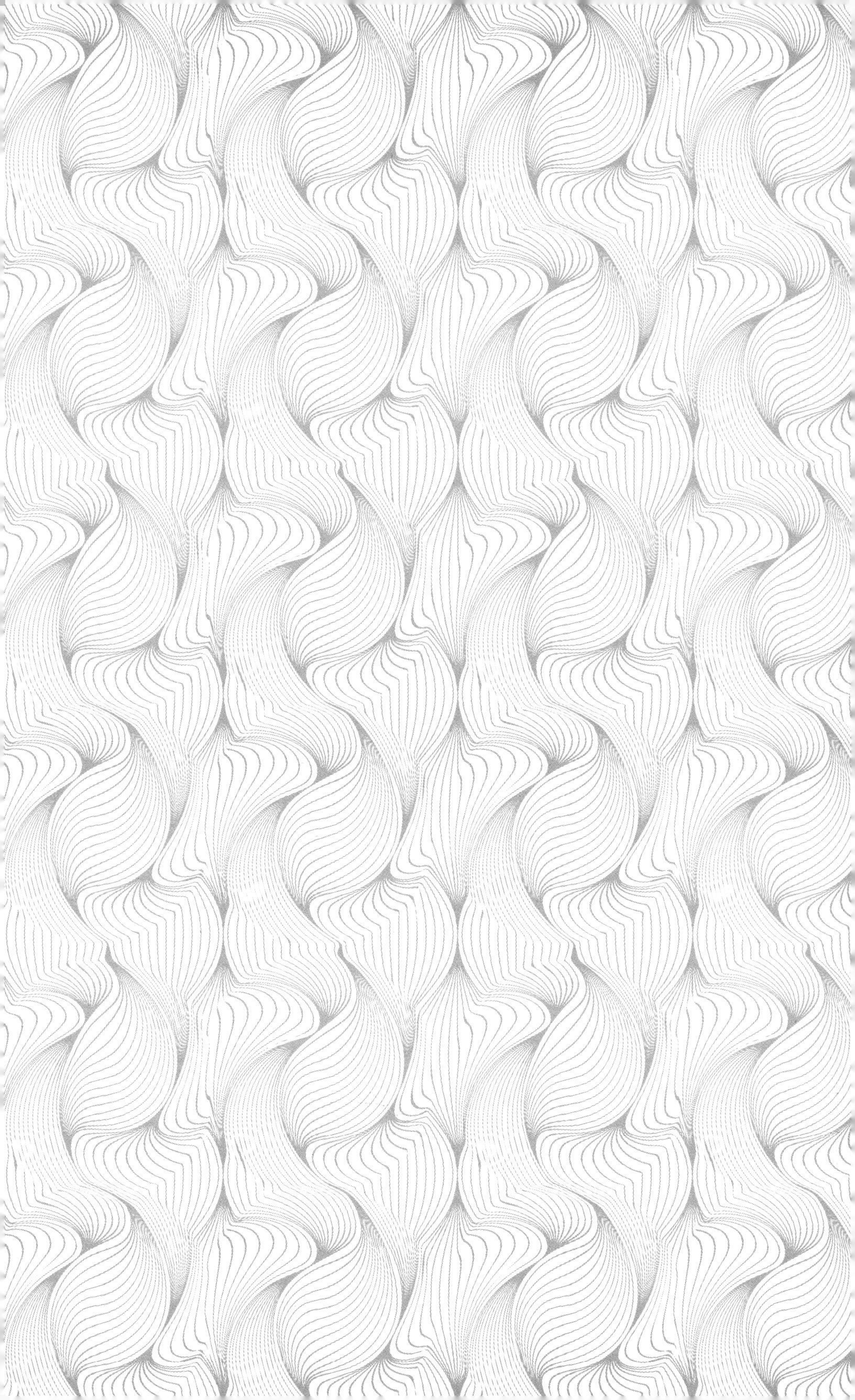

Famine, Sword, and Fire: The Liberation of Southwest China in World War II

Daniel Jackson

Schiffer Publishing Ltd®
4880 Lower Valley Road • Atglen, PA 19310

Other Schiffer Books by the Author:
The Forgotten Squadron, ISBN: 978-0-7643-3537-2

Other Schiffer Books on Related Subjects:
Flying Tiger to Air Commando, ISBN: 978-0-7643-0690-7

Published by Schiffer Publishing, Ltd.
4880 Lower Valley Road
Atglen, PA 19310
Phone: (610) 593-1777; Fax: (610) 593-2002
E-mail: Info@schifferbooks.com

For our complete selection of fine books on this and related subjects, please visit our website at www.schifferbooks.com.
You may also write for a free catalog.

This book may be purchased from the publisher.
Please try your bookstore first.

We are always looking for people to write books on
new and related subjects. If you have an idea for a book, please contact us at proposals@schifferbooks.com.

Schiffer Publishing's titles are available at special discounts for bulk purchases for sales promotions or premiums. Special editions, including personalized covers, corporate imprints, and excerpts can be created in large quantities for special needs. For more information, contact the publisher.

Copyright © 2015 by Daniel Jackson

Library of Congress Control Number: 2015938048

All rights reserved. No part of this work may be reproduced or used in any form or by any means—graphic, electronic, or mechanical, including photocopying or information storage and retrieval systems—without written permission from the publisher.
The scanning, uploading, and distribution of this book or any part thereof via the Internet or via any other means without the permission of the publisher is illegal and punishable by law. Please purchase only authorized editions and do not participate in or encourage the electronic piracy of copyrighted materials.
"Schiffer," "Schiffer Publishing, Ltd. & Design," and the "Design of pen and inkwell" are registered trademarks of Schiffer Publishing, Ltd.

Designed by RoS
Cover design by Molly Shields
Type set in Swiss921 BT/Adobe Caslon Pro

ISBN: 978-0-7643-4838-9
Printed in China

Contents

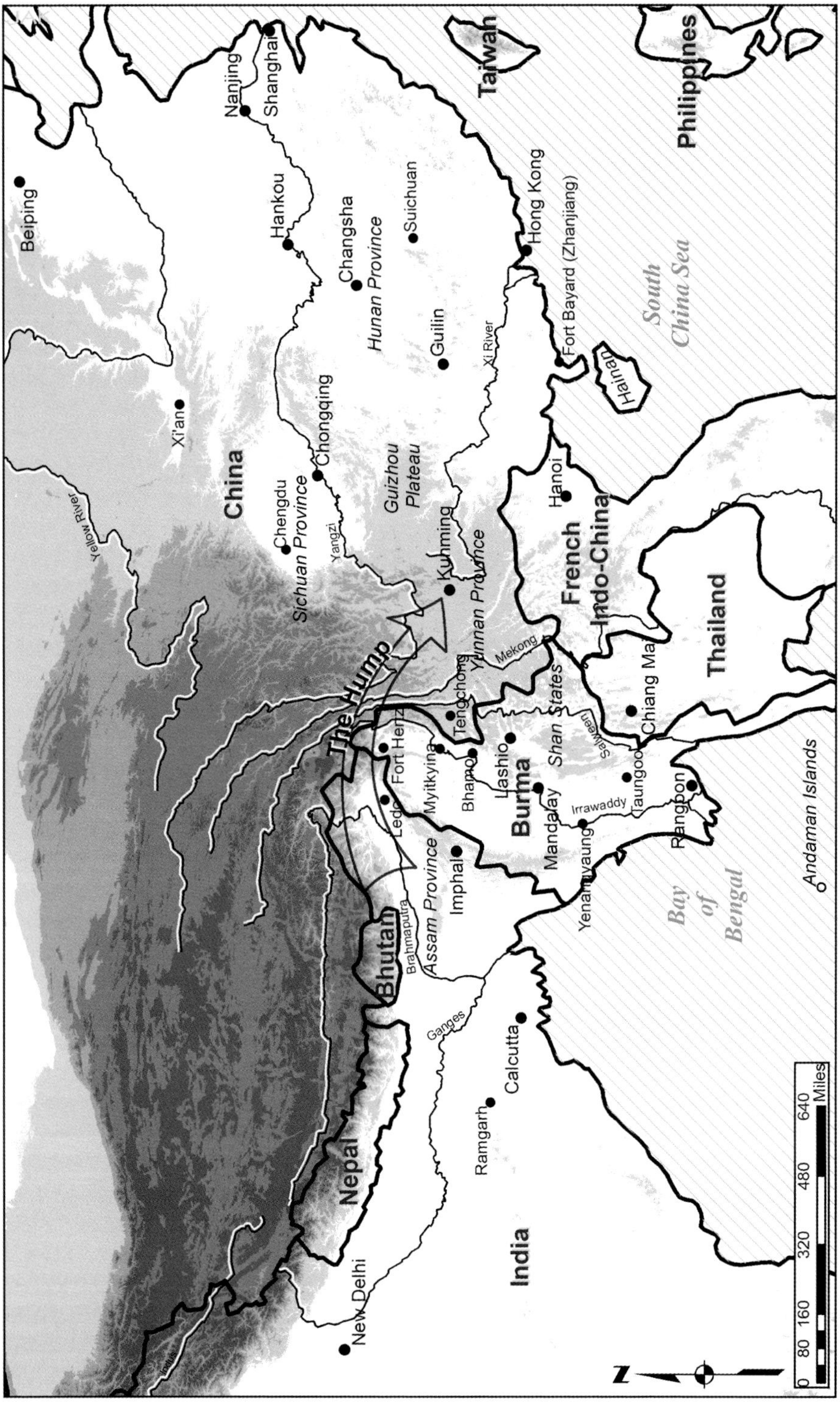

The China-Burma-India Theater

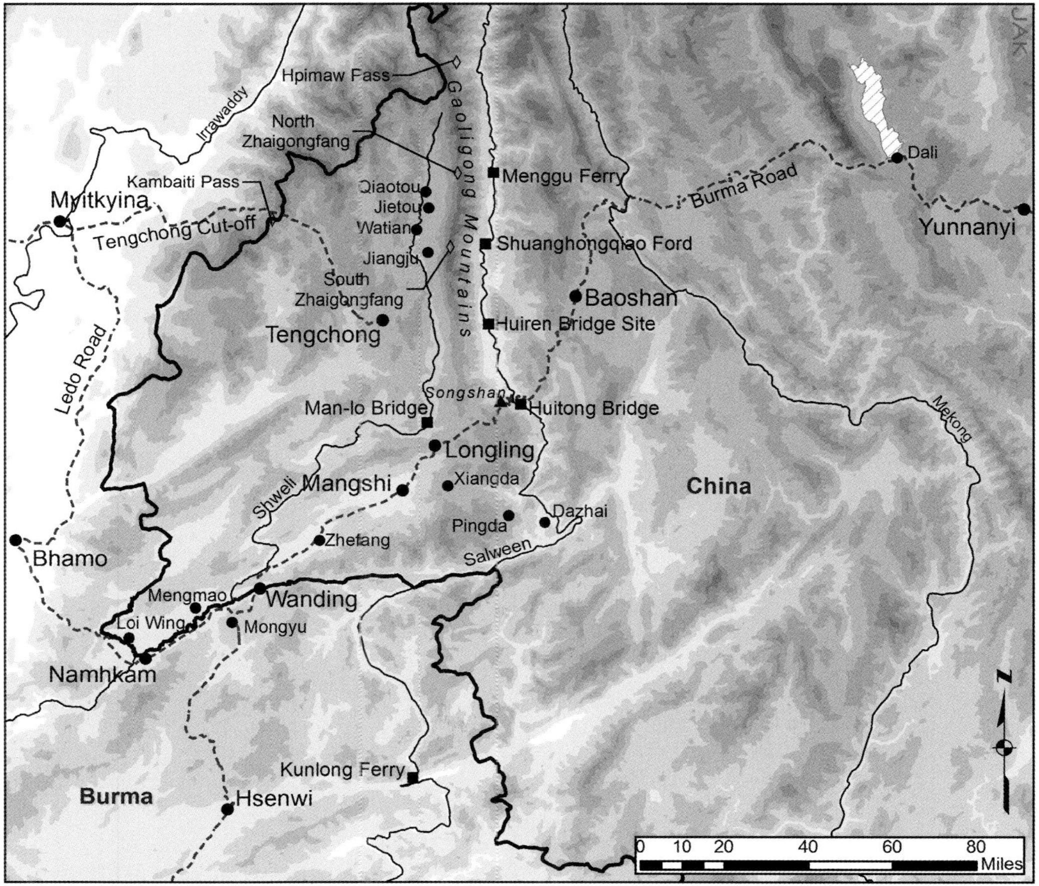

The Salween Front

Author's Note

This book focuses primarily on the relationship between the Chinese and Americans as they fought to retake the frontier west of the Salween River during World War II. There are relatively few sources from the Japanese perspective, in part because so few survived, but also because it was something even fewer wished to remember. In my research, I found the interplay between the Chinese and Americans to be the richest source of material and, perhaps more significantly, full of important lessons for the modern era. While most of the American sources regarding the Salween Campaign use the Wade-Giles Romanization of people and place names, I decided to use the modern Pinyin system. This is partly because I used a fair number of Chinese sources. It is also because the Wade-Giles spellings often vary. Pinyin provided an easy method of standardization. The exception to this is when the Wade-Giles version is so prevalent as to make the Pinyin confusing—Chiang Kai-shek, for example—when the Pinyin was unavailable, or when giving the names of Chinese veterans from Taiwan, where Pinyin is not used.

I owe an extraordinary debt of gratitude to a great many people who made this book possible. First and foremost, I thank the veterans whose story this is; I depended heavily on their support and assistance. Dave Hayward from the 22nd Bomb Squadron Association, Sterling Barrow and Art Clark from the 35th Photo Reconnaissance Squadron, and Bob Passanisi from the Merrill's Marauders Association were particularly helpful. In Taiwan, Samuel Hui, editor of the *Want China Times*, and Pan I-jung provided invaluable assistance working with the ROC's Veterans Affairs Council to track down and interview Chinese veterans. My coworkers Ron Boisvert and Andrew Kimmel patiently listened to me drone on and provided helpful comments on the manuscript. Andrew also made excellent maps to accompany the text. My aunt waded through reams of documents at the Hoover Institution on my behalf. Hak Hakanson provided valuable information from Thailand. Jeff Greene, Director of the Sino-American Aviation Heritage Foundation; Colonel John Plating, author of *The Hump: America's Strategy for Keeping China in World War II*; Peter Harmsen, author of *Shanghai 1937: Stalingrad on the Yangzte*; Carl Molesworth, author of several books about the air war in China; and Professor Rana Mitter, author of *Forgotten Ally: China's World War II, 1937-1945*, all provided helpful input and advice. My wife Brianna let me bounce ideas off her, provided great advice on form and readability, and pulled from her extensive background in human behavior and psychology to help me flesh out the personalities of key individuals. Throughout the course of working on this project, God has grown me as a writer and given me insight and perspective on war and the human experience. None of this would have happened without His grace, the help and patience of my wife, and the insights and adventurous spirits of David Corpman, Jesse Long, Anthony Mascaro, and James Tippets. Thank you.

Prologue: Author's Odyssey

A flight of four P-40 Warhawks raced up the valley from the southeast at 250 miles per hour. They flew low, just above the rice paddies, one after another in trail formation. Each had a single 500-pound bomb slung under its belly. The fortress walls of Tengchong rose sharply in front of them. As the walls loomed close, the lead pilot released his bomb and wrenched back on the stick, barely clearing the top. Tracers from Japanese machine guns followed him as he zoomed skyward. His bomb exploded in a geyser of rock, dirt, and flame, marking the spot for the planes that followed. One after another, the fighters flung their bombs into the wall, hammering out a breach through the stone ramparts. Chinese infantry ran forward from their trenches and laid bamboo ladders against the rubble. They climbed into the teeth of intense fire from machine guns and small arms. Through the breach, they surged into the city. The siege of Tengchong, in China's rugged Yunnan Province, was one of the most fascinating and strangely anachronistic battles in history. In the midst of World War II, Chinese soldiers fought a medieval siege while the most modern American warplanes roared overhead, supporting them from above. It was a battle that would stand among few in history in which the Chinese retook territory from the Japanese invader. Working together, Chinese and Americans fought to liberate the occupied frontier of western Yunnan.

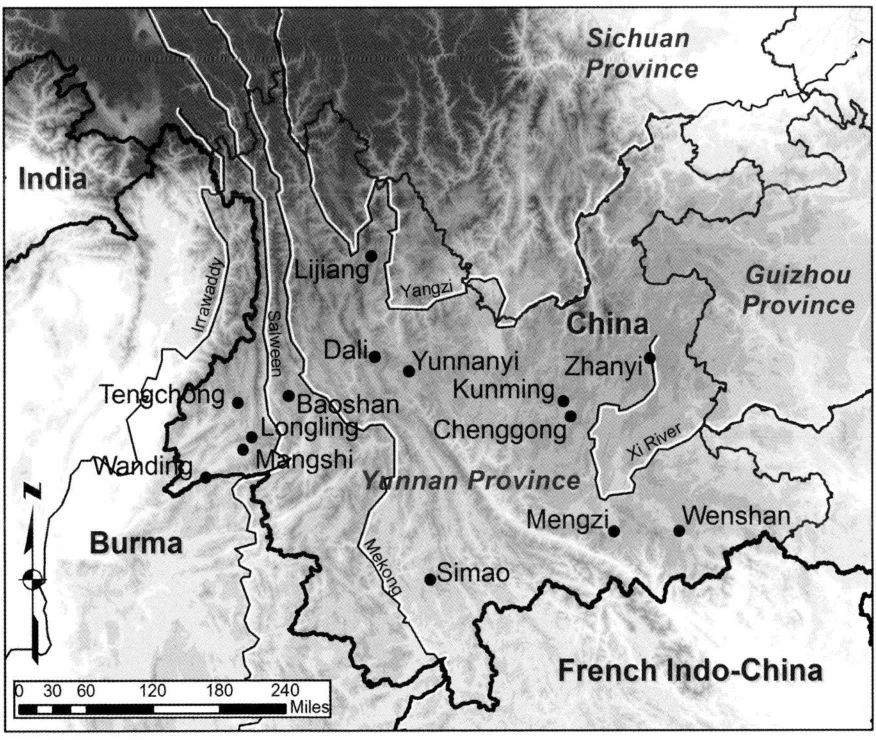

Yunnan Province

My first glimpse of Yunnan was from the window of a commercial airliner on June 26, 2008. I could not yet see the ground as we began our approach into Kunming Wujiaba International Airport. Beneath us, brilliant white clouds stretched to the horizon. The jet descended and its wingtips played along the ragged edges of the tops before it sank fully into the murk. The vibrant blue sky above us faded to dull gray. The billowing cumulus gave way to a disorienting maze of clouds and mist. Lower still, and jagged, dark green mountains appeared ominously in the haze. It was an awesome sight. I watched this scene unfold from the relative safety of a state-of-the-art jetliner. At that moment, I wondered at how terrifying it must have been during World War II for a young, inexperienced pilot to attempt to pierce this gloomy veil in an unsophisticated aircraft without modern navigation aids.

Yunnan forms China's southwest frontier, bordered by Burma to the west, Laos to the south, and Vietnam to the southeast. It is a geographic and cultural crossroads; a frontier with a human and natural diversity found nowhere else in China. During World War II, it was a frontier the Japanese intended to occupy in the course of their aggressive conquest. It was a frontier the Allies had to cross to carry aid to China in opposition to that conquest. It was a frontier that proved perilous for both sides. The famous traveler Marco Polo visited Yunnan—known to him as Carajan—in 1278. "The country is wild and hard of access," he wrote, "full of great woods and mountains which 'tis impossible to pass."[1] From humid lowlands in the southeast, the terrain rises abruptly to towering mountains in the north and west. The few cities, towns, and villages are nestled deep within valleys or perched high atop plateaus. Literally translated, Yunnan means "the land south of the clouds." With its unique culture and forbidding geography, some interpret its name to suggest a remote wilderness, a "land beyond the clouds." Our airliner continued beyond the clouds on final approach into Kunming. Skyscrapers suddenly appeared from the mist. Kunming is the provincial capital, and though it is small compared to China's east coast metropolises, its population of more than six million makes it large by American standards.

My trip to Yunnan was part of a study abroad program for American students learning Mandarin Chinese, including stops in Beijing, Shanghai, Nanjing, Xi'an, Guilin, and Lijiang. We changed planes for Lijiang in Kunming. Taking off to the south, we banked to pick up a northerly heading and passed over a massive lake that stretched out on either side of the airplane. Dark hills and mountains hemmed its shores. The city of Kunming bounded it to the north. This was Lake Dian. Every American that passed through Kunming during the war remembered it as the singular geographic feature of the valley. We left the lake behind, flying 180 miles north to Lijiang, near the northwest border of the province. It was a short flight, but by the time we arrived it was dark. I looked out the window; the cloud layer was lower and thinner here. The moonlight reflected softly off the clouds and the tips of dark mountains jutted through. As we descended into the airport it started raining.

I was excited to finally visit this part of China—more so than anywhere else on our itinerary. At the time, I was working on a book about the 449th Fighter Squadron, an American unit that fought in China during World War II. Though the war spanned the entire Asian continent, Yunnan Province was the center of American operations in China. It was the entry terminal for Allied aid arriving by air, as well as the headquarters of Claire Chennault's Flying Tigers—the American Volunteer Group, China Air Task Force, and 14th Army Air Force. In fact, the first reference I saw to the Flying Tigers in China was outside of Lijiang. I was hard pressed to find anything about them even at museums and bookstores in Beijing, Shanghai, and Nanjing. I thought this might be due to the fact that America's wartime relationship was with China's Nationalist government, now exiled to Taiwan. However, I discovered my first clue to the true nature of this relationship in a coffee shop at the base of Jade Dragon Snow Mountain, *Yulongxue Shan* (玉龙雪山), an imposing eighteen-thousand-foot peak at the north end of the Lijiang Valley. Our student group planned to ride the cable car partway up the mountain. While we waited to depart, I saw a sign depicting an American pilot holding a cup of coffee and standing in front of a shark-nosed P-40. The sign read "Hump Coffee Shop" in English and Chinese. I was surprised at this casual reference to something I could barely find in bookstores on the east coast. The "Hump" was what American pilots called the epic spur of the Himalayas that juts south into Burma, dividing China and India. It was over these mountains that American aid came to China via air transport. Lijiang was situated at the northern end of this route and had an auxiliary airstrip for transports unable to reach Kunming because of weather or malfunction. According to Jeff Greene, director of the Sino-American Aviation Heritage Foundation, an old Irish missionary kept watch over the field and occasionally, transports landed and brought him coffee—the inspiration for the coffee shop. I told one of the workers I was writing a book about the Flying Tigers and he gave me an illustrated menu to keep as a souvenir.

Our climb up Jade Dragon Snow Mountain was breathtaking—both because of the beautiful scenery and lack of oxygen! From the cable car we saw stout, squat pine trees spread below us with blue, flower-like pine cones. It was a steep hike from the cable car platform to an overlook fifteen thousand feet above sea level. Granite outcroppings jutted majestically from beneath ice and snow. It was windy, overcast, and cold. I labored to breathe and my pulse pounded in my head. As we turned to head back down, the clouds parted and we could see the valley spread before us. The view from this imposing mountain was incredible. It made me wonder again how terrifying it must have been to cross this range in bad weather without modern navigation aids. Aircrews called it the "Aluminum Trail" because of the many airplanes that crashed or disappeared. My own experience flying in terrible weather over similar terrain in Afghanistan would prove very challenging even *with* modern equipment.

I had an opportunity to meet Jeff Greene in person a few days later. Our student group had a day-long layover in Kunming before departing Yunnan Province. I had corresponded with Jeff for months regarding my book on the 449th and he offered to show me some of the sights around Kunming. We visited monuments built to memorialize the Hump Airlift and the Burma Road. We toured Chenggong Airfield, where a Chinese major showed us an old stone paving roller. He explained to us that Chinese workers once used it to make gravel airfields for American airplanes. To him, it represented the wartime friendship and cooperation between the United States and China. We went to General Chennault's old headquarters, still standing not far from the Kunming airport. As I walked up the steps, Jeff spoke the names of some of the legendary figures who stood there before: "Tex" Hill, "Casey" Vincent, Joe Stilwell. Every step felt like an electric connection to those heroes of the past. By the end of my stay I had resolved to return. Besides its history, Yunnan had great food and friendly people. The climate and terrain were similar to where I was from in Colorado, though the mountains seemed larger and the valleys narrower—almost a caricature of the Rockies. I knew I was just beginning to learn about epic events that happened in this epic place.

I received a grant from the Olmstead Foundation to discover the history and visit the battlefields of Yunnan Province in March 2009; David Corpman, Jesse Long, Anthony Mascaro, and James Tippets accompanied me. All four were conversant in Chinese. Dave had actually lived in Kunming for a year. This time, instead of flying north from Kunming to Lijiang, we flew west to Dali and drove from there to the small town of Yunnanyi. On March 27, we found ourselves standing on the old American airfield there, about 130 miles west of Kunming. The crushed gravel runway was decayed, but still apparent. It was oriented southwest to northeast with the prevailing winds, which blew steadily. Hills and mountains rose only a few miles away in every direction. We wandered through the fields of winter wheat which would be replanted with rice in the summertime. Not far from the derelict landing strip were several large revetments: barricades made of compacted earth that once protected American warplanes. In 1944, Yunnanyi hosted a task force of airplanes supporting the Chinese Expeditionary Force (CEF) as it crossed the Salween River to liberate the Japanese-occupied frontier. Some of the revetments were over ten feet tall and fifty feet across. Rather than attempt to level the sturdy barriers, Chinese farmers simply planted wheat on top of them.

Kunming, the capital of Yunnan Province, is home to six million people. It is situated on the north shore of Lake Dian and surrounded by mountains. During World War II, it was the center of American operations in China. ***Author's Photo***

Running north of the airfield was the old Burma Road. The road opened in December 1938. Over one hundred thousand Chinese workers built it by hand after the Japanese occupied the coast. It was once China's lifeline, carrying supplies from the railhead at Lashio, Burma, to Kunming. I imagined it looked much the same over sixty years ago as it did now: one lane wide, crudely paved with rocks, with dilapidated trucks rumbling through, belching smoke. On the far side of the road from the airfield was a narrow stone street. A town official walked with us and explained that the first building on the left was one of the 14th Air Force hostels where pilots and ground crew had lived. It was one story tall, made from crumbling mud bricks. It had wooden doors and window shutters and a steep tile roof. I felt as if I were walking into a fog of history as we continued up the lane. My eyes lingered on the rough textures and sepia colors of the old buildings. The smell of wood cook fires, mildew, and garbage mixed together into a strange symphony of odors. I was overwhelmed. The official explained to us in his thick Yunnan accent that Chiang Kai-shek, Madame Chiang, and Claire Chennault had walked this very path, and that the American pilots drank coffee at a cafe that used to be up the lane a ways. He led us into the courtyard of an old two-story house-turned-museum. The downstairs rooms were filled with old photos with captions written in Chinese. A big room at the end had a sand table demonstrating the layout of the airfield during the war. One wall of this room was painted floor-to-ceiling with an American and a Nationalist Chinese flag side-by-side. Upstairs were various artifacts from the war and more photographs. I found the dusty old place encouraging. It was not made for Americans, but for Chinese. They made this place

Jade Dragon Snow Mountain, *Yulongxue Shan* (玉龙雪山), is an imposing 18,360-foot tall mountain north of Lijiang. During World War II, it marked the northern edge of the Hump airlift route. *Author's Photo*

because they wanted to pass on the history of the Sino-American resistance against Japan to their children, and their children's children. As we walked back to the van, the town official told us: "Most Americans do not know where Yunnan Province is, let alone Yunnanyi. Now you have been here." As we drove away, James told me he had gained a new appreciation for his heritage as an American and as a military officer.

The next day we drove further west to Baoshan. It was less than one hundred miles by air, but much further on the twisting mountain roads. Between Yunnanyi and Baoshan were mountains, one after another without respite. We drove through passes, along narrow valleys, and over deep, rocky draws. During the war, Baoshan was the headquarters of the CEF and featured a small grass airfield that supported the campaign. The valley's suitability for such a field was immediately apparent; as the road brought us in from the north, the valley opened before us—a broad, flat oasis after travelling through a jungle of highlands. Most of the land was devoted to farming. Vivid green rice paddies covered the valley floor. Sunlight spilled over the mountaintops to the west, illuminating a low haze. The town of two million was nestled up against the mountains. We stayed the night in Baoshan and toured a museum with a display about the CEF's campaign across the Salween River.

The next day we crossed the Salween ourselves. The modern highway was built onto the sides of mountains. Lofty bridges spanned deep, narrow valleys and long tunnels burrowed through steep ridges. We crossed the river at a relative wide point, but even so, the mountains came down almost to its banks. Salween is the Burmese name for the river. The Chinese call it *Nujiang* (怒江), or "Angry River." It was an apt name; the river's rapid waters plunged through a mile-deep chasm carved between two steep, colossal ranges. The forbidding geography made it a natural barrier. It was here, on the banks of this violent river, that Chinese soldiers and American airmen stopped the Japanese column surging up from Burma in May 1942. It was the farthest limit of enemy occupation in southwest China and, consequently, the point from which the Allies launched their campaign of liberation.

From the river, the Gaoligong Mountains were just visible through the cool, humid mist. They were dark and imposing, impossibly tall and ominous. We crossed the river at 2,100 feet above sea level. The Gaoligong Range rises to twelve thousand feet on the other side. The ascent was perilous. The road was often not wide enough for two vehicles as it zigzagged up the steep slope. We saw smoke billowing from the brakes of trucks passing us in the opposite direction. To pass vehicles ahead of us, our driver honked twice, stomped on the gas, and hoped to get by before someone sped around the next blind curve. The ground dropped away sharply beside us. There was nowhere to pull over. I was in awe of the tens of thousands of Chinese soldiers that crossed this terrain on foot during the monsoon while fighting the Japanese. It was the highest, most rugged battleground of World War II.[2] As we crossed to the west side of the range, the mist grew thicker. We found ourselves in a rainforest of towering broad-leaved evergreens, bamboo groves, and beautiful rhododendrons. At high altitude, the air was cold and damp. Chinese farmers had carved rice terraces into the sides of some of the mountains. We ate lunch at a small village alongside the Shweli River, called the Longchuan River in Chinese. From there it was another hour to our destination.

Our journey took us to Tengchong, the focal point of the campaign to retake China's southwest frontier. Tengchong is situated in a valley six-and-a-half miles long north to south and three miles across—5,500 feet above sea level. It is smaller than Baoshan, with

The Graveyard of the National Heroes in Tengchong, where 3,346 Chinese soldiers that died in the 1944 battle are buried. ***Author's Photo***

a population of only seventy thousand. It is famous for its jade markets and historic trade routes travelled by Marco Polo, linking it with India through Burma. Laifengshan, "the mountain where the phoenix comes," rises five hundred feet above its southwest corner. During the war, the town was still surrounded by its Ming Dynasty walls, making it an imposing fortress.

Our first stop on the morning of March 30 was the Graveyard of the National Heroes, near the base of Laifengshan. Amongst the stone murals, statues, and exhibit halls commemorating the war, we found nineteen stone markers. Each had purple writing in both English and Chinese honoring the Americans who died in the campaign. It was a monument to American sacrifice in an out-of-the-way frontier town in China. The U.S. Army brought most of the dead heroes home after the war, but the five of us felt profoundly moved to be standing before a foreign monument to our fallen countrymen. Just behind the monument a small hill rose, shaded by lofty trees and covered with a forest of stone markers for the 3,346 Chinese soldiers buried there. We reverently ascended the steps to the top, where we found a tall monolith honoring the costly sacrifice of the CEF in liberating the town. The scene was almost too much to take in—too much loss, too much sacrifice. We needed to blow off some steam, so we asked our driver to take us to the base of Laifengshan.

The five of us trekked up the stone steps and dirt path to the top of the mountain. It was a tiring hike—five hundred feet vertical up a steep slope. The physical effort was just

The author provides first aid to a Chinese man who cut his leg open with a machete. ***Courtesy of Anthony Mascaro***

what we needed. The face of the mountain was covered in tall, dark trees. Decaying leaves covered the ground. Several old tombs dotted the face of the hill. Occasionally, we saw what appeared to be a bomb or artillery crater. At the top of the mountain was a tall, white pagoda commanding a view of the entire valley. We climbed to its highest level and surveyed the scene before us. The sky was dark gray, the distant mountains shrouded in mist. Standing where the Japanese had stationed their artillery in 1944, an image of the battle suddenly became vivid in my mind's eye. The siege of Tengchong reminded me of the epic sieges of antiquity—like the Israelites at Jericho, the Achaeans at Troy, or Henry V at Harfleur. I could see the P-40s and B-25s racing up the valley from the south, hurling their bombs at the mighty wall while waves of Chinese infantry scaled the breaches with bamboo ladders. Fire and smoke would have cast a pall across the scene as the weather did now. The valley must have echoed with the harsh staccato of machine guns and the loud report of crashing artillery and exploding bombs. "Once more unto the breach!" Henry cried to his English soldiers at Harfleur.[3] I imagined Chinese officers yelling the same challenge to their men as they surged into the city.

Our journey to discover the epic history of a battlefield forgotten to all but those who lived or fought there was shaping into an adventure in its own right: our drive across the Salween and over the mighty Gaoligong, our visit to the graves of forgotten heroes, and the scene of battle playing before our eyes from the top of Laifengshan. Later that day, we met with a Chinese World War II veteran and two men who witnessed the war as children. Their local dialect was difficult for me to follow, but with the help of my friends and a translator I was able to understand. Lu Caiwen—a young intelligence officer during the campaign—told us, "We could not have won the war without American support. … It was extremely lucky for us to have the United States as our ally. Whenever we talk about the war, we always mention American help. We can never forget their help."[4] It was humbling to hear those words from someone who witnessed the terrible sacrifice the conflict demanded of his own people.

Dave, James, Anthony, and I decided to return to Laifengshan after dinner on our last night in Tengchong. We walked from the hotel and climbed the north face of the mountain. There were no paths here, as we had found on the east side. The slope was very steep and covered in pines and cypress. We scaled the first part using the step-like structure of a stone drainage way. From there, we moved from tree to tree to make it up the slope. Finally, we made it to an area that appeared to have once been terraced for rice, but was now overgrown with pines. Old yellowed needles covered the ground, as did the occasional tree felled for logging. We walked along a path on the terrace. After a short time, we came across an old man with one blind eye and tan, weather-beaten skin. He was clearing brush with a machete. Rather than slashing away from himself, horizontally, he slashed vertically, toward himself. Unfortunately, he cut his leg open and laid it bare to the bone. He was not bleeding profusely—somehow he managed to miss any significant vein or artery. He definitely needed stitches, though. I happened to have a first aid kit in my backpack, so I disinfected and bandaged the wound. We told him in Chinese to go to the hospital (*Ni bixu kanbing!*). "*Weishenme?*"(why?) he asked. "You took care of it." We tried to impress upon him the short-term nature of our repairs before he turned to walk up the hill toward his home and we continued along the path back to Tengchong. It was a strange encounter. Somehow it made us feel like we were connected to this place.

By the following week we were back in the United States. Our adventure seemed like a vivid dream—something unreal, something out of place in the world we inhabited. It was clear to me I needed to tell the story of the desperate struggle to stop the Japanese at the Salween in 1942, and the subsequent campaign to liberate Tengchong and the rest of the frontier west of the river in 1944. In eight brutal years of war, the Salween Campaign marked China's first successful attempt at removing the Japanese from occupied territory. It played a role in clearing the Japanese from the Burma Road, opening a land line of communications from India and allowing air transports crossing the Hump to fly further south over less-dangerous terrain. It was a story of Chinese and American cooperation: the Chinese Expeditionary Force used American supplies, advisors, technicians, and air support. In the present era of constrained military budgets, the United States may find its ability to respond to contingencies around the world limited, just as the demands of World War II limited its efforts in China. Lessons from a campaign in which American advisors and aircraft helped a Chinese peasant army defeat a battle-hardened, modern enemy can be applied today. Additionally, with the bilateral relationship between China and the United States becoming increasingly important, the story of past cooperation can serve as common ground for mutual respect and understanding. Most important of all, the soldiers and airmen who died for the cause of freedom deserve to have their story told, as was that of the English at Harfleur and the Achaeans at Troy. This is their story.[5]

1

Stopped at the Salween

Burma was in flames as the month of May dawned in 1942. British and Chinese resistance fell to pieces as the Japanese advanced north from Rangoon. Lashio, the link between the railway from Rangoon and the road to China, fell on April 29. Six Chinese divisions retreated into China. Lieutenant General Shojiro Iida, the commander of the Japanese 15th Army, directed the 56th Division to pursue them along the Burma Road. All but two of the retreating divisions were intact, but with their tanks and trucks the Japanese moved with such speed and struck with such ferocity that the Chinese could not pull together an effective defense. Colonel Claire Lee Chennault, commander of the mercenary American Volunteer Group (AVG)—better known as the Flying Tigers—recalled the rout in Burma and the Japanese advance into southwest China as "the darkest hour since the fall of Nanjing."[1] All that stood between the devastating enemy offensive and Free China were the ragged, war-weary remains of Chennault's fighter group and the disorganized and defeated Chinese troops fleeing Burma. Together, they would make a last desperate stand in the steep chasm of the Salween River gorge.[2]

Chennault was a retired U.S. Army Air Corps captain forced from the service because of his failing health and radical views on pursuit aviation. He was bold and dynamic, with black hair, dark eyes, and a hard, angular jaw set firm in defiance of anything —or anbody—that stood in his way. The intense energy of his active mind was focused inward; he was observant, reflective, analytical, and decisive. His ideas were central to his identity and he took criticism very personally. To those who embraced his ideas and followed him he was warm and fatherly. To those who opposed him he was stubborn and icy. He grew up in rural Louisiana and was self-conscious of his humble origins. From an early age he was largely self-taught and a voracious reader, especially from his grandfather's extensive library on the American Civil War. His heroes were the daring cavalry leaders of the Confederacy. While the backwoods of Louisiana deprived him of a first-class education, it gave him an appreciation for nature, in which

Claire Lee Chennault became an advisor to the Chinese Air Force after retiring as a captain from the Army Air Corps in 1937. In 1942, he was brought out of retirement to command the China Air Task Force of the U.S. 10th Air Force, and in 1943, he was promoted to the rank of major general to command his own numbered air force, the 14th. *National Archives*

he found his sanctuary. Throughout his life he found restoration and peace in the outdoors. In China, he could often be found wandering the rice paddies, shotgun in hand, looking for duck.[3]

Chennault was a school teacher in Louisiana until the First World War prompted him to join the Army in 1917. He wanted to be a pilot, but his applications for flight training again and again met with rejection. Yet he remained persistent and eventually his persistence paid off. He finally graduated flight school in April 1919—too late to see combat in the war. He became a fighter pilot in an Air Corps struggling to survive in peace time. As he grew in confidence and experience, he thought about how better to fly and fight in the air. His ideas formed crossways to the general trend of the service. Most of his compatriots came to think of the fighter as outmoded and the bomber as invulnerable. While stationed at the Air Corps Tactical School at Maxwell Field, Alabama, in the early 1930s, Chennault advocated the use of fighter aircraft to intercept and defeat bombers. His 1933 study titled *The Role of Defensive Pursuit* did not sit well with the bomber-minded Air Corps brass. However, it and Chennault's own stunt flying with the Three Men on a Flying Trapeze—a forerunner to the Thunderbirds—attracted attention in China. In 1937, Generalissimo Chiang Kai-shek was trying to unite China under his Nationalist regime, while simultaneously keeping it from disintegrating in the face of Japanese imperialism. Key to Chiang's strategy was developing a modern air force. His wife, Song Meiling—known to the public and press as Madame Chiang—hired Chennault as an advisor upon his retirement from the Air Corps. The job offered $12,000 a year—a lot more than his salary in the service and enough to take care of his wife and eight children back in Louisiana. More importantly, it offered him an opportunity to prove his ideas. He arrived in China on May 31, 1937. Five weeks later, war broke out with Japan.[4]

China could only field a hodgepodge fleet of obsolete airplanes against the state-of-the-art Japanese air force. Chennault realized that for the outclassed Chinese to be able to hold their own, they needed to ambush the enemy at a time and place of their choosing. It was a difficult problem when one considers that airplanes are not constrained by geography in the same manner as armies or navies. Formations of enemy bombers were not restricted to predictable avenues of approach as they carried out their devastating raids on Chinese cities. Furthermore, it took time for intercepting fighters to climb to an altitude from which they could attack with an advantage. The fighters had to determine the exact point in space where the enemy would be at a future time when they could arrive with enough altitude to attack. Such a forecast required careful planning and accurate and continual intelligence. Chennault immediately began assembling a network of observers around the Nationalist capital at Nanjing. The observers used radios and telephones to report enemy aircraft to a command center that plotted the course of the raids, determined their target, and coordinated the response of Chinese fighters. The network enjoyed some early success. In July 1937, the Japanese lost fifty-four planes in three raids over Nanjing. By October, they had learned to provide ample fighter escort. According to Chennault, "With inferior planes and training and without replacements [the Chinese] were doomed to early extinction."[5]

Chennault often stood outside during bombing raids, smoking a Camel cigarette, watching the Japanese and studying their tactics. His notes would later prove valuable, but he was not content merely to observe and advise. He went to China to prove his ideas. To some extent he already knew he was right; defending fighters could decimate formations of unescorted bombers. Chennault was a man of deep emotion though, even if he did not always show it on the outside. He empathized with the suffering of the Chinese people. He knew he was probably the most experienced fighter pilot in China and he wanted to make a difference. His sense of duty and yearning for adventure propelled him into the sky. He asked Madame Chiang to purchase a Curtiss Hawk Special for his personal use. During the desperate air battles over Nanjing, he got his "first taste of Jap flak and fighter tactics" flying the blunt-nosed, fixed-gear fighter. Nobody knows the true extent of Chennault's participation in combat; he kept the details to himself. As an American citizen, it was illegal for him to participate in a foreign war not sanctioned by the U.S. government. Even long after the war he only wrote about it in general terms. It remains a mystery as to whether he regularly challenged the Japanese in combat, or if his encounters with the enemy were incidental to his observing, directing, and reconnoitering. Whatever the case, he reported that he quickly discovered the difference between the Hawk, which "was built ruggedly with maneuverability sacrificed for heavy firepower, durability, and diving speed," and the Japanese "featherweight monoplanes ... that sacrificed everything else for incredible maneuverability. In a turning, tail-chasing dogfight they were poisonous." His Hawk "acquired some bullet holes much too close for comfort as I learned very, very early in the game that trying to turn with Jap fighters was non-habit forming."[6]

With air and ground resistance crumbling, Nanjing fell on December 13, 1937. The Nationalist government retreated westward, trading space for time, determined to resist. They moved the capital first to Hankou, in Hubei Province. When that city fell in October 1938, they moved again to Chongqing, in the remote Sichuan Province. The Japanese bombed them relentlessly. In May 1939, they began massive air raids, making the new Nationalist capital the most-bombed city in the world until London stole the infamy during the Battle of Britain. The Chinese Air Force (CAF) continued intercepting the raids, but in August 1940, the Japanese unleashed their new A6M Type Zero Carrier Fighter. The "Zero" was far superior to anything the CAF could field and achieved complete air dominance. The Chinese withdrew what was left of their air force from combat to preserve a core of experienced pilots. By December 7, 1941, Japan controlled China's skies, along with ninety-five-percent of its industry, one-fourth of its area, and half its population. Millions of refugees fled in terror and lived in squalor, ever fearful of coming under the guns of the Japanese army or air force. "The Japanese fighters and bombers never stopped attacking us," recalled Luo Chih-tsai, a Chinese Army veteran who as a child fled his home in Hubei Province. "I remember a Japanese fighter that flew low enough for me to see the pilot's face. If I threw a rock at the airplane, I think it would have likely hit it ... the Japanese were unopposed wherever they flew."[7]

In November 1940, Chennault accompanied the CAF's director of operations to the United States on a mission to request five hundred planes and pilots to defend China. President Franklin Roosevelt was sympathetic to the cause. He felt his family had a special connection to China. His maternal grandfather, Warren Delano, had been a partner in a company sailing clipper ships for the China trade. His mother even spent several years of her childhood in Hong Kong. In October 1937, during the bloody Battle of Shanghai, Roosevelt warned about "the epidemic of world lawlessness" and called for concrete steps to be taken against Japanese aggression.[8] After they invaded Indochina in 1940, he imposed an embargo on oil and steel and closed the Panama Canal to Japanese shipping. In response to Chennault's mission, he authorized military aid to China and verbally approved the formation of a group of volunteers to man a one-hundred-plane fighter group. It was a significant—if clandestine—demonstration of the United States' support. The first contingent of volunteers arrived by ship in Rangoon on July 28, 1941.

Chennault began indoctrinating the pilots in his methods of aerial warfare at a British airfield near Taungoo, 150 miles north of Rangoon. "All my life I have been a teacher," he wrote, "ranging from the one-room schools of rural Louisiana to director of one of the largest Air Corps flying schools, but I believe that the best teaching of my career was done in that teakwood shack at Taungoo."[9] He taught his men to use a two-ship element to provide mutual support in hit-and-run attacks, exploiting the high diving speed and superior firepower of their Curtiss Hawk 81-A2s. The fighters were the export version of the P-40B Warhawk, Curtiss' liquid-cooled evolution of the Hawk Special Chennault flew in 1937. He warned his pilots to strictly avoid turning combat with the maneuverable Japanese. He reinforced his teaching with a simple rhyme: "It's better to fight and run away, and live to fight another day."[10] For their part, the pilots came to respect the "Old Man," with his low Cajun drawl, weather-beaten face, and almost uncanny ability to outguess the Japanese.

The American Volunteer Group met the Japanese Army Air Force (JAAF) in December 1941 as the latter supported the Japanese advance into Burma. In one raid on Rangoon, Christmas Day 1941, the Flying Tigers claimed twenty-four enemy airplanes destroyed for the loss of only two of their own. In fact, the Japanese reported losing only ten planes, but virtually every

A Curtiss Hawk 81-A2 from the American Volunteer Group lands at Kunming. The Hawk 81 was the liquid-cooled evolution of the Hawk Special Chennault flew in 1937. It was faster and more heavily armed and armored than the Japanese Ki-27 and Ki-43 fighters, but not nearly as maneuverable. *National Archives*

The Huitong Bridge crosses the Salween River in a steep, narrow gorge at 2,100 feet above sea level. The Gaoligong Mountains rise up to twelve thousand feet to the west. It took twenty miles of road in thirty-five hairpin switchbacks to traverse the one mile slope down to the bridge. *Hoover Institution*

one of their bombers suffered damage and several returned with dead or wounded crewmen. Over-claiming was common during confusing air battles; that same day, the Japanese claimed thirty-six planes shot down when Allied losses amounted to only two AVG Hawk 81s and five RAF Buffalos.[11] What was clear was that the AVG gave better than it got, though it could not single-handedly prevent disaster on the ground. When Rangoon fell on March 6, 1942, the group fell back to Magwe. They continued to retreat as the Japanese advanced northward. The group's assembly and repair depot at Loi Wing, on the China-Burma border, was supposed to have been well behind the front lines. By May 1, the tide of the enemy advance forced them to evacuate.

AVG pilot Charlie Bond, stationed with the 1st Squadron at Kunming, remembered when "all of the pilots from Loi Wing came barging into Kunming" on May 1. "They were an ugly-looking bunch—dirty and unshaven. We did all we could to help them get their junk unloaded and off to their barracks." The next day, Bond's squadron commander, Bob Neale, informed him and six other pilots they would move to the grass airfield at Baoshan, 220 miles west on the Burma Road. Bond wrote in his diary: "The Baoshan field is not too good, just a grass aerodrome, no runways, but adequate to land on and take off from in a P-40." They landed and refueled, waiting to escort CAF bombers on a mission into Burma. "They finally appeared," Bond wrote, "nine bombers in a loose formation heading south. We scrambled and took up a position to escort them." The Russian-built SB-3s were supposed to bomb a bridge near Kutkai, 140 miles down the Burma Road from Baoshan, but to Bond's amazement, "they flew right over it without dropping bombs and headed on down to Lashio, where they attempted to bomb the railroad yards. One bomb hit within the yards, but no fires resulted."[12] The Chinese bombers turned for home and the AVG fighters returned to Baoshan.

AVG pilots Peter Wright, Ben Foshee, and Erik Shilling evacuated Loi Wing in trucks full of supplies and equipment. The onset of the summer monsoon and the flood of refugees hindered traffic along the Burma Road. "The road turned into a quagmire," Shilling recalled, "looking like thick opaque red molasses and just as sticky. Our trucks did not have four wheel drive, and it was damn difficult driving in mud almost up to our hubcaps." They made slow progress and became separated in the heavy traffic. Shilling spent the nights in Mangshi and Longling, finally arriving at the Salween River on May 3. "Rounding a bend I had a clear view of the Salween suspension bridge," he later wrote. "The road presented an amazing sight. From my position all the way to the bridge, the mountain was almost perpendicular, a half tunnel had been dug into the side in order to build the road." It took twenty miles of road in thirty-five hairpin curves to traverse the one vertical mile from the top of the gorge to the Huitong Bridge. Traffic was backed up for miles. "Since it was a one-way bridge and traffic was headed in both directions, crossing it was a painfully slow process," wrote Shilling. He spent that night on the east bank of the river and continued on to Baoshan the next day. He was still ten miles from the city when he heard the rumble of dozens of airplane engines. He quickly pulled to the side of the road, jumped out of the truck, and took cover in the woods. From the trees, he could see several waves of Japanese fighters and bombers.[13]

At the Baoshan aerodrome, Charlie Bond was cleaning his pistol when Bob Neale burst in and yelled for everyone to get to their ships. "We dashed out to the planes," Bond recalled, "and by the time I had started my engine I looked up and saw the Jap bomber formation high above, heading toward our field." The bombers were twin-engine

Ki-21 Type 97 Heavy Bombers—Allied codename "Sally"—from the 12th and 98th sentais. A Japanese sentai was equivalent to an American group. A chutai was equivalent to a squadron. Bob Neale fired his pistol in the air to get everyone's attention and directed them to take cover in a nearby ditch. Bond was the only pilot in an airplane. He paused for a moment to consider. By himself, with the enemy already overhead, he was in considerable danger. Taking off would make him an easy target. The safest course of action would be to take cover and wait for the raid to pass. But Charlie Bond did not choose the safest course of action. He decided to go for it. He shoved the throttle forward, expecting bombs to start exploding around him at any moment. Luckily for him, the Japanese bypassed the field and bombed the city. As he climbed after them, he quickly strapped into his parachute and safety harness and looked at the town below. "The bombing was almost perfect," he noted, "right in the middle of the city."[14]

Bond kept after the Japanese and finally got into position at eighteen thousand feet—one thousand feet above the trailing wave of bombers. "I made a diving left turn and pulled up into the right rear quarter of the outside flank of the formation," he recalled. "I closed in on the outside bomber and squeezed the trigger. My bursts completely enveloped the fuselage, but I saw no smoke or fire." Using Chennault's hit and run tactics, Bond dove and attacked three times before his target went down. "I saw his right engine disintegrate and ignite into a flaming torch. He went down and through the overcast." Bond turned his attention to the next bomber in the formation, but his guns quit firing. He panicked. Tracers from the enemy bombers streaked toward him. He thought his guns had jammed, but he soon discovered he was out of ammunition. "I pulled away sharply and made a diving 180 turn to head back," he wrote. The 98th Sentai reported losing one bomber. Two more returned with a total of three wounded crew members aboard.[15]

Bond celebrated his victory with a slow roll over the field. He tried to contact the airfield controller on the radio, but to no avail. He decided to make a wide turn to enter the landing pattern, examining the town as he passed overhead. "What a sight," he remarked. "Before, the city had been spilling with evacuees, and now they were jammed all over the place. The Japanese bombs had caught them without warning. Fires engulfed the city. Many buildings and houses were blown to bits." As he lined up on final, Bond suddenly heard several loud explosions behind him. At first he thought there was a malfunction with his hydraulics, but as he looked back, he saw a trio of Japanese fighters on his tail. They were Ki-43 Army Type 1 Fighters—Allied codename "Oscar"—from the 64th Sentai. The explosions he heard were bullets hitting the armor plate behind his seat. What Charlie Bond did not know was that the Oscars stayed behind after the bombing raid to strafe the seven Hawk 81s still on the field. From his vantage point in the woods Erik Shilling witnessed the attack. "I wondered what the hell was he doing? He must be nuts doing a victory roll with a Jap fighter right on his ass sending a stream of tracers into his plane." The bullets slammed into the fuselage fuel tank of Bond's airplane, setting it on fire. He unhooked his harness, abruptly climbed, rolled inverted, and bailed out. According to Shilling, "the chute opened, and a second later he hit the ground." Bond was terrified the Japanese would strafe him under canopy and prayed fervently for his life. He landed in a cemetery a mile and a half from the field and immediately took cover. He was burned, but alive. Many in Baoshan were not so lucky.[16]

Erik Shilling returned to his truck and drove the rest of the way to the town. "It was a sickening sight," he reported. "The frigging Japanese had hit the city, although there wasn't a damn military target in all of Baoshan." He was appalled by the grotesque sight and smell. "The dead and dying littered the streets," he wrote, "and the cries of the wounded were everywhere. In some places, the gutters ran red with human blood."[17] Prior to the attack, crowds of Chinese civilians filled the streets celebrating the May Fourth Movement, a historic anti-imperialist protest that swept across China in 1919. The bombing left an estimated ten thousand people dead. Yizhi Yuan was a Muslim Chinese expatriate living in Burma before the Japanese invasion. She and her family escaped to Baoshan, only to have a Japanese bomb fall through her roof and kill her husband, younger brother, and younger sister. Yuan herself was wounded. Despite her injuries and her devastating grief, she worked tirelessly to help other victims of the bombing.[18]

Shilling decided not to stay in Baoshan, but to continue down the Burma Road. What he did not know was that AVG pilot Ben Foshee was included amongst the wounded. Pete Wright had made it to the hostel at Baoshan airfield ahead of Shilling and woke up to the sound of engine noise overhead. He watched as the bombs fell and the blasts enveloped the city. After the attack, a Chinese man arrived and told him to come quickly, there was an injured American in the hospital. It was Ben Foshee. He had been driving on a narrow stretch of the Burma Road that wound its way through the city. When the bombers arrived overhead there was nowhere for him to go. He was in the center of the chaos. The world turned to flame around him. Shrapnel tore open his leg. Wright arrived at the hospital to find his friend dying before his eyes. There was nothing he could do but watch. It was too late.[19]

With the Japanese advancing into China, Chennault's air raid warning net quickly fell to pieces. He ordered 1st Squadron to withdraw from Baoshan to Kunming. Ground crews worked feverishly to get the damaged fighters into flying condition and four of the Hawk 81s departed that afternoon. Two were written off after the strafing attack, putting the AVG down by a total of three fighters, including Bond's. The last Hawk 81 departed Baoshan that evening. Chennault guessed the Japanese would try to capitalize on their success with an attack the next day. "I sent nine P-40s to Yunnanyi at dawn to refuel and await further orders," he wrote. David Lee "Tex" Hill—a tall, lanky southerner and AVG ace—led six new shark-nosed P-40Es from 2nd Squadron, along with three Hawk 81s from 1st Squadron, 130 miles west to Yunnanyi. At 0915 hours, the code room in Kunming intercepted a message that a group of bombers had taken off from Mingaladon, near Rangoon, and another group was preparing to depart Chiang Mai, Thailand. Chennault calculated they would arrive over Baoshan at approximately 1230. He ordered his fighters to launch from Yunnanyi to intercept.[20]

"Tex" Hill had engine trouble. By the time he took off, the rest of the formation was out of sight. He arrived over Baoshan at twenty-one thousand feet. He had no idea where the rest of the AVG fighters were. He had no idea where the Japanese were. He was completely alone. Suddenly, below him, he saw a formation of seven single-engine airplanes. They were not P-40s. He could see their blunt radial engines and big red "meatballs" on the wings. He dove right into the middle of them, one against seven. Bringing one of the Japanese airplanes into his sights, he let loose a hail of bullets from his six .50-caliber machine guns, shooting it down with a three-second burst. It was his tenth victory. Continuing his dive, he saw an explosion out of the corner of his right eye; the cavalry had arrived. The rest of the AVG fighters dove into the fight, vectored to the enemy by an AVG radioman on the field. Frank Lawlor led them in the attack. On his wing, Frank Schiel reported: "Lawlor got a flamer on his first run … On my first rear attack I got in a good burst. When I looked back the plane was burning in a spin."[21] The AVG claimed eight Japanese fighters shot down over Baoshan. They believed the bombers must have turned back when they saw their fighter escort ambushed and destroyed. In fact, the Japanese bombers were single-engine Ki-30 Type 97 Light Bombers—Allied code name "Ann"—from the 27th Sentai. The 27th reported losing two bombers and the 11th Sentai reported losing three Ki-27 Type 97 Fighters—Allied codename "Nate."[22]

While the AVG and JAAF fought for the skies, Major General Shizuo Sakaguchi led three regiments of the 56th Division to the west bank of the Salween River. The Japanese were hard-pressed to advance quickly and capitalize on the Chinese retreat. They could not afford to pause and consolidate their gains as they thrust up the Burma Road. Japanese troops lived off the land, used captured British and Chinese trucks, and used ammunition and supplies captured at the Chinese depots around Lashio. Under these conditions, Chennault believed "the Japs were in no condition to fight a sustained battle against determined opposition, but they were ideally equipped to scatter light resistance and advance almost as fast as their mechanized equipment could carry them." He feared that if they crossed the Salween without encountering any resistance they would continue to Kunming, and it would be "the end of the war for China."

The Chinese fought brief delaying actions at Kutkai—approximately thirty-five miles north of Lashio—and Wanding, on the China-Burma border. By May 5, they had fallen back to prepared positions on the east bank of the Salween River, demolishing the Huitong Bridge behind them. The Japanese stood opposite them on the west bank. Though only ordered to pursue the Chinese to the Salween, it seems clear that at the very least, Sakaguchi intended to establish a bridgehead across the river. Once across, it is possible he hoped to continue his advance.[23]

According to Chennault, the decision to attack the advancing enemy column was a difficult one, as the Burma Road was still packed with refugees. He sent a telegram to Madame Chiang:

> LATEST REPORTS SAY JAPS ON WEST BANK SALWEEN RIVER 1500 HOURS 5 MAY STOP BRIDGE DESTROYED STOP JAPS MEETING NO OPPOSITION ANYWHERE AS SOLDIERS AND CIVILIANS PANIC STRICKEN FLEEING EAST ALONG ROAD STOP CONSIDER SITUATION DESPERATE AND JAPS MAY DRIVE KUNMING IN TRUCKS UNLESS ROAD AND BRIDGES DESTROYED AND DETERMINED OPPOSITION DEVELOPED STOP DUE TO FACT MANY CHINESE TRUCKS WEST OF SALWEEN PRESUMABLY IN HANDS OF ENEMY REQUEST AUTHORITY HIS EXCELLENCY THE GENERALISSIMO TO ATTACK TARGETS BETWEEN SALWEEN AND LONGLING CITY

Madame Chiang replied: "Generalissimo instructs you send all available AVG to attack trucks boats etc between Salween and Longling city."[24] That same day, the CAF launched six SB-3s to bomb the Japanese truck convoys moving toward the river, but the pace of operations and poor maintenance had taken its toll. The bombers returned to Kunming in too poor a condition to fly any more missions.[25]

To hamper the Japanese advance, Chennault formulated a plan to bomb the Burma Road where it descended into the Salween gorge. With the road blocked, the motorized Japanese regiments would find it difficult to move their forces down to the river. Chennault called "Tex" Hill into his office. "Remember when you gave me a lesson on dive-bombing?" he asked. Prior to joining the AVG, Hill had been a dive-bomber pilot on the USS *Ranger*. "It's time for the real thing," Chennault told him. "I want you to pick three other pilots." Hill picked Ed Rector, Frank Lawlor, and Tom Jones, all former U.S. Navy dive-bomber pilots. "I haven't done any dive-bombing since I left the fleet!" Jones complained after Hill briefed them on the mission. "It's a cliff wall a mile high," Hill reassured him. "You can't possibly miss."[26] The flight of dive-bombers flew the AVG's new P-40E Warhawks, which came equipped with under-wing bomb racks. Armorers Roy Hoffman and Chuck Baisden also improvised a centerline rack so they could carry Russian surplus 570-pound high-explosive bombs.[27] Arvid Olsen from the 3rd Squadron led a flight of four Hawk 81s—which could not carry bombs—as top cover.

Eight AVG fighters took off from Kunming in miserable weather the morning of May 7. It was pouring rain while they refueled at Yunnanyi. The hundred miles from Yunnanyi to the Salween gorge was difficult flying. The formation struggled to dodge thunderheads as they tried to remain beneath the weather. Then Hill spotted a gap in the clouds and all eight fighters broke through into clear, sunlit skies. The deep chasm of the Salween was before them. Trucks and troops of the Japanese 56th Division were strung out along the road from the bottom of the gorge to the horizon. Hill noted a group of engineers readying a pontoon bridge across the river. He put his P-40 into a steep dive, aiming for where the road met the top of the gorge. According to 3rd Squadron pilot R.T. Smith, the P-40 had a tendency to pick up excessive speed in a dive and it was "far from being satisfactory" as a dive-bomber.[28] Hill and his flight restricted their dive angle to between fifty and sixty degrees and kept their throttles back. Each of the P-40Es was armed with clusters of 35-pound fragmentation bombs under the wings and a 570-pound demolition bomb on the centerline rack. Hill's demolition bomb hit the side of the gorge and sent an avalanche of rocks crashing onto the road below. One after another, the other Warhawks in his flight followed him, making the road impassable. Coming back around, Hill fired a burst from his machine guns to keep heads down and dropped his frags over the Japanese column. Rector, Jones, and Lawlor did likewise and the four of them peeled off in different directions. As Hill wheeled around over the other side of the river, he could see Chinese soldiers "beside themselves—firing their rifles into the air, shouting encouragement, and dancing for joy along the shoreline."[29] Hill's flight made pass after pass with their machine guns. When they were out of ammunition, they switched with Olson's top cover flight, which continued strafing.

Tom Jones returned to the gorge the next day with another flight of P-40Es. R.T. Smith flew with the eight Hawk 81s in the top cover element. "Jones and his gang did the dirty work while we stayed on top," he reported. "They blasted about 50 trucks." The weather on the ninth prevented another mission, but the attacks left the Japanese off balance and allowed the Chinese to counterattack. The 36th and 87th divisions of the Chinese 71st Army crossed the Salween north of the Huitong Bridge site and attacked

Longling. The Japanese drove them back, but the attack signified a definite shift; the Japanese had lost their momentum. R.T. Smith was part of a sweep with six Hawk 81s and six P-40Es strafing and bombing trucks beyond Longling the next day. "It seems the Chinese are driving the Japs back down the road now," he noted. "Hope it continues that direction."[30] Chennault kept up the aerial pressure, making sure that "every town and village along the road that could serve the Japanese as shelter or a supply depot was bombed and burned."[31] Meanwhile, the Chinese ground troops worked to disrupt the Japanese, taking advantage of the rough terrain and onset of the monsoon to inhibit their road-bound enemy. By the end of May, the situation settled into confused fighting in the area between Longling, Tengchong, and the Huitong Bridge site.

The desperate stand of the Chinese Army and the AVG worked, even though there was no system of air-to-ground coordination. Efforts by American airmen and Chinese troops were entirely independent of each other. The Chinese used the terrain and prepared positions to their advantage. The AVG, under the daring and imaginative leadership of Claire Chennault, blocked the road and hammered relentlessly at the enemy column. Together, they managed to stop the Japanese at the Salween River. It was precisely the miracle China needed in its "darkest hour."

David Lee "Tex" Hill, former U.S. Navy dive-bomber pilot and double ace in the American Volunteer Group, led the first mission to bomb the Burma Road in the Salween River Gorge. This photo shows him as commander of the 23rd Fighter Group during his second tour of duty in China. *National Archives*

2

Stilwell's Walkout

It was something of a controversy that Lieutenant General Joseph W. Stilwell was absent and incommunicado during the crisis at the Salween River. He was the commander of U.S. Army forces in China, Burma, and India (CBI), as well as the chief of Chiang Kai-shek's Allied staff. He arrived in Burma just in time to watch the defense crumble around him. British and Chinese troops retreated in disarray. It was a disaster. Nothing could stop the enemy advance. The violence of battle and the hopelessness of defeat were overwhelming. While the Japanese drove up the Burma Road toward China, Stilwell and his staff embarked on an epic escape on foot, through the jungle, racing against the Japanese and the monsoon to make a last-ditch stand in North Burma or, failing that, to reach the safety of India.

Stilwell was a tough, wiry man of medium height and slight stature. He kept his graying hair cut short. Round, steel-rimmed glasses framed his dark, active eyes. Unlike Chennault, he was from an upper-middle class family in Yonkers, New York, though he was by no means a typical Army officer. He ended up at West Point almost by accident. He excelled at physical activity and competition and planned to play football at Yale. After several incidents of misbehavior in high school though, his father thought the Army would give him a badly-needed sense of discipline and pulled strings to get him an appointment to the U.S. Military Academy. His father was wrong. The Army never subdued him, but he excelled in spite of it. He found he had a natural talent for foreign languages and placed number one in French during his second year at the Academy. He ran cross country and track and is credited with introducing basketball to West Point. Despite his slight stature, he lettered in varsity football. When he returned to his alma mater on two later tours, he not only taught Spanish, French, and History, but also coached football and basketball.

Stilwell held himself to a high standard. He was active and purposeful, a man of emotion rather than reflection—a doer. He threw out the rule book. He once told a subordinate, "Don't give me that 'regulations' crap! You know goddam well I've never read a regulation in my life!"[1] As a regimental and division commander in the early 1940s, he was known for the speed and surprise of his swift flanking movements and hit and run attacks on training maneuvers. His men saw him constantly crisscrossing the battlefield on foot, directing, encouraging, and cursing. He was driven. He was also disgusted with anything less in others and could not bring himself to be civil to someone he did not respect. When faced with incompetence, he was impatient and caustic. It was after he gave a particularly brutal critique of an exercise at the Infantry School at Fort Benning that a subordinate christened him with the nickname "Vinegar Joe." It stuck. His motto was *Illegitimati non carborundum*, which he translated as, "Don't let the bastards get you down."

Stilwell's knowledge of China—its language, culture, military situation, and politics—was without parallel in the U.S. Army. He first visited while on leave from his second tour in the Philippines. It was 1911, during the height of the revolution against the decrepit Qing dynasty. He returned in 1920 as a language student in Beijing and became well acquainted with a China fractured by imperialism and competing warlords. From 1926 to 1929, he served as a battalion commander in the 15th Infantry regiment at Tianjin and witnessed the rise of the Guomindang (Nationalist Party) and Chiang Kai-shek's aggressive Northern Expedition to unite the country. As military attaché from 1935 to 1939, he observed the first years of war with Japan. He watched as the Chinese suffered defeat after defeat. He was not particularly impressed with Chiang or his army. In his opinion, their poor battlefield performance was not just because of a lack of modern equipment, as Chiang claimed, but could be attributed to their ignoring fundamental military principles. He thought their command and staff procedures were unsound, their use of supporting weapons improper, their intelligence indifferent, their communications poor, and maintenance of weapons and vehicles virtually nonexistent. He was impressed by the ordinary Chinese soldier though, whom he saw as tough and uncomplaining, despite being subjected to terrible conditions and terrible leadership. He followed the Chinese government as it withdrew to Hankou and then to Chongqing before he finally returned to the United States in 1939.

After America entered the war in December 1941, Roosevelt and the Allies declared Chiang the Supreme Allied Commander of the China Theater. It was more symbolic than anything else, since China had been at war with Japan since 1937. Chiang requested an American chief of staff to coordinate aid; command U.S. forces in China, and any Chinese forces that may be assigned to him; represent the United States on Chinese war councils; and manage the Burma Road. Secretary of War Henry L. Stimson recommended Lieutenant General Hugh Aloysius Drum for the position. Drum was commander of the 1st Army in New York and was the most experienced line officer in the U.S. Army. When he was summoned to Washington, he expected to be sent on an important mission to Europe. He was shocked and disappointed when he was asked to go to China instead. He wanted the pomp and glory of a *real* combat command, not to head some tedious liaison mission in a forgotten backwater. He also pointed out that he had no experience in the Far East. Stimson did not seem to think this would be a problem, but General George C. Marshall, Chief of Staff of the Army, disagreed. He was concerned after Chiang sent a letter assuring President Roosevelt that the officer he sent "need not be an expert on the Far East," and that "military men who have knowledge of Chinese armies when China was under warlords, operate at a disadvantage." To Marshall, it looked as if Chiang wanted a naïve lackey to do his bidding and become a tool to manipulate the American government. He thought Drum's ignorance would be a liability. When Stimson and Marshall finally fell out with Drum over their many differences, Marshall proposed Stilwell in his place.[2]

Marshall had served with Stilwell in the 15th Infantry at Tianjin and at the Infantry School at Fort Benning, and was well aware of his expertise on China, as well as his personal and professional strengths and weaknesses. In a letter about him in 1944, Marshall wrote:

> Frankly, I have found him uniformly through long years of personal command relations, irritating and intolerant of slow motion, excessive caution, and cut-and-dried procedure. On the other hand, he will provide tremendous energy, courage, and unlimited ingenuity and imagination to any aggressive proposals or operations. His mind is far more alert than almost any of our generals and his training and understanding are on an unusually high level. Impatience with conservatism and slow motion is his weakness.[3]

In contrast to Drum's egotism, when Marshall asked Stilwell if he would accept the job, he simply said, "I'll go where I'm sent." Marshall directed him to proceed immediately to the Far East. He hoped that in addition to taking up duties as Chiang's chief of staff he could smooth out relations between the British and Chinese in Burma. There was a long history of antipathy between the two countries. Since the Opium Wars of the nineteenth century, imperial Britain had taken advantage of China's political chaos to gain special privileges and territorial concessions. Despite this, Chiang offered to help reinforce Burma in the face of the Japanese threat, if for no other reason than to keep the road open to China. The British responded with haughty contempt. Sir Archibald Wavell, British Commander-in-Chief in India, refused Chiang's offer, but was more than willing to plunder Chinese lend-lease supplies from the docks at Rangoon. The result was a diplomatic deadlock that played into Japanese hands.[4]

Stilwell assembled his staff, many of whom had also served as language officers in China. This included Major Frank Dorn, his aide. Dorn had dark blonde hair, blue eyes, and often a rather mischievous look. He was studying in China when Stilwell was the military attaché there and he very much appreciated the latter's outlook and temperament. Both Stilwell and Dorn hated "stuffed shirt" politicians and generals. When, much to his own surprise, Stilwell became a general in 1939, he approached the topic carefully with Dorn. "I know damned well what you think of generals," he began. "They're a lot of stuffed shirts and ..." Dorn interrupted in embarrassed protest, but Stilwell silenced him with a wave of the hand. "Let me finish," he insisted. "I don't think too highly of generals myself. Furthermore, I know what you think of aides—generals' aides, that is—nothing but door openers, coat holders, and tea hounds."

"I sure do," Dorn replied, feeling confident on this point. "A lot of boot-licking fancy-Dans."

"Well," said Stilwell, "I see that we pretty much agree on just how useless most generals and aides really are."

"Aides in particular," Dorn said helpfully.

"Okay," Stilwell said after a short pause, "how would you like to be my aide-de-camp?" Dorn was flabbergasted. He stumbled and stammered a few words of awkward protest, but Stilwell stopped him. "How's this for a proposition," he said. "I'll be a new kind of general and you be a new kind of aide. We might make a pretty good team on that basis."[5]

More than two years later, Dorn was still the general's aide and boarded the airplane in Miami with him and the rest of his staff. They departed the United States on February 13, 1942—twenty-four days after the Japanese invaded Burma. They arrived in India on February 24—only ten days before the fall of Rangoon. Stilwell conferred with the British staff in New Delhi and then travelled to China. On the morning of March 4, he met with Chennault in Kunming. He intended to induct the mercenary AVG into the U.S. Army and was nervous the grizzled old airman would not agree with him, nor recognize his authority. To his relief, Chennault assented. In his diary he wrote: "To airfield to wait for Chennault. Had a talk. He'll be OK. Met a group of pilots, they look damn good."[6]

Stilwell continued on to Chongqing for several days of meetings and conferences about Burma. By this time, the situation was critical. If the Japanese completed their conquest of Burma, not only would they cut off China, but they would be in the perfect position to invade India. If they invaded India, they could link up with the Germans pushing from North Africa through the Middle East. It was a nightmare scenario that appeared all the more likely after the Japanese brushed aside the British troops defending Rangoon. Wavell in India and General Harold Alexander, the British field commander in Burma, finally requested Chinese help. Chiang sent an expeditionary force of nine divisions from the 5th, 6th, and 66th armies. It was the first sortie abroad of a Chinese army since the Sino-Japanese War in the 1890s. Chiang did not trust the British and relations were still strained. On March 11, he finally told Stilwell to go down and take charge. "I told those army commanders not to take orders from anybody but you and to wait until you came," he said. Arranging things as best he could in China, Stilwell departed for Burma.[7]

The China-Burma-India Theater stretched from the Arabian Sea to the east coast of China—an area greater than the entire United States. The ports at Karachi, Bombay, and Calcutta—through which Allied war material had to flow after the fall of Rangoon—were twelve thousand miles from North America. Burma itself was larger than Texas. Rugged, jungle-covered mountains split the country into three roughly parallel north-south valleys: that of the Salween River in the east, the Sittang River in the center, and the Irrawaddy River in the west. The rough terrain made east-west travel very difficult. By mid-March, the fighting was one hundred miles north of Rangoon. Two British divisions—the 1st Burma and the 17th Indian—held at Prome, in the Irrawaddy Valley. Eighty miles to the east, the elite Chinese 200th Division, under the command of Dai Anlan, held at Taungoo, in the Sittang Valley. The rest of the Chinese 5th Army was still hundreds of miles to the rear. The 6th Army was moving forward along the Salween River through the Shan states toward the Thai border in eastern Burma. Two divisions of the 66th Army held at the China-Burma border while the third slowly made its way toward Mandalay.[8]

Stilwell wanted to use all three divisions of the 5th Army and two divisions of the 66th to oppose the Japanese at Taungoo, but the Chinese were slow to move forward and Chiang pressured him to make a stand at Mandalay instead, two hundred miles to the rear. Chiang was a notorious micromanager. Even though he instructed Stilwell to take command of the Chinese Expeditionary Force in Burma, he continued to issue orders of his own. It was confusing for the Chinese troops. Stilwell ordered them forward to Taungoo. Chiang ordered them to concentrate at Mandalay. Meanwhile, the Japanese 15th Army, under the command of Lieutenant General Shojiro Iida, had four divisions devoted to the conquest of Burma. Lieutenant General Genzo Yanagida's 33rd Division drove up the Irrawaddy Valley toward Prome. Lieutenant General Yutaka Takeuchi's 55th Division drove up the Sittang Valley toward Taungoo. Lieutenant Generals Sukezo Matsuyama and Renya Mutaguchi commanded the 56th and 18th divisions, respectively, and held in reserve.[9]

Yang Chi-kuo was a lieutenant with a tank platoon assigned to the 200th Division. As the fighting raged at Taungoo, his unit was strung out along the road from Kunming to Lashio. Yang was the son of a shop owner in Wuchang, Hubei Province. His father died when he was a child, leaving his mother to raise him alone. "This was very difficult for a woman at that period of time in China," he recalled. When violence flared up after the Marco Polo Bridge Incident in 1937, he decided he wanted to serve his

Yang Chi-kuo was a lieutenant with one of the 200th Division's tank regiments. He was a veteran of the epic Battle of Kunlun Pass, when the 200th stopped a Japanese advance aimed at Nanning. His regiment deployed to Burma and evacuated back to China without meeting the enemy in combat. *Courtesy of Samuel Hui.*

country against the Japanese. He was in high school. He passed the exam to join the 5th Regiment of the Military Police, but since he was the only boy in the family, his mother refused to let him go. Without her knowledge, he secretly took the exam to join the Chinese armored corps. He passed and joined the 200th Division. The 200th was the only mechanized division in the Chinese Army. Two of its four regiments were tank regiments.

After basic training, Yang moved to Xiangtan, Hunan Province, where Chinese and Russian instructors taught him the basics of armored warfare. "Before driving a tank, we were trained how to drive regular cars," he remembered. "Since we did not have enough gas for training, eleven trainees from our twelve-man squad would have to push the car while one of them drove with the instructor next to him." Yang completed training in April 1938 and joined 1st Platoon, 3rd Company, of the 1st Battalion. He became a technical sergeant and served as the driver for the platoon leader's Fiat tank. As with every branch of the Chinese military, the armored corps had a hodgepodge of equipment, including the Italian Fiat, the Russian T-26, and the French Rennault. The main battle tank in the Chinese Army was the T-26, which had a 45-millimeter cannon and three machine guns. The Fiat did not have a cannon, only machine guns, but it had better armor than the T-26 and was therefore assigned to the platoon leader. "It was a very old tank," remembered Yang, "and I still remember that we had to start the engine with our hands." By the time the 200th Division deployed to Burma in 1942, Yang was a veteran of the battles of Shanggao and Kunlun Pass and had risen to the rank of second lieutenant. His unit drove from Kunming to Lashio on the Burma Road and loaded their tanks onto a British train bound for Pyinmana, sixty miles north of Taungoo.[10]

The Russian T-26 was the main battle tank of the Chinese Army in 1942. It had one 45-millimeter cannon and three machine guns. *National Archives via Samuel Hui*

The Fiat Tank in Chinese service. It did not have a cannon like the T-26, but was assigned to the platoon leader because of its heavier armor. *National Archives via Samuel Hui*

The Japanese increased the pressure at Taungoo. The 56th Division marched almost two hundred miles in three days to join the 55th in pushing the Chinese back to the walled city. Often visiting the front with Stilwell, Frank Dorn witnessed the action: "As the battle seesawed back and forth, the enemy succeeded in taking a corner of the wall," he wrote, "but on the same day were dislodged by a savage hand-to-hand fight."[11] On March 26, the Japanese 112th Regiment entered the city. The fighting became increasingly desperate. Dai Anlan asked to withdraw his division. In a telegram to Du Yuming, commander of the 5th Army, he wrote, "I am willing to die in Taungoo, but what is the value in this?" The Japanese remembered the battle as the most difficult of the campaign. The Chinese fought resolutely, but could not stem the overwhelming tide of the enemy advance. After three days' hard fighting in the city, Dai managed to withdraw his division intact.[12]

Stilwell saw an opportunity to use the 200th Division's skillful retreat to get the other Chinese divisions into the fight and surprise the Japanese. The 22nd Division, under the command of Liao Yaoxiang, arrived at the front too late to save Taungoo, but now its troops threw themselves between the Japanese and the 200th. Stilwell decided to have the 22nd make a fighting withdrawal toward Pyinmana, where the Chinese tanks and the 96th Division were already arriving and to where the 200th could fall back and reassemble. The 22nd would then draw the Japanese into a massive counterattack by all three divisions. It would be the hallmark of classic Stilwell, a swift, unexpected flanking attack to win the battle in a single stroke. The thing that bothered him most about the plan though, was that it depended on the British holding in the Irrawaddy Valley to the west. His liaison officer to the British Army—tall, heavyset, and bespectacled Major Frank Merrill—warned, "Things don't look too good at Prome ... The troops are scared to death of Jap road blocks. Their morale is shot to hell." He was right. On April 6, the British announced they would withdraw toward Yenangyaung, over one hundred miles north. "Good Christ!" exclaimed Stilwell. "After only one day's half-hearted defense? That leaves the Chinese flank wide open." The trap at Pyinmana was no longer feasible. The Japanese chased the retreating British and at midnight on April 16, struck the 1st Burma Division at Yenangyaung.[13]

Chiang still wanted to marshal his forces for a decisive battle at Mandalay, but General Alexander sent a frantic plea for the Chinese to help his troops at Yenangyaung. They were completely surrounded and were running short of water and supplies. Sun Liren, commander of the Chinese 38th Division, 66th Army, rushed to their aid. His men attacked on the morning of April 18. Over the next two days, they bravely engaged the Japanese in bloody combat and pushed them back. The confusion gave the British enough time to escape. Unfortunately, even as the Chinese rushed to help the British, the Japanese struck a mortal blow in the east. From Taungoo, the 56th Division veered east—cross country—and broke through the lines along the Thai border, virtually destroying two divisions of the Chinese 6th Army and opening the road to Lashio. Du Yuming ordered the 200th Division east to stem the tide, but it was too late. On April 18, Stilwell recorded in his diary, "All our plans knocked to pieces."[14]

Yang Chi-kuo's tank platoon never made it to Pyinmana. When the rout became apparent, they withdrew before ever meeting the enemy in battle. They joined a flood of British and Chinese soldiers fleeing the front lines. Lashio was in flames when they passed through on their way back to China. Local partisans eager to be rid of their British colonial masters set fires and performed acts of sabotage. They did not yet know they were trading one colonial regime for another, much more brutal administration. Yang's tanks crossed the Huitong Bridge on April 28. "There were a lot of people and vehicles jammed on the Burma Road," he remembered. "If a vehicle turned off its engine, Chinese soldiers pushed it off the road… it was chaos." His unit made it back to Kunming without any losses. They deployed to Burma and withdrew without seeing any action. "We were very lucky," Yang recalled. The two other tank companies deployed to support the division at Taungoo took heavy losses.[15]

As the British fell back from Yenangyaung, Stilwell had no choice but to pull the Chinese troops at Pyinmana back eighty miles north to Meiktila, then seventy-eight miles further north to Mandalay, and finally fifty miles northwest to Shwebo. According to Dorn: "With that plan blown sky high, once the momentum of retreat got under way, there was no stopping it."[16] The north-south geography of Burma meant that when Lashio fell on April 29, it blocked the troops at Shwebo from retreating into China. Six divisions of the Chinese Army reached Yunnan, including the two divisions of the 66th Army still moving along the Burma Road between Kunming and Lashio, three divisions of the 6th Army falling back from the Thai border, and most of the 200th Division, though Dai Anlan was mortally wounded; Gao Jiren, the deputy division commander, took over in his stead. Sun Liren's 38th Division retreated from Yenangyaung with the British into India. Stilwell decided to make a last stand with the 22nd and 96th divisions at Myitkyina, 220 miles north of Shwebo.[17]

Colonel Caleb Haynes—a veteran pilot and commander of the Assam-Burma-China Ferry Command—landed a C-53 (a troop transport version of the DC-3) at Shwebo on the twenty-ninth to evacuate Stilwell and his staff. Stilwell refused. "I'm going to Myikyina," he announced. "That is where most of the Chinese troops will be, and I belong with them." He selected those members of his staff he felt would not be physically capable of making the arduous trek to North Burma to depart with Haynes. When the overloaded transport finally struggled off the field, only twelve men remained behind. Among them were Colonel George Sliney, an artillery officer who had been part of the American Military Mission to China prior to Stilwell's arrival and then became a liaison to the Chinese 5th and 6th armies; Major Frank Merrill, Stilwell's liaison to the British, who had lived in Japan as a language officer and had come to Burma from the Philippines after Pearl Harbor; and of course Frank Dorn, Stilwell's aide. "As we turned away, a strange feeling of loneliness swept over me," Dorn recalled. "I wondered if I'd ever see those men in the plane again."

"Well that's over," Stilwell said simply once the plane was out of sight. "Now to work."[18]

Stilwell's party started north from Shwebo the morning of May 1. Besides the twelve members of his staff, there were twelve other American officers and enlisted men; one American reporter; a missionary; Dr. Gordon Seagrave, an American medical missionary who attached himself to the Chinese Army after the Japanese invasion, along with another doctor and nineteen Burmese nurses; sixteen Chinese guards; seven British Quakers from an ambulance unit; twenty British officers and civilians; and nine Burmese, Indian, and Malayan cooks and porters. Several days later they were joined by fifteen British commandos. From the dozen members of his staff that watched the plane disappear from the runway, Stilwell's group swelled to 114 refugees. He was determined to bring them all to safety.[19]

The way ahead was not easy. Stilwell complained of the "bitch of a 'road'" from Shwebo.[20] It was covered in dust and rocks and deeply rutted from decades of use by bullock carts. The throng of retreating British and Chinese kept the pace excruciatingly slow. Abandoned carts and wrecked trucks littered the roadside. Dorn remembered: "Motor transport, no longer able to run, was pushed into ditches or overturned. Trucks lay on their sides, sprawling like great wounded beasts with bellies exposed, their upraised wheels slowly spinning."[21] Major Merrill led the party in a jeep. Following him was Stilwell's sedan—driven by the recently-promoted Lieutenant Colonel Dorn—two other sedans, several jeeps, and several trucks carrying Seagrave's unit.

The pace improved somewhat when the British traffic turned west toward Kalewa and Stilwell's party and the Chinese continued north. Traffic improved, but the road got worse. According to Dorn, "Shortly after leaving Pinde, the route became no more than the barest excuse for a road." Finally, on May 4, they emerged onto a paved highway that carried them into Kawlin, eighty-five miles north of Shwebo. From there, Stilwell hoped to take the railway north to Myitkyina, but a wrecked train blocked the line. They would have to keep to the roads for the time being.[22] In his diary Stilwell wrote: "reconnoitered Katha Road for an hour. Looked good. We'll go that way."[23] They made steady progress, but Colonel Holcombe—leading the party from Merrill's jeep—took a wrong turn and they went six miles out of their way before anyone realized it. Driving through a muddy draw, Stilwell's sedan got stuck. "To hell with it!" he exclaimed. "You've put it in the soup for good, Dorn. There's no time to fool with it. Probably wouldn't get much farther anyway. Set it on fire." One of the officers fired his pistol into the gas tank and it erupted in flames. Dorn admitted to getting lost several times. "That maze of side trails simply invited errors," he wrote. They finally got back on the proper route and after twelve miles of decent road, arrived at a British bungalow at 2030.[24]

On May 5, the party continued on to Meza, thirty-three miles northeast of Kawlin, where they found the bridge was out. Stilwell and Dorn, both of whom spoke Mandarin, managed to convince a group of Chinese Army engineers to make temporary repairs. They crossed and continued ten miles to In Daw. Again, they hoped to find a train northward, but the railway was hopelessly jammed. They continued by road. In Man Si, twelve miles northeast of In Daw, they learned the Japanese were already on the Bhamo-Myitkyina Road. It was unlikely they could make it to Myitkyina by any mode of travel before it was occupied. In fact, the Japanese took the town only three days later, on the eighth.[25] Burma was lost. Stilwell gave up his hope of organizing a defense at Myitkyina. His new focus was to make it out alive. The only chance for his disparate group of refugees was to reach the old British fort at Imphal, in the Manipur Province of East India. The manager of a teak company in Man Si gave them a map and advised they head one hundred miles northwest to Homalin, on the Chindwin River. "After you reach the west side of the Chindwin, General, there's a good trail over the mountains to Imphal," he told them. "But it's very steep most of the way. Very steep indeed, sir." The party had to abandon their trucks soon after entering the jungle outside Man Si. A native guide led them on foot and the few remaining jeeps followed behind.[26] They sent a request via radio for help and supplies to meet them at Homalin. The batteries were dying. "This is our last message," they reported. Then they smashed the radio with an ax and burned their code books.[27]

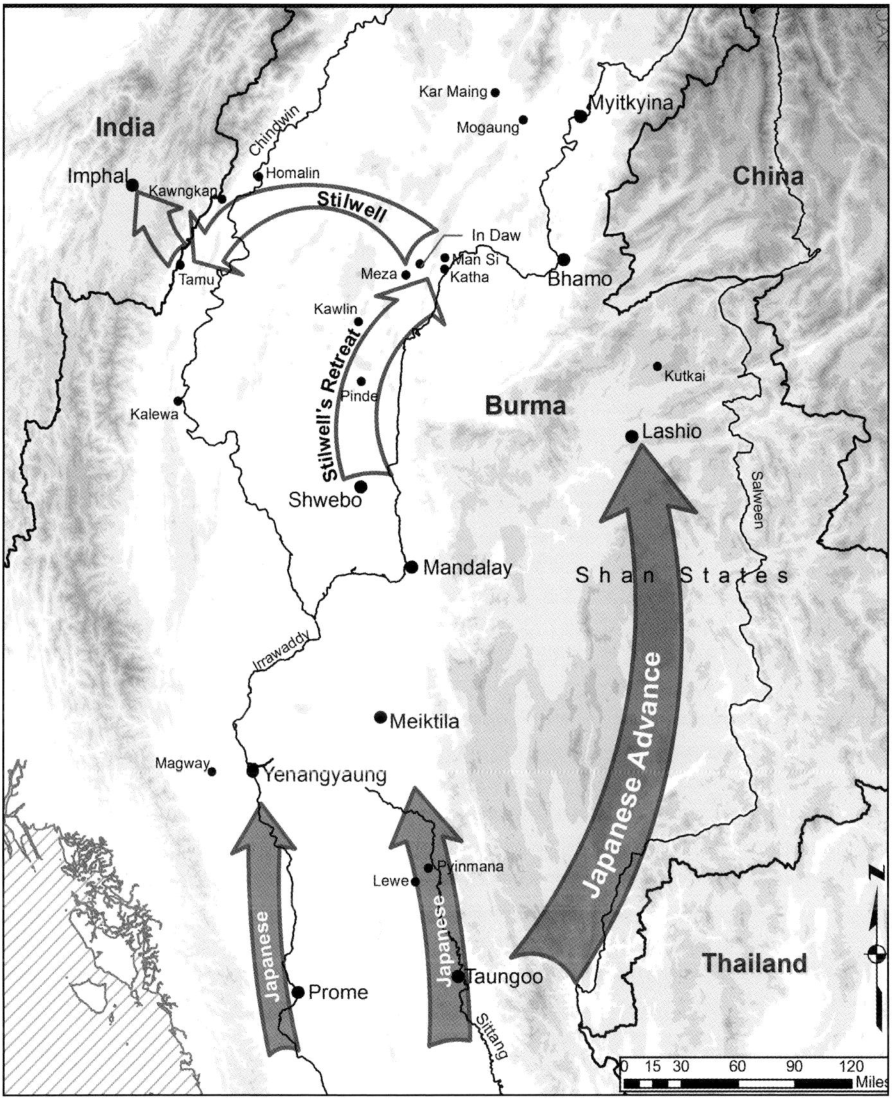

Stilwell's Walkout

It was tough going. They had to ration their supplies. Most everybody walked. One by one the jeeps broke down. Luckily, within a few days the party came across two Chinese men leading a string of mules. They promptly requisitioned the pack train to carry their supplies. When they arrived at the Uyu River, they fashioned thirteen rafts to float west to Homalin. Most of the party was exhausted and Stilwell hoped floating the river would provide a welcome reprieve from the endless march. An RAF transport plane sighted them on the river and made a supply drop. It was an encouraging sign. On May 12, Stilwell wrote: "mountains now in plain view." They arrived at Homalin at noon that day. It was nearly deserted. There was no one to meet them there. Their spirits sank. After a lengthy search, they found a Burmese clerk who agreed to find them a way across the Chindwin the next day. That night they hiked to a village about three miles away, where they slept on the concrete floor of a Buddhist temple.[28]

The next morning, Stilwell led them to the banks of the Chindwin. They waited for some time, nervous that nothing would appear to ferry them across. Finally, five dugout canoes and a small freight boat came into view around the bend to the north. The clerk was true to his word. According to Stilwell, from the west shore of the Chindwin they "took it easy over good trail, but the sissies are pooped out. They can't take it." By 1700 "everybody was tired and snappy," so they stopped and camped for the night.[29]

The next day's journey was even more taxing. They departed the campsite at 0715 and climbed steadily upward. Somehow, despite his age and slight frame, Stilwell led from the front, pushing onward, never faltering. According to Dorn, he was "a solid rock, a torch of leadership and example … a soldier in the real sense, insistent on that understanding discipline which inspires men to fix their eyes on a goal."[30] The rest of the group struggled, wilting in the heat. They gasped for air at the steadily increasing altitude.[31] That evening they made it to Kawngkan, twenty-one miles southwest of Homalin, in pouring rain. Waiting for them were rations, doctors, pack animals, and

Stilwell began his epic walkout from Burma on May 1 and finally reached Imphal on the twentieth. His group swelled to 114 refugees, all of whom he brought out to safety. Here, he leads the column in his characteristic World War I campaign hat. Frank Dorn is following right behind him. ***Hoover Institution***

Exhausted, members of Stilwell's party take a break during the walkout. From left to right are Major Paul Jones, Lieutenant Colonel Frank Merrill, Colonel Robert Williams, and Colonel Adrian St. John. ***Hoover Institution***

Tim Sharpe, a thirty-one year old tall, blond, blue-eyed British guide who was to escort them the rest of the way to Imphal. For Stilwell it was "quite a relief."[32] Sharpe told them about the recent fall of the Philippines and that while many of the Chinese troops made it to the Salween, most of the 5th Army retreated toward India through the Hukawng Valley, in North Burma. Scores of men perished battling disease, starvation, and monsoon rains in the hostile jungle. Of the forty-two thousand soldiers from the 5th Army that deployed to Burma, 7,300 died in battle. More than twice that number died retreating though the Hukawng Valley. American reconnaissance planes eventually located several groups and Allied transports airdropped over two hundred tons of supplies. Though unorthodox at the time, air supply kept the Chinese from completely wasting away in the jungles of North Burma. Still, less than half of the 5th Army made it out alive.[33]

On May 15, Sharpe led Stilwell's group up the Manipur Hills, passing from the humid jungle into the cooler highlands. "The cream puffs are doing better," Stilwell noted in his diary. Naga tribesmen came out to greet the party as they passed through each village. The Nagas were rumored to be cannibals and headhunters, but Sharpe was familiar with them and they were friendly to Stilwell's party. Sharpe's knowledge of the area and the supplies he sent forward when he first set out to find Stilwell proved crucial.[34]

Later that day, when the front of the column reached the top of a high ridge, Sharpe stopped and turned to Stilwell. "General, you're on the international line right now," he told him, "Burma to the rear, India ahead." Stilwell paused, leaning on his tommy gun and looking over the mountains of East India, catching his breath. He turned to Dorn and said, "Might as well let the column catch up with us."

"If that's India," Dorn said disappointedly, "It doesn't look any different from Burma to me."

"To me either," Stilwell said smiling. "But I don't suppose any border areas look different at their boundary lines. That is, unless men build a fence or a wall." They stood thoughtfully for a moment.

"General," said Dorn. "As we cross the line, you ought to make some world shaking statement for future quotation."

"Ok Dorn," Stilwell answered. "How about, 'the higher a monkey climbs, the more you see of his backside?' That's to the point, and it fits the pickle I'm in right now."

"I was thinking of something more like Caesar's 'The die is cast' when he crossed the Rubicon," Dorn told him.

"All right, mine will be 'The dice was loaded.' Now let's see you send that gem charging down through the pages of history."[35] With that, Stilwell stood upright and continued onward. Though Imphal was due west, they turned south, through the rough terrain of the Naga country. On May 19, they arrived at Tamu, a British outpost forty miles southwest of Kawngkan. Tamu was connected by road to Imphal, fifty miles to the northwest. Seven trucks arrived for them the next day. It had rained all night and the road to Imphal was a muddy quagmire. "A road in name only," Dorn wrote. "No more than a half-flooded route across the flat valley." When they finally arrived at Imphal's old stone fort, they learned that the Japanese had been in Homalin for a week, arriving just after they passed through. The next day, they went by truck to Dimapur and boarded a train for Dinjan. There, Stilwell conferred with his staff and with the British commanders Wavell and Alexander. Lewis Brereton, commander of the new India-based U.S. 10th Air Force, then flew them in his personal C-53 to New Delhi.[36]

Stepping off the airplane at 1630 on May 24, Stilwell was met by a flock of newsmen and photographers. He pushed through the crowd, telling them he would hold a press conference later that evening. Arriving at the Imperial Hotel, Stilwell and his staff washed up. Stepping on the scale, Dorn discovered he weighed only 118 pounds—thirty-two pounds less than when he left Shwebo. Stilwell had lost twenty pounds.[37]

At 1900, the press gathered for the promised conference. American, British, and Indian correspondents crowded into the room. Stilwell walked briskly to the podium. He stood straight and alert, but Dorn thought that beneath it all, he looked tired and ill. He began taking questions. After about an hour, a British correspondent caught his attention and began asking about the terms Wavell and Alexander used to describe the disaster in Burma: "an heroic, voluntary withdrawal, and a glorious retreat." Stilwell quickly cut him off. "In the first place," he said angrily, "no military commander in history ever made a voluntary withdrawal. And there's no such thing as a glorious retreat. All retreats are ignoramus as hell. I claim we got a hell of a beating. We got run out of Burma and it's humiliating as hell. I think we ought to find out what caused it, go back and retake it." With that, he abruptly ended the press conference and left the room.[38]

The U.S. press gave the conference a positive spin. The newspapers on May 26 described Stilwell as "Still full of fight after a 'hell of a beating,' in Burma and a weary march of 140 miles through wild Burmese jungles." That same day, Stilwell penned a letter to his wife, telling her "everything O.K." despite the fact that he was "a little underweight.... To be quite truthful I look a good deal like the guy in the medical book with his skin off, showing the next layer of what you have." He reassured her he was "eating it on again fast." He cautioned her about the news articles: "We had quite a trip, which I suppose will now be exaggerated, as usual, till it's unrecognizable." As far as he was concerned, his only achievement was getting his entire party out alive. He did not lose a single one, though Merrill suffered a mild heart attack. Stilwell told his wife that he was "damn glad to get my gang out of the jungle," though "most of them now consider me more of a mean old s.o.b. than ever."[39]

In marked contrast to the American press, Chennault thought Stilwell's walkout was completely irresponsible. Though he admitted it was "an amazing feat of physical endurance for a man nearing sixty," he believed Stilwell left the Chinese armies "to shift for themselves" and remained incommunicado for three weeks "while the fate of China teetered precariously on the rim of the Salween gorge." When Stilwell refused to evacuate Shwebo in Haynes' C-53, he considered his primary responsibility to lead his staff to safety—ideally to Myitkyina, where he hoped to organize a defense. He thought if he allowed Haynes to fly him out, it would be "one more defeat, one more surrender. I could not command the Chinese again."[40] Chennault thought he should have evacuated to China or India, from either of which "he would have been in a position to direct the reorganization of Chinese resistance wherever the need was most acute." Chennault thought Stilwell's actions were appropriate for a company, battalion, or regimental commander, but "for a man with the tremendous burden of the ranking American officer in Asia and Chief of Staff of the Chinese Republic, it was a startling exhibition of his ignorance or disregard for these larger responsibilities." Chennault penned these words after the war, influenced by years of bitter feud, but he marked the point as significant. According to him, after the debacle in Burma, Chiang questioned Stilwell's judgment and never again fully trusted him with Chinese troops.[41] The misgivings were mutual. Stilwell did not understand why Chiang put him in command, only to issue contradictory orders. He felt betrayed. The seeds of mistrust were sown, and not just between Chiang and Stilwell. Both men resented the British for abandoning their positions and leaving the Chinese to fight by themselves. The rout in Burma left a dark cloud over the Allies at a time when they most needed to stand together. The road ahead would not be easy, but infighting and dissension could make it impossible.

3

Enemy Occupation

While Stilwell walked out through the jungles of Burma and the Chinese troops and AVG fought the Japanese in the Salween River gorge, the people of western Yunnan faced the terrible new reality of living under enemy occupation. The area was no stranger to conflict, but the deprivations of the Japanese were particularly harsh. For the local people it was a nightmare—a struggle for survival. Women hid in the hills, village leaders created guerilla groups to fight the Japanese, and young men escaped east to join the Chinese Army. All hoped someday for salvation. To the rest of Free China, the Japanese thrust into Yunnan was like a knife cutting through the last ropes of their bridge to the outside world. While the Salween River acted as a barrier, keeping the enemy from getting in, it could also be seen as the wall of a prison in which the Japanese hoped to contain China until it withered and died. In the chaotic months following the defeat in Burma, the United States threw a precarious lifeline over this barrier in the form of an airlift. It was a small ray of light shining into an otherwise dark, doubtful future.

The confused fighting west of the Salween continued for several months after the Chinese Army and AVG stopped the 56th Division. Having lost their forward momentum, the Japanese focused on consolidating their positions. They fanned out to capture the towns and villages north and south of the Burma Road. Lu Caiwen grew up in Tengchong and witnessed the Japanese invasion as a teenager. "For several days everything was in chaos," he remembered. "Some wounded soldiers of the Chinese Army and civilians who fled Burma took refuge in the city."[1] Long Chunwu—Superintendent of the Tengchong Frontier Zone and son of Long Yun, the governor of Yunnan—had three battalions of provincial troops—one thousand men in all—at his disposal. He ordered them to retreat. They looted all the jade, silk, opium, and artwork they could carry and then departed, leaving the people of Tengchong to fend for themselves. The people felt betrayed. The "warlord soldiers" had bullied and taxed them, but when the enemy came, they disappeared without firing a shot. Qiu Tianpei, the county magistrate, also fled.[2]

It was by no means the first time western Yunnan bore witness to the horrors of war. Throughout history, the region saw several rebellions by ethnic minorities and civil wars during the transitions between Chinese dynasties. In 1277, during the reign of Kublai Khan, the King of Mien invaded from central Burma with an army mounted on elephants. Mongol archers joined with local militia to defeat the intruders in a savage battle. "Right fiercely did the two hosts rush together," wrote Marco Polo. "God might have thundered and no man would have heard it!"[3] After the Opium Wars in the nineteenth century, both Britain and France sought to expand their influence in Yunnan. They encroached on the border—the British from Burma and the French from Indochina—and forced trade concessions, including the construction of the Hanoi-Kunming Railroad.

Civil war, rebellion, elephant-borne expeditions, and imperial intrigue—the Japanese invasion in 1942 was of an entirely different nature. Never before had a foreign army made such a forceful and determined assault. With the provincial troops in full retreat, a detachment of only three hundred Japanese soldiers stormed Tengchong on May 10, 1942. "We could hear the Japanese shouting and firing guns," remembered Lu. "We didn't know what to do or where to hide." He saw soldiers wearing steel helmets. "Chinese soldiers didn't wear steel helmets," he said. "The Japanese had arrived."[4] The Nationalist Army tried to send help. On May 15, the 2nd Reserve Division crossed the Salween and set up headquarters at Jietou, thirty miles north of Tengchong in the Shweli Valley. The division advanced to the south and west, but its poorly-equipped troops could not hope to push back the Japanese. In desperation, they fought a savage guerrilla campaign, taking every opportunity to harass and annoy the enemy. Local fighters joined with the 2nd Division troops in a few sharp actions around the villages of Lunma and Danzha, thirty miles northwest of Tengchong near the Burma border. Mr. Guo, a resident of Lunma, was eleven years old in 1942. He witnessed a fierce battle in which he saw local guerrillas and Chinese troops fight side by side against the invaders. But despite their every effort, the 2nd Division was outnumbered and overwhelmed. Ultimately, the Japanese pushed them back across the Salween.[5]

Zhang Wende was the elderly magistrate of Tengchong. With thinning white hair and a wispy beard, he looked like an old Confucian sage. His frail exterior belied an indomitable spirit. When his superiors fled, he remained with the people, leading them into hiding in the mountains north of the city. The Japanese captured a town empty of people and provisions. Having advanced so quickly up the Burma Road, they had outpaced their supply lines and were desperate for food. They were also eager to exact revenge on the Chinese—especially after enduring the stubborn guerrilla attacks of the 2nd Division. Magistrate Zhang recounted how in the wake of the fighting, patrols of Japanese soldiers terrorized the countryside. They plundered rural villages of rice and grain. They took any chickens, cows, pigs, and other livestock they could find from local farmers. They tortured and killed any persons suspected of being guerrillas or spies, and many others besides. Japanese soldiers often competed with each other to devise creative ways to kill the Chinese. Sometimes they would tie them to trees and practice bayoneting them until they bled to death. All the pent up rage they harbored from months of hard fighting in Malaya, Singapore, Burma, and southwest China they took out on the people.

Most of the residents of Danzha fled as soon as they heard the Japanese were coming. One man tried to escape after they occupied the village. Enemy soldiers caught him and bayonetted him to death. They forced another man by the name of Bao Cai to cook for them. They bayonetted him to death as well after he accidentally dropped a cooking pot. In Lunma, the Japanese accused the locals of aiding the Chinese guerrillas. They set the village on fire as punishment. All forty houses burned to ashes. In Bapai, eight miles southwest of Tengchong, a patrol of twenty Japanese soldiers came to steal horses. According to Mr. Li, who was ten years old at the time, "We were poor and had nothing valuable but the horses, so they just took our horses away." While this was going on, the soldiers came across a sixty year old woman who was too old to run away. A few of them decided to rape her. According to Li, "She resisted and screamed. Her old husband tried to save her, but both of them were killed." Sadly, this sort of incident was not uncommon. Theodore White, a correspondent for *Time Magazine*, wrote: "In some of the districts through which I passed, every woman caught by the Japanese had been raped without exception. The tales of rape were so sickeningly alike that they were monotonous unless they were relieved by some particular device of fiendishness."[6]

The horrific violence was only the beginning. Determined to hold what they had gained, the Japanese conscripted townspeople and farmers to help them build fortifications. Afterward, they shot some of these conscripts to prevent them from giving information to the Chinese Army. They shot workers who tried to escape the labor gangs.[7] Li Zhengzao—a civilian who lived near Songshan, between Longling and the Huitong Bridge site—remembered being forced to work in a labor detail. In his case, the Japanese did not allow the workers near the elaborate defenses they constructed. "You could see nothing," said Li. "They asked us to help them carry boxes… We worked for four or five months. We carried boxes every night. When we carried boxes to the mountain pass, we were stopped. Japanese soldiers took over the boxes and carried them away." In some areas, the Japanese imported workers from Burma to keep the Chinese from learning about their fortifications. Likewise, they sent Chinese workers to help build fortifications in Burma.[8]

The campaign of terror and exploitation forced the civilians to take measures to protect themselves. Magistrate Zhang formed guerrilla groups throughout the countryside, as did Sun Chengxiao, Na Qizhong, and Liu Chongshan, all of whom became famous resistance leaders. These "self-defense brigades" harassed the Japanese any time their patrols ventured into the countryside and warned villagers of approaching foraging or punitive expeditions. On a few occasions, they killed dozens of Japanese soldiers in elaborate ambushes. On one particular raid, Sun, Na, and Liu's groups joined forces to inflict an estimated forty-two casualties on the enemy. Unlike many guerrilla groups across Europe and even elsewhere in Asia, the partisans in western Yunnan received almost no outside assistance. What they did, they did on their own. It was their own initiative carried out with their own meager resources.[9]

The brutality of Japan's occupation of western Yunnan was consistent with the reputation its Army had built for itself since the Rape of Nanjing in 1937. My understanding of these atrocities was purely academic until I visited the Nanjing Massacre Memorial in 2008. Some of the mass graves of murdered Chinese civilians had been partially excavated and I could see the piles of human skeletons stacked several feet high. Some child-sized skulls were crushed, apparently smashed in by the butts of Japanese rifles. Other bones were scarred by the sharp blades of bayonets. The International Military Tribunal of the Far East estimated that at least 260,000 people died in six weeks of terror at Nanjing. That is more than died in the atomic bombings of Hiroshima and Nagasaki combined. Some in Japan deny these atrocities, but the evidence is as overwhelming and undeniable as is that of the Holocaust in Europe. Some of the most damning testimony can be found in the wartime journals of the Japanese troops themselves or in Japanese newspapers, which covered the atrocities as if they were sporting events.[10]

The cruelty of the Japanese was self-defeating. Their atrocities only served to encourage further resistance. Eventually, they attempted to improve their image by putting a Chinese face on their administration. They set up a puppet government for occupied Yunnan in Longling and hired mercenary Chinese to police the countryside in "security brigades." It was similar to the lackey regime under the traitor Wang Jingwei in Nanjing. They found allies in some of the local elites who formed "preservation associations," called *weichihui* (维持会), which sought to maintain order by cooperating with the occupation. Cooperation and collaboration were not black-and-white issues. Motivations ranged from the purely selfish, to those desperately hoping to prevent another "Rape of Nanjing." The Japanese also reopened schools and made attendance mandatory. They replaced the Chinese curriculum with propaganda promoting the "Greater East Asia Co-Prosperity Sphere." To contain the sexual depravity of their troops, they brought in hundreds of "comfort women," a sick euphemism for girls forced into prostitution. These women were often taken from their homes in Korea, Taiwan, and other occupied territories to live a life of sexual slavery. Each soldier in Tengchong had two vouchers a week to use at government brothels. Each woman had to sleep with an average of sixty soldiers per day.[11]

A Chinese guerrilla on the Salween Front. During the brutal Japanese occupation, local leaders such as Zhang Wende formed guerrilla groups to protect Chinese civilians and harass the enemy. ***Hoover Institution***

To force residents to return to Tengchong, the Japanese posted notices declaring that any house found empty would be burned to the ground. Many reluctantly returned to avoid losing everything they owned, though most of the women remained in hiding. The new policies were not successful at putting an end to the terror. The Japanese still required the puppet government to deliver quotas of workmen and food to their depots. If the quotas were not met, soldiers still marched into the countryside and pillaged what they needed. The puppet administration also forced Chinese farmers to plant tobacco and other cash crops, which they then heavily taxed to offset the expense of occupation. The result was a chronic food shortage. They also forced the subjugated peoples to use a paper currency printed by the Japanese Army. Everyone had to use it except for the Japanese soldiers, who continued to seize what they needed without payment. According to Mr. Sun, who was a boy of eleven in 1942, when a column of one thousand Japanese soldiers passed through his village, they "took everything edible from the villagers and … consumed most of our livestock." The policies decimated the local economy, which never fully recovered until well after the war.[12] The Japanese claimed to be following in the footsteps of Western colonialism. They were quickly proving to be the most brutal practitioners of an enterprise not known for its humanity.

In August 1943, the chief executive of the Japanese administration in Tengchong invited Magistrate Zhang to the city for negotiations. "I admired you so much that I came from far away to seek your wisdom," he wrote. Citing the "suffering of the people," he proposed the two of them sit down and talk about ways to "overcome our difficulties." He requested Zhang come without any weapons or armed escort. The old magistrate thought the invitation was an obvious trap. His written reply is immortalized on a stone monument at the military cemetery in Tengchong: "You propose to talk about easing the suffering of the people," he wrote, "but events ... have swept away the foundation on which I could give my consideration." He went on to explain to the executive the true nature of his peoples' suffering:

> Fathers have lost their sons. Wives have lost their husbands. People do not have shelter against the wind and rain and do not have any means of making a living. They are hungry and cold, waiting to die. Some have been enslaved by you and your men, beaten up or sent to be cannon fodder in Myitkyina. I would also mention the outrageous atrocities committed against our women. What blessings you have brought us! You seem at a loss as to how to deliver Tengchong and its people from misery and suffering. I, as a Chinese citizen and official, have no obligation to help you. To fulfill your so-called goodwill, I can only suggest you go back to Tokyo and stop harassing the people of Tengchong. Leave us alone. When justice is done, when we have normal relations, I will fly to Tokyo, without guards as you have required, and thank you for bringing an end to my peoples' suffering. I will even go to your Shrine to pray for your dead, hoping Heaven will forgive their crimes. However, if you remain here, please excuse my efforts to fight against your crimes. Soon you will not have such a favorable impression of Tengchong. The time will come when you will yield to my people. Therefore, with respect, I decline your suggestion to meet. I have more important matters to attend to. My people suffer, but we will deliver ourselves from suffering.

Zhang's reply reinforced his reputation as a legendary leader of Chinese resistance and became a rallying point for his oppressed countrymen. He would not negotiate. He would continue to fight.

Following Zhang's example, many of the young men in occupied Yunnan felt they must find some way to resist. Besides those that joined the guerrilla bands or self-defense brigades, many escaped across the Salween to join the Nationalist Army. Shao Ying-jen was twenty years old when the Japanese captured Tengchong. The fall of his hometown was another chapter in a life filled with tragedy. His father had died when he was three and his mother when he was ten. His two older brothers raised him and took care of him. When the Japanese invaded, they burned down Shao's family home and killed and ate all his mules and horses. He had nothing left to lose. He fled to Jietou, where he trained to be a political officer with the 2nd Reserve Division. After a month, the division sent him to the Cadre Training School in Dali, one hundred miles east of occupied Yunnan, for another year of training in regular and guerrilla warfare. He graduated as a lieutenant in 1943.[13]

Like Shao, Lu Caiwen fled east and took the entrance exam for the Huangpu Military Academy. The Academy was a prestigious institution. Chiang Kai-shek was famously its first commandant. Its rolls were filled with the names of prominent men who led both the Nationalist and Communist militaries during the Chinese Civil War and World War II. At one time, both He Yingqin, the Chinese Army Chief of Staff, and Zhou Enlai, future Premier of the People's Republic, were instructors there. Originally established in Guangzhou, the Academy relocated to Nanjing after Chiang's rise to power, and then to Chengdu after the Japanese captured Nanjing. In an echo of Dante's warning on the gates of Hell, a sign hung in front which read: "Enter not this gate, you who are afraid of death." Considering the many thousands of company grade officers that died in the war, it was not hyperbole.[11]

In August 1942, Chiang opened a branch of the Academy in Yunnan. "The

Liu Cheng-hua grew up in a rich peasant family in Hubei Province. After the Japanese invasion forced his family to flee, he decided to join the Chinese Army and attended the Huangpu Academy in Yunnan. He became an infantry officer in 1944. *Courtesy of Samuel Hui*.

Lu Caiwen at an interview with the author in 2009. Lu graduated from the Yunnan branch of the Huangpu Academy and became an intelligence officer, leading a plainclothes intelligence team behind enemy lines to Tengchong. *Courtesy of Anthony Mascaro*.

teaching was intense," remembered Lu. During the war, the course of study was compressed from the normal three years down to only one. One of Lu's classmates was Liu Cheng-hua. Liu was from a rich peasant family in Mianyang, Hubei Province. With the help of an uncle who was educated in Japan, he was able to attend elementary school in the city of Wuhan. The war began before he could finish; Wuhan fell to the Japanese in October 1938. Liu and his classmates escaped to Changsha under the guns of the Japanese air force. Later they moved to Enshi, where they continued their studies. En route to Changsha, Liu was approached by the Communists, who wanted to recruit him. "Since I was from a family of local elites," he related, "we were always told how terrible the Communists were when we were little." He declined their invitation. Instead, he joined the Youth League of the Three People's Principles, an organization dedicated to the ideals of Dr. Sun Yixian (Sun Yat-sen), the founding father of the Nationalist Republic and loyal to Chiang Kai-shek as his political heir. "For this reason, I believed what I was told to die for my country and leader," he explained.

Though Liu was from a wealthy family that could afford to exempt him from conscription, he decided that he wanted to serve. In 1941, he travelled to Hengyang to take the entrance exam for the Huangpu Academy. He passed and was assigned to the branch in Yunnan. "We spent about three months walking to Kunming from Hengyang," he remembered. "A lot of cadets starved to death en route." When the weary and emaciated young men reached Kunming, they boarded trucks to take them to basic training in Dali, 170 miles further west. The alcohol-fueled trucks broke down frequently, adding more time and hardship to Liu's already long and arduous journey. They finally arrived and began training in February 1943. Liu became an infantry officer in mid-1944. Lu Caiwen became an intelligence officer.[15]

When I met Lu he was eighty-four, a retired teacher and head of the Yunnan branch of the Huangpu Alumni Association. His weathered face looked as if it were chiseled from stone. His stoic features testified to a strength of character that still inhabited his old frame. He spoke with pride about his service in the war. After he graduated from the Academy, he led a plainclothes intelligence team behind enemy lines back to his home town. "We had to investigate everything possible related to the Japanese," he told me. "We carried a radio with us so we could report to our headquarters." Lu's team received little direct support from the Chinese Army. His superiors told him to use his knowledge and talents to live off the land. He and his team often depended on the assistance of local guerrilla groups.

In the small village of Dadong, Lu met with Sun Zhengbang, the leader of a security brigade working for the puppet government. Sun's actions branded him as a traitor, but Lu's contacts indicated he might be willing to work with the Nationalists. Sun's compound was surrounded by Japanese soldiers and Lu had to sneak in barefooted. "I was very tense," he admitted. When he got inside he did not mince words. He told Sun that the Chinese would one day return to Tengchong. "You're serving the Japanese," he told him. "What kind of an end will you come to? Think about your family, your property, and your life. You can't protect them!" Lu was right; if the Chinese returned, Sun would be run off or probably even executed. He could hedge his bet by remaining where he was, but agreeing to pass information to the intelligence team. Lu still had to make it past the enemy soldiers on his way out of the compound. "After I had walked over a hundred meters and nothing happened, I felt relieved and wiped the sweat from my face," he said. This was just one example of Lu's efforts to undermine the Japanese and collect useful intelligence for future operations.[16]

In Tengchong County alone, the Japanese killed over thirteen thousand civilians, burned down more than twenty thousand homes, and stole more than sixty thousand tons of grain and over fifty thousand livestock throughout the course of their occupation.[17] Tengchong's experience was not unique. Countless towns and villages suffered similar fates across Japan's newly-won territory. By January 1943, they held a one hundred-mile front along the west bank of the Salween River. From the Salween, the line of occupation stretched 120 miles northwest through Myitkyina to Kar Maing, then over four hundred miles southwest through Kalewa to the Akyab Peninsula. The Hukawng Valley in North Burma remained unoccupied—a no man's land between the Japanese lines and the Allies in India.

The occupation completed the blockade of China. Between 1937 and 1939, the Japanese seized China's seaports. In 1940, they occupied Indochina and closed the railway from Hanoi to Kunming. By 1941, all that was left was the Burma Road—though it was largely symbolic; corruption and inefficiency drastically reduced its effectiveness. Before the fall of Burma, lend-lease officials learned that traffic figures at Lashio were higher than at Wanding, on the China-Burma border. Traffic figures at Wanding were fifty percent more than at the road's terminus in

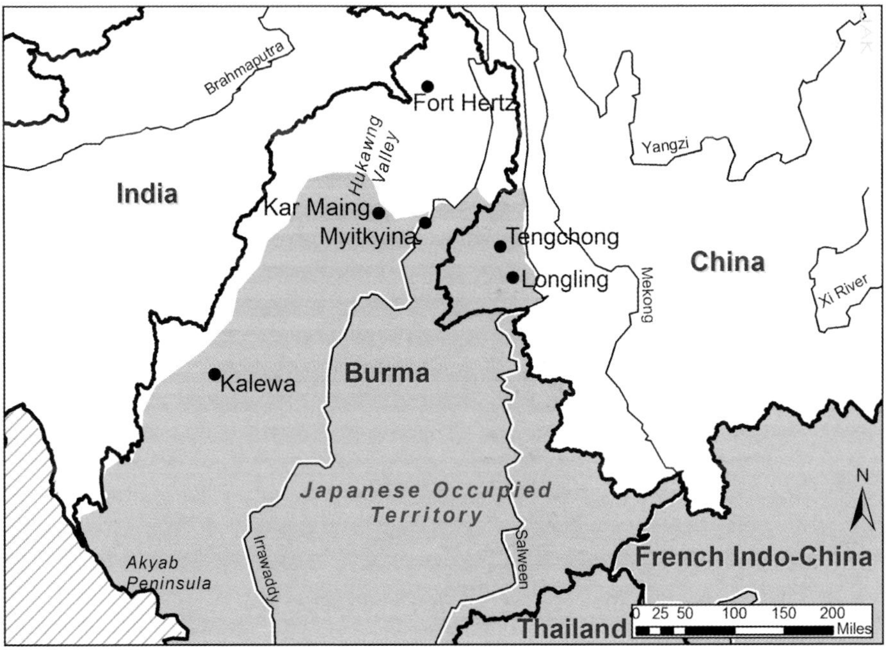

Japanese Occupation

Kunming. The unmistakable implication was that goods destined for China's war effort were disappearing into the countryside for private profit—a common practice due to runaway inflation and widespread poverty called "the squeeze." In addition, the road from Lashio to Kunming was inadequate. The rail line from Rangoon delivered more to Lashio than the road could handle. Consequently, supplies piled up. The China National Aviation Corporation (CNAC)—later joined by a small contingent of the U.S. Army Air Forces—began an airline from Burma into China to provide emergency relief for this bottleneck. Chiang Kai-shek thought it might be helpful to build a new road across North Burma from Ledo, India, through Myitkyina. He radioed Washington the proposal on January 1, 1942, claiming it would take Chinese workers only five months. Roosevelt backed the proposal, but planners in the War Department advised him that such an undertaking would take over two years to accomplish. Construction hardly began before the capture of Burma not only put that project on hold, but also closed the last remaining land route to China.[18]

The Nationalists estimated their war reserves would last only three months. An emergency airlift from India over the Hump was their only link to the outside world, and it was a tenuous link at best. The Allies had only limited air transport capability and Japanese fighters at Myikyina forced them to travel far north of the direct route. In October 1943, for example, the Japanese launched Operation Tsuzigiri, or "Street Murder." They shot down five Hump transports in two weeks. The northern route avoided the enemy fighters, but took the airplanes over the rugged Himalayas, where the terrain and weather fought as proxies for the Japanese. American transports only delivered seventy-seven tons of supplies to China in July 1942.[19] With the airlift as the only source of outside aid, the situation appeared truly desperate. For the people of Tengchong and the other towns and villages of western Yunnan, there was no end in sight to the bitter suffering they endured at the hands of the enemy occupation.

4

Plans and Politics

In the wake of the disaster in Burma, the Allies began discussing what to do next. There was no greater proponent of immediately turning around and plunging back into Burma than General Stilwell. In Chennault's opinion, he was obsessed with "wiping out the stain of his defeat."[1] Of course, Chennault had his own agenda, which was to further prove his ideas by prosecuting the war from the air. A sharp divide emerged between him and Stilwell, and it came to dominate every debate about the CBI Theater. According to *Time* correspondent Theodore White: "The great feud between Chennault and Stilwell rocked the entire American Army in China. You could be either a Stilwell man or a Chennault man; to be friendly with both meant walking a tight-rope. Both were dynamic, hard-hitting fighting men."[2] Chennault's plan was enticing to Chiang Kai-shek, who would prefer the American air force fight for him rather than commit his own troops; and to Winston Churchill, who would rather focus on the recapture of Singapore and Hong Kong than go back into the fetid swamps of Burma. It was even enticing to President Roosevelt, who wanted the most expedient way of showing moral support to keep China in the war. Besides his own staff and General Marshall back in Washington, it seemed Stilwell had no one in his corner. Rather than swift action to retake Burma, the coming months would see him embroiled in a titanic political struggle.

Stilwell began thinking about how to retake Burma even before his epic walkout. As the defense was crumbling around him, he proposed moving one hundred thousand Chinese troops to India. There, unhindered by Japanese blockade, he would furnish them with lend-lease equipment and train them into an elite force that would form the core of a new Chinese Army. He believed that properly trained, the Chinese soldier could be as good as any other. Chiang approved, activating the training center at Ramgarh, in the Bihar Province of India, on August 26, 1942. He required that at least half the senior officers be Chinese and warned that his troops must not be used to maintain India as a British colonial possession. He gave Stilwell the authority to create two full divisions, three artillery regiments, an engineer regiment, ten artillery battalions, and to allocate 1,500 instructors to train the Chinese army in Yunnan. The initial contingent was composed of Sun Liren's 38th Division and the remnants of the 5th Army that escaped to India after the fall of Burma.[3]

In July 1942, Stilwell formally submitted his grand plan. In it, he described the U.S. and Britain taking Rangoon in an amphibious assault and invading Burma from India with five to seven divisions. While they attacked Rangoon and Mandalay, between fifteen and twenty Chinese divisions would advance through Yunnan to Lashio. He proposed the offensive begin in the spring of 1943. Allied air superiority was a prerequisite, as was the capture of the Andaman Islands and control of the China and Java Seas to cover the landing at Rangoon. Stilwell saw the conquest of Burma and the reopening of an overland supply route to China as the foundation for any future operations. With communications reestablished, he would shift operations east across the Guizhou Plateau and Hunan toward an attack on Hankou, in central China.[4]

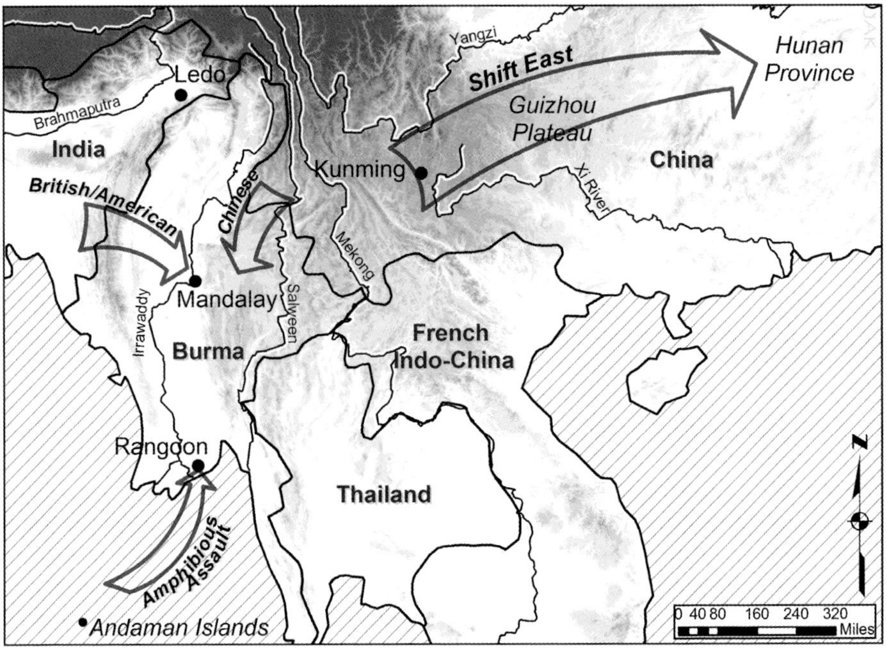

Stilwell's Plan

Chiang gave Stilwell his approval, but Chennault soon suggested a plan of his own, and it differed greatly from what Stilwell intended to do. Stilwell focused on retaking Burma so as to permit land operations in China. He wanted Chennault to remain on the defensive, protecting the Hump airlift and supporting the ground effort. Chennault saw things much differently. He saw no reason to remove the Japanese from their possessions. Much as T.E. Lawrence cut the railroads and isolated the Turks in Medina during the First World War, he wished to cut Japanese supply lines and make them prisoners of their own conquests, languishing without provisions in China and Southeast Asia. He wanted to go on the offensive, destroying the Japanese air force in China, sinking Japanese shipping, and eventually bombing Japan itself—all without a major ground effort. He thought using the limited Hump supplies to support a small air force would be much more effective and efficient than using them to reform and equip the Chinese Army. He worked hard to reduce his logistical footprint. A Chinese organization called the War Area Service Corps (WASC) provided food and lodging for his airmen, allowing his air force to operate at half the troop strength and one-quarter the supplies it would normally require.[5] The American Volunteer Group had far exceeded expectations in the Burma Campaign. Chennault believed airpower was responsible for stopping the Japanese at the Salween River and he had confidence that airpower could halt future land drives by the Japanese.

Stilwell did not share Chennault's beliefs. He thought aggressive air action would only provoke retaliation, as was the case with the Doolittle Raid. In the wake of the raid, Japanese troops killed over two hundred thousand Chinese men, women, and

Generalissimo Chiang Kai-shek (third from left) reviews troops of the Chinese Youth Army in 1945. To the right of Chiang is Marshal Wei Lihuang, who figured prominently in the Salween Campaign. ***National Archives via Samuel Hui***

children and captured several outlying airfields in Jiangxi and Zhejiang (Chiang Kai-shek's home province). Chennault countered that he was not ready to fight in Jiangxi and Zhejiang because nobody bothered to tell him about the raid before it happened—something for which he blamed Stilwell. Chennault, a firm apostle of airpower, was squaring off against Stilwell, a dyed-in-the-wool infantryman. "In every case, the damage has been severe, but no decision has been gained," Stilwell wrote in a memo to Chiang on July 7, 1942:

> This is because of the limitations of the airplane. It can do a great deal of damage, but it is still only an auxiliary of the ground forces, indispensable if a decision is to be reached, but incapable of reaching that decision by itself. The great limitation is that although it can neutralize an area, or deny it to the enemy for a time, it cannot hold ground. Only the troops on the ground can do that, and only by doing so can a decision be reached.[6]

It was the beginning of a feud that came to define the CBI Theater. Colonel Philip Cochran, commander of the 1st Air Commando Group—which arrived in CBI during the fall of 1943—commented on it: "I have the impression that there wasn't much of a meeting of the minds there at all," he said. "Chennault was the consummate airman," while "Stilwell was the epitome of the ground person, the old infantry slug-it-out, slosh-through-the-marshes kind of tough effort, and I just don't think that their personalities had much in common at all." Cochran made a reputation creating close cooperation between his air group and the British commandos he supported on the ground. In his opinion, "There wasn't a great deal of team effort at all" between Chennault and Stilwell. "I think Chennault had a strong idea of what his role was, and it was to support the Chinese in any way he could. Boy, he did it and, of course, that wasn't Stilwell's role. Stilwell's main compulsion was to take back what he had lost ... Burma. ... He was stubborn." Having worked with Stilwell personally, Cochran reported, "I really don't believe that General Stilwell understood the use of air."[7]

That Stilwell did not understand airpower was certainly the view Chennault held. During the collapse in Burma, Stilwell ordered him to send his Hawk 81s on low-level tactical reconnaissance missions. From Stilwell's perspective, it made perfect sense: he needed information on the enemy and Chennault had airplanes that could fly overhead and get that information. But the P-40 was not built for reconnaissance and the dangerous low-level missions left them exposed to ground fire and vulnerable to Japanese fighters. The order almost caused a mutiny in the AVG. The pilots argued the missions had no real benefit and were merely to "show the flag" to demoralized Chinese troops. Ordering his men on pointless suicide missions was not something Chennault took lightly and the incident made him question Stilwell's judgment.

He also questioned his integrity. Stilwell had agreed that Chennault would be brought out of retirement to be the senior air officer in China. After everything he had accomplished with the AVG, he felt it was his due. Stilwell *did* make him the senior air officer *in China*, but subordinated his entire command to Brigadier General Clayton Bissell in India. Bissell was one of Chennault's old enemies from the Air Corps—a fighter ace in the First World War who had since aligned himself with the Air Corps' bomber doctrine. He did not agree with Chennault's ideas about pursuit aviation. He did not like Chennault personally. Worst of all, he lacked tact. Chennault hoped to incorporate most of the AVG into an Army Air Force fighter group when it disbanded on July 4, 1942; Bissell ruined it. He refused to let any of the pilots or ground crew return to the United States for leave, despite their having served in combat for over six months. He so badly offended the pilots and mismanaged their induction that only five stayed in China with the AAF. Frank Dorn admitted that Stilwell made a mistake in selecting Bissell. "For one thing," he wrote, "he was intensely disliked by most air officers ... Shifty-eyed, with sallow, slightly mottled skin and narrow, rounded shoulders, in appearance Bissell was a hell of a long way off from the image of a dashing fly-boy."[8] At the Casablanca Conference in January 1943, AAF Chief of Staff General "Hap" Arnold warned Secretary of State Harry Hopkins that Bissell was "very antagonistic to Chennault."[9]

Stilwell and Bissell were not the only antagonists, though. Rather than using proper channels, Chennault sent his ideas about what he thought airpower could accomplish in China directly to President Roosevelt. It was a flagrant breach of military protocol and angered Stilwell and Marshall, whom he bypassed. And while Chennault, in his very all-or-nothing way, accused Stilwell of being anti-air, he was wrong. Stilwell might not have understood it at the level of a professional airman, but he was quite

From left to right: Lieutenant General Henry "Hap" Arnold, Brigadier General Chennault, Lieutenant General Stilwell, Sir John Dill, and Brigadier General Clayton Bissell meet during Arnold's inspection trip to China in 1943. ***National Archives***

progressive when compared to most ground officers. Perhaps Cochran was on to something when he pointed to differences in their personalities, rather than just their backgrounds, as a source of conflict. Many observers thought Stilwell and Chennault did not get along because they were so similar. Certainly they were both assertive, independent, and stubborn. But Chennault resented Stilwell because he criticized his ideas and denied him freedom of action. Stilwell hated Chennault because he got in the way of a swift return to Burma. For Chennault, it was about the black-and-white, right-or-wrong belief in the power of his ideas. For Stilwell, it was about the movement, the result—getting things done. It was a tragedy, because they could have made a great team. Stilwell needed Chennault's imagination and ideas. He was a tactical genius and possessed an incredible technical knowledge of what airpower could accomplish. Chennault needed Stilwell, though, to balance his overstated, single-minded belief in airpower and incorporate it into the bigger picture of planning and logistics.[10] Sadly, it was not to be.

Even more important than Stilwell's relationship with Chennault was his relationship with Chiang, which began to disintegrate with the evaporation of Allied promises to China. American strength was already minimal in CBI. In December 1942, there were only 17,091 American personnel in-theater, including supply, air forces, and ground personnel. This amounted to the equivalent of little more than a

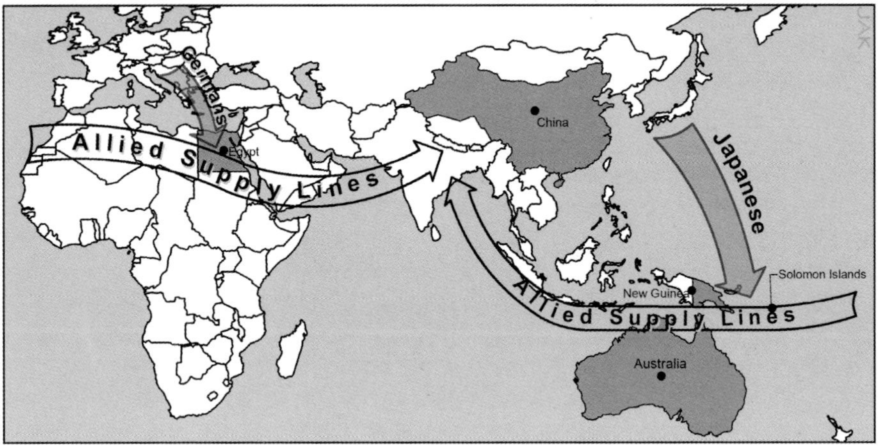

Allied Supply Lines

single infantry division. With America's global commitments expanding and the fighting in North Africa, Europe, and the Solomon Islands taking priority, it became increasingly clear that promised resources would not be available for operations in Burma or China. In fact, on June 23, 1942, the War Department notified Stilwell that it was moving most of the 10th Air Force from CBI to the Middle East to help stem the tide of Rommel's drive into Egypt. "Now what can I say to the G-mo?" lamented Stilwell in his diary. "We fail in all our commitments and blithely tell him to carry on." The reallocation of resources from CBI to North Africa and the Pacific was frustrating, but American resources would have been cut off from reaching China altogether were Rommel to continue his advance into Egypt and the Japanese toward Australia. Chiang was not privy to Allied planning, nor did he participate in making decisions or setting priorities. He requested that China be included on the Combined Chiefs of Staff (CCS) in April 1942. The U.S. and Britain rejected his request because they decided China's demands would far outweigh any possible contributions it could make. It was an insult and a loss of face to the Chinese leader, who increasingly became frustrated with Stilwell as the bearer of bad news.[11]

Stilwell was in an impossible situation. He was responsible to Chiang as the Chief of his Joint Staff; he was responsible to Roosevelt as his representative in Chongqing; he was commander of U.S. forces in China, Burma, and India; and he was in charge of administering lend-lease aid. In theory, the only way this arrangement could have worked would have been if the U.S. and China reached a consensus and then jointly issued orders. In reality, Washington often tried to secure Chiang's cooperation *through* Stilwell. It was frustrating for all parties involved, but completely impossible for Stilwell. T.V. Song,[12] the generalissimo's brother-in-law and foreign minister, wrote to President Roosevelt about some of the problems with Stilwell's arrangement:

> At present he is Chief of Staff of the China Theater and has independent command of the U.S. Air Force in China, India, and Burma. He also commands the SOS [Services of Supply] in India and China, Air Transport Command

The Generalissimo, Madame Chiang, and Stilwell pose for a photograph. The smiles for the newsmen mask a bitter antagonism growing between them. *Hoover Institution*

between India and China, and the Chinese Ramgarh divisions, and has some undefined authority over the Chinese Expeditionary Troops now in Yunnan. In addition he had been given authority by the War Department, without the concurrence of China, over the Chinese lend-lease program. The straddling of authority over such multifarious spheres is making for friction which may dangerously imperil future campaigns.

Song recommended that the Supreme Commander of China and the Chief of Staff both be Chinese with American deputies, and again asked that China be represented on the CCS.[13]

Already plagued by increasing friction and limited resources, Stilwell learned that Britain vetoed his plan to retake Burma. Churchill wanted to bypass the country altogether in favor of retaking Singapore and Hong Kong. He did not believe the recapture of Burma was an important step toward the defeat of Japan. Nor did he think the Burma Road could provide for all of China's military supply needs. The CCS recommended that Stilwell's grand plan be scrapped. In its place, they suggested limited operations in North Burma to establish a modest land line of communications and capture Japanese airfields menacing the Hump.

Chiang was outraged by the change of plans. In a letter to Roosevelt on January 8, 1943, he wrote: "I am convinced that the attempt to retake Burma must be a combined overland and seaborne operation." He believed an offensive limited to North Burma would allow the Japanese to concentrate against his armies there. "Owing to the weakness of our supply lines, we shall not be able to match the Japanese concentration," he argued. In his judgment, it was "possible, and even likely, that in an advance restricted to North Burma our armies would ultimately be exposed to the risk of defeat." Though he was as eager as anyone to reopen supply lines to China, "another failure in Burma would be a disaster for China so grave that the results cannot now be predicted." Stilwell still pushed for the limited offensive, but Chiang excused his Yunnan divisions for the time being and suggested the Allies "muster satisfactory numbers" and "wait a few months longer, or even until the monsoon season end next autumn."

The postponed offensive became a topic of discussion at the Casablanca Conference a week later. No representative of China was privy to the discussion or present at the conference. In response to Chiang's concerns, the Chiefs of Staff recommended a revised plan to capture Burma starting on November 15, 1943. Before the general offensive, the Allies would establish a submarine blockade of Rangoon while the Chinese moved to jump-off positions in Yunnan and the British secured the Akyab Peninsula and bridgeheads across the Chindwin. In November, eleven Chinese divisions would drive south from Yunnan, Stilwell's Ramgarh forces would advance from Ledo, three British-Indian divisions would advance on Mandalay, and amphibious landings would take Taungup, Sandoway, and Bassein in December. The timeline projected the assault on Rangoon to take place in January 1944. They forwarded the proposal to Chiang and, as it contained all his prerequisites for participating in Burma operations, he approved it on February 6.

Meanwhile, with several months to go before the operation began, Chiang requested that Roosevelt call Chennault to Washington to talk about his air plan.

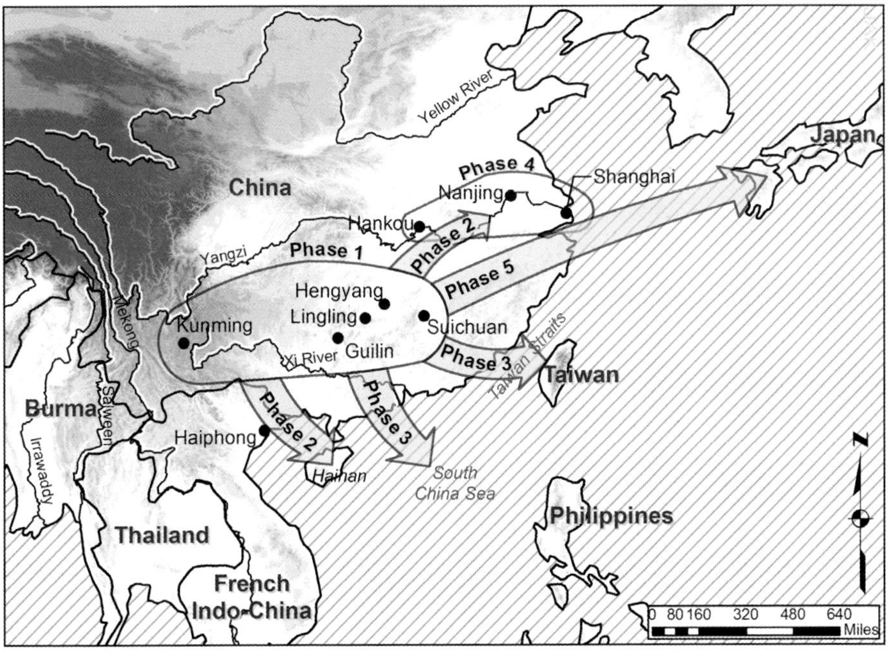

Chennault's Plan

General Marshall was concerned when he heard about the request; it seemed his friend Stilwell was being bypassed again. He radioed him for comment. Stilwell replied that he had no knowledge of any new plans and did not know why Chennault was bypassing him and dealing directly with Chiang. He angrily called Chennault and accused him of going over his head with new plans. Chennault told him that his plan was the same he had presented in October 1942 and that he had no knowledge of Chiang's request for him to discuss it with Roosevelt. Stilwell was not convinced. He suggested that Bissell and himself be brought to Washington with Chennault to discuss operations. Marshall passed this suggestion on to the president, noting: "to call in Chennault and ignore Stilwell, which is the probable purpose of the generalissimo's proposal, would create such a definite division of authority in the China Theater as to necessitate Stilwell's relief and Chennault's appointment to command of ground and air, which so far as I am concerned would be a grave mistake." Roosevelt agreed, and though he excluded Bissell, he brought both Chennault and Stilwell to Washington in April 1943.

The thought of the two great rivals sharing the same airplane for the four-day flight back to America is almost comical. They sat at opposite ends—Stilwell with cigarette holder in hand, Chennault lighting-up a Camel—an air of icy indifference between them. Chennault worked on refining his plan en route, using his briefcase as a desk. When they got to Washington, he made his pitch first. He told the president that the Japanese did not want to fight in China, particularly in the air, and therefore should be made to do so. He outlined a plan which began in July 1943 with a two-month campaign to seize air superiority. In late August, he would move his B-25 medium bombers forward to Guilin to hit Japanese river traffic along the Yangzi and shipping off Haiphong and Hainan Island. In September, they would stretch out to cover the Taiwan Straits and the South China Sea. He told the president that with ten thousand tons over the Hump each month he could sink one million tons of Japanese shipping. Roosevelt banged his fist on the desk. "If you can sink a million tons, we'll break their backs!" he exclaimed. With the anti-shipping campaign underway, Chennault would then begin strategic bombing of Japanese lines of communication and direct his B-24 heavy bombers to hit Taiwan and Japanese strongholds in the Shanghai-Nanjing-Hankou triangle. By the end of 1943, he hoped to bomb Japan itself.

In contrast to Chennault's passionate delivery, Stilwell sat hunched over in his chair and mumbled his presentation. Roosevelt thought he was sick. His penchant for understatement was up against Chennault's dramatic exaggeration. His irony and sarcasm fell flat next to the force of Chennault's burning conviction. He conceded that Chennault's plan could cause considerable damage to the Japanese, but pointed out that they would practice swift retaliation as they had after the Doolittle Raid. He estimated Japan could muster over half a million troops to root out Chennault's air force. The only way to hold the bases from which to attack Japan was to develop a strong ground force. The only way to develop a strong ground force was to open supply lines through Burma.

He told the president he could improve the Chinese Army and cited his progress with the Ramgarh divisions as evidence. A continuing flow of supplies to the Yunnan divisions—or Y Force as he called it—was necessary to ensure its readiness for operations in Burma. If tonnage allotted to the Y Force was diverted to Chennault, he doubted the Chinese could advance into Burma before January 1944. He further told the president that Chiang's championing of Chennault's plan was to avoid his commitments to provide promised manpower to the Allies. He recommended that Hump allotments not change and that Chiang be informed Chennault's air force would no longer bypass the American chain of command. He was adamant that the Chinese be held to their commitments in Burma. If they reneged, lend-lease supplies should be withheld. Roosevelt disagreed with this quid-pro-quo approach. "My first thought is that Stilwell has exactly the wrong approach in dealing with Generalissimo Chiang," he wrote to Marshall. "All of us must remember that the Generalissimo came up the hard way to become the undisputed leader of four hundred million people—an enormously difficult job ... one cannot speak sternly to a man like that or exact commitments from him the way we might do from the Sultan of Morocco."[14]

To the president, Chennault addressed the possibility of a Japanese ground offensive powerful enough to occupy central China. He told him that if such an offensive were to be made, it would have to be in such force as to dangerously reduce the enemy's strength in other theaters. Furthermore, T.V. Song delivered a letter from Chiang that gave his "personal assurance that in the event the enemy attempts to interrupt the air offensive by a ground advance on the air bases, the advance can be halted by the existing Chinese forces." Given his army's experience stopping the Japanese at Changsha in 1939, 1941, and 1942, he probably genuinely thought this was possible. Chiang asked for more Hump tonnage to be given to Chennault, claiming that "such a concentration of resources on the air effort need not, in the Generalissimo's opinion, interfere with the program of ground action." Of course, for that to be true, the airlift would have to deliver at least seven thousand tons a month. Roosevelt promised ten thousand tons a month by September, even though only three thousand made it over the Hump in March.[15]

Chiang was not necessarily trying to discredit Stilwell personally; rather, he thought an air offensive would buy him time to consolidate political and military power. Roosevelt was right that Chiang had "an enormously difficult job," but his leadership was far from "undisputed." Stilwell believed he was not doing what was necessary to increase the efficiency of the Chinese Army or reform the Nationalist political structure. He thought he was trying to *use* the United States to fight the war *for* him whilst marshaling his forces to defeat the Communists and other political rivals. To some extent this was true. Chiang was a somewhat Machiavellian leader trying to hold on to power. Though he claimed to be the president of a free and democratic China, his "emergency powers" as Chairman of the Supreme National Defense Council allowed him to do whatever he thought was necessary for the survival of the nation. In effect, these powers made him a virtual dictator. He presided over a one-party state, having outlawed all other political parties. He claimed the Guomindang alone held the government in sacred trust for the people until such a time as they were ready to fully participate in a democratic government. He promised freedom of speech and of the press. He promised the end of dictatorship. He promised to abolish his secret police force. But first he must triumph over the Japanese and overthrow the warlords and the Communists. He was especially concerned about the Communists, whom he referred to as "a disease of the heart," as opposed to the Japanese, who were merely "a disease of the skin."[16]

Like Stilwell though, Chiang was in an impossible situation. When the Japanese evicted him from China's east coast, he lost the industry, banks, and merchants in the nation's wealthiest cities that made up his power base. What was left was an assortment of warlords and semi-autonomous provincial governments whose loyalty and cooperation were not guaranteed. From the outside looking in, there seemed to be enough troops and equipment on paper for Chiang to consolidate over three hundred divisions into a smaller number of effective fighting units. In reality, reforming the army and providing manpower to the Allies was much more problematic. Nationalist China was not a nation in the Western sense; it was more a fragile coalition. Each governor or division commander's troops represented his wealth and power. It was a commander's privilege to distribute his troops' pay, and though he often secreted away a substantial portion for himself, it meant his men owed their loyalty to him, not to the central government. Thus, any loss of troops or equipment to battle or otherwise represented a loss of that commander's wealth and power, predisposing him to avoid direct action. In order to keep his tenuous grip on power, Chiang could not impose too many reforms or ask for more than he knew the warlords and provincials were willing to give him. To do otherwise would precipitate a crisis highlighting how little control he truly wielded. It was much easier for him to command the loyalty of Chennault and his air force than to navigate the turbulent world of Chinese politics.

Roosevelt appreciated Chennault's imagination and Chiang's judgment and told Stilwell to limit operations in Burma. The air campaign would boost Chinese morale and have a more immediate effect than a "tedious ground buildup." He asked Chennault to write to him directly, bypassing Marshall and Stilwell. Chennault now officially had a direct line to Roosevelt and, in July 1943, Chiang asked for Bissell to be recalled and for Chennault to be made his Air Chief of Staff, giving him a direct line to the generalissimo as well. Roosevelt thought it was a good idea. Marshall, on the other hand, still supported his friend and warned that it would set a bad precedent to reduce Stilwell to irrelevancy. Roosevelt decided on a compromise. Chennault became Chiang's Chief of Staff for the Chinese Air Force, but his American command remained under Stilwell's authority. He recalled Bissell and appointed Brigadier General Howard C. Davidson as commander of the 10th Air Force in India. Chennault's air task force became its own numbered air force—the 14th—in March 1943.[17]

Stilwell became increasingly frustrated. Throughout 1943, his diary entries became more and more bitter. He referred to Chiang as "Peanut," a sarcastic term he had used before to describe "millionaires, politicians, and social darlings."[18] Though he was usually respectful in person, stories of his caustic, disrespectful comments made their way back to Chongqing.[19] Since he had a thorough knowledge of Chinese culture and understood the idea of "face," it is hard to believe this was entirely unintentional. Was he trying to provoke some sort of response? Did he think Chiang could be shamed into action? As the leader of China, he was already humiliated at having to depend on a foreigner.[20] General Somervell in India wrote Stilwell that he thought "it was very unfortunate for you to refer to the Generalissimo in the way you have and to make some other remarks which have caused unnecessary friction."[21]

Chiang's reaction was to ask for Stilwell to be recalled. When Stilwell found out, he was furious. When he confronted Chiang though, the generalissimo offered to retract his request if he would just promise to follow orders and function as a chief of staff, rather than trying to undermine and manipulate him.[22] Stilwell's ideas and policies were certainly less convenient for Chiang than Chennault's. However, Chiang's opposition probably had more to do with the manner with which Stilwell treated him and privately disparaged him. Stilwell and Chennault were both difficult, stubborn men, but Chennault treated Chiang with respect, both in public and private. Stilwell's denigration of Chiang amongst his staff was infamous. He worked against the generalissimo instead of trying to find common ground. As 1943 wore on, Stilwell's plans seemed to be continually frustrated in favor of Chennault's. The theater split into two distinct and mutually hostile camps, and any sense of goodwill and cooperation rotted away. The unfortunate effect of this clash of personalities, in addition to limited resources, was to divide Allied leadership and delay operations in the CBI.

5

The Y Force

Stilwell was not happy about the shift in priorities toward Chennault's air plan. He was, however, privately relieved when Chiang postponed the spring 1943 offensive. In his opinion, the Y Force—or the Chinese Expeditionary Force (CEF), as the Chinese called it—was not up to the task. The delay until November gave him time to get things into shape. He made Frank Dorn his Deputy Chief of Staff for Operations on the Salween Front and charged him with overseeing training and liaison. He opened schools for artillery and infantry and pressured the Chinese War Ministry to assign competent officers. Given the fragmented state of the Chinese Army, the corruption, the abuses, and the war-weariness, transforming the divisions in Yunnan into a capable, modern fighting force amounted to quite a task.

Brigadier General John Magruder reported in 1941 that the Chinese Army had considerable potential, but was a heterogeneous force lacking training and discipline. Magruder was commander of the American Military Mission to China (AMMISCA) prior to Stilwell's arrival. He did not believe the Chinese Army was an army in the Western sense. In his opinion, it served primarily as a tool of the warlords and provincial officials to dominate the peasantry. On paper there were 324 divisions, plus over one hundred independent brigades and guerrilla units. According to Stilwell, instead of the usual ten thousand men, the average division had only five thousand. The troops were often unpaid, unshod, and unfit. They had little to no training and their equipment was old and unserviceable. Tu Chi-liang—a conscript from Hubei Province—recalled that his squad had only four rifles and one machine gun. "Most of us used whatever we could find," he said. "My weapon at that time was a shovel." Even Chiang's German-trained divisions, considered his best, were mediocre by Western standards. When Chiang threw them into the bloody fighting around Shanghai in 1937, they stubbornly resisted the Japanese but were decimated in the process. Administratively, Chiang divided the army into war areas, which for the most part conformed to provincial borders and acknowledged the de facto organization of the warlords and provinces. As a consequence, military commanders were often also political leaders. Chiang ensured the obedience of what troops he had direct influence over by appointing commanders loyal to him. Loyalty was more important than competence. The result was an ill-equipped, ill-trained rabble led by incompetent, self-centered politicians.[1]

Newly-promoted Colonel Frank Dorn arrived in Kunming in January 1943 as Stilwell's deputy chief of staff. "With one officer ... and one room in the main building of Hostel One, I was in business," he wrote. In some respects he was a lot like Stilwell: highly opinionated, a results-oriented doer, and a hater of "stuffed shirts." He grew up in an upper-middle class family in San Francisco. His father was a lawyer. He wanted to be an artist. He attended the San Francisco Institute of Art during high school and impressed his instructors with his passion and natural talent. Then the First World War changed the course of his life. His father convinced him to apply for West Point so he could go to war as an officer, rather than being drafted. The war was over by the time he was accepted, but his father redoubled the pressure and he gave in. He graduated with the Class of 1923.[2]

Frank Dorn, promoted to brigadier general in late 1943, took charge of training and advising the Chinese Expeditionary Force as Stilwell's representative in Kunming. ***Hoover Institution***

Assigned to the Field Artillery, Dorn, like Stilwell, was eventually posted to the Philippines. But while Stilwell was morally upright and scrupulously proper in his personal life, Dorn almost destroyed his career through multiple indiscretions with other officers' wives. Stilwell led a Spartan life and rarely had much alcohol; Dorn enjoyed parties enormously and often got roaring drunk. Yet he had a serious intellectual side, as evidenced by an article he wrote about the language and culture of the Negrito people in the Philippines, complete with a 3,300-word dictionary. He first saw China while on leave in July 1928. "I felt completely at home," he later wrote:

> I belonged here… the stupendous palaces, temples, treasures of arts and crafts, quiet courtyards, walled gardens, and the easy elegance of life for foreigners convinced me that I had to live here. But there was only one way that I could swing that—get assigned as a Chinese language officer. Okay, hell or high water, I would get ordered here. I'd learn the crazy language.[3]

After applying three times, he finally got his dream assignment and reported to Beiping in October 1934. It was the next summer he met the new military attaché for the first time: Colonel Joseph W. Stilwell. That summer was the beginning of a professional relationship and deep personal friendship that would last until Stilwell's death in 1946.

After Stilwell returned from Washington, DC, in May 1943, he consolidated all the organizations working with the CEF into the Y Force Operations Staff (YFOS) under his command, with Dorn as chief of staff. He told Dorn he believed "the Chinese, with training and modern equipment, can press an offensive—and win." He gave him informal orders on April 29 and officially announced the mission on June 18. Dorn was to advise the Chinese and provide training and logistical support. He was to obtain lend-lease equipment (including arms, ammunition, and medical supplies) from the U.S. Army Services of Supply (SOS) and issue it to the Chinese troops. He was also to assist the CEF in operational planning. His authority did not include any function of command. "The official mission of the U.S. Army in China is to increase the combat efficiency of the Chinese Army—and nothing else," wrote Dorn. "The Americans could recommend," he explained, "they could persuade; they could cajole, but they could not command the Chinese."[4]

Stilwell envisioned a two-pronged approach to training the Y Force. American instructors at training schools in Kunming would provide six-week courses in artillery, infantry, and signals, preparing groups of officers and men to return to their units and pass on their training. American liaison teams attached to each division would then supervise unit-level training, provide technical and professional aid, and organize and outfit units with American equipment as it arrived. The liaison teams would make sure the Chinese soldiers were proficient with their weapons and equipment and would organize training that stressed offensive tactics. In Dorn's words, this would ensure "training is continuous, progressive, and uniform." The Chinese War Ministry wanted to disperse all of the American instructors throughout the CEF, but Stilwell resisted. He believed the training would be more effective with most of the instructors concentrated at the schools in Kunming.[5]

Dorn charged into his new duties with characteristic energy. He set up two main supply depots at Kunming and Yunnanyi, as well as five advanced depots along the front lines. His organization expanded rapidly. When YFOS officially stood up in June he had only four officers. By January 1, 1944, he commanded 654 officers and 1,629 enlisted men. The language barrier was a problem, so he established a school for interpreters in Kunming. The school eventually trained 808 Chinese interpreters, 235 of which were assigned to YFOS. The rest went to Chinese units in India, or to assist the American air force or other functions in China.

When he arrived in Kunming, Dorn heard the common Chinese adage, "Never use good iron for nails, nor good men for soldiers." He found this rather discouraging, given that his mission was to transform the CEF into a modern and effective fighting force. He hoped he could show instead, "that just as fine steel can be made from old iron when smelted with proper ingredients, so, with proper training and tempering under fire, a good soldier can be developed from the lowliest conscripted coolie." Considering the sorry state of the conscription system in China, this amounted to quite a task.[6]

A 1945 memo from Lieutenant General Albert Wedemeyer to Chiang Kai-shek described Chinese conscripts as "entirely useless." They were less soldiers than a "source of income for officials." For the peasants, conscription was a disaster—like famine or flood—though according to the memo it came "more regularly—every year twice—and claims more victims. Famine, flood, and drought compare with conscription like chicken pox with the plague." Press gangs roamed the countryside, snatching men from their fields and homes. "Hoe and plough rust in the field," wrote Wedemeyer, "the wife runs to the magistrate to cry and beg for her husband, the children starve." Often, conscription officers ran a racket with the local government. For every man a county magistrate had to provide he arrested ten. Nine of them could buy their way out of jail, but the poorest would remain until the conscription officer came for him.

Shen You-chih was from a poor peasant family in Huangchuan, Henan Province. He was seventeen when war broke out in 1937. His family did not feel the impact of the conflict for some time, since they lived deep in the interior, and Shen managed to make a living working as a laborer for a rich family. In the summer of 1939 he was conscripted. Once a conscription officer secured his men, he often herded them to training camps a considerable distance away. Sometimes, they found themselves marching hundreds or even thousands of miles. "Over endless roads they walk," described Wedemeyer, "billeting in small hamlets, carrying their rice and rations and nothing else." Many escaped during the first few days of the march. Those that did not were soon too weak to run. If caught, the runaways were cruelly beaten. Their bruised and battered bodies would be carried along, their wounds festering with infection, until finally death released them from their suffering. Their bodies were left behind, but their names lived on to pad division numbers. According to Wedemeyer: "His rice and his pay become a long-lasting token of memory in the pocket of his commanding officer."[7]

It took Shen about a month to reach Luoyang, where he went through basic training. He received no pay for the first three months of his life as a soldier. "The treatment of us ordinary soldiers in the beginning was very bad," he remembered. "When I was taken by the conscription officers, they tied me up with other conscripted soldiers together on the march. When I told them it was unnecessary to tie me like that, they answered that it was a method to prevent us from escaping." The recruits could only shuffle down the road like a chain gang. "Each of us was given one rice bag to be carried on our shoulders and began to march," said Shen. When he finally arrived in Luoyang, he became an infantryman and later a machine gunner in the 47th Division, 9th Army.[8]

Conscription was an unmitigated disaster. Conscripts were poorly trained. They were physically and mentally broken. Chances were they would die from disease or malnutrition long before facing the Japanese. At the other end of the scale, Dorn complained that "Chinese officers, particularly higher commanders (regimental and up), are not too good as a rule. However, there are notable exceptions. Many of the higher commanders hold their positions through political maneuvers, rather than military ability." Though several officers in the CEF were of fair quality, or showed improvement, too large a number were "not so hot" or "not competent."[9] China's army was broken at all levels. At the bottom, the soldiers struggled to survive. At the top, politics, competing loyalties, and money-hungry corruption prevented cohesion and a sound command structure.

Stilwell submitted a suggestion for organizing the Y Force, but given the sorry state of affairs, he did not expect the Chinese to implement it. It was to his astonishment then, when the War Ministry told him they had adopted his plan. There would be thirty-two divisions with 10,300 men each, organized into eleven armies (a Chinese army was equivalent to an American corps). Chiang appointed General Chen Cheng to command the CEF on February 17, 1943.[10] This was good news for the Americans. Chen was a heavy hitter in the Nationalist military-political establishment. He was one of the first graduates from the Huangpu Academy. He caught Chiang's attention during the Northern Expedition in the late-1920s and was one of his top aides during the Battle of Shanghai in 1937. He went on to command Chinese armies at the battles of Wuhan and Changsha, among others. His postwar career included Premier of the Republic of China on Taiwan from 1950 to 1954 and 1958 to 1963, as well as vice president from 1954 to 1965. According to Dorn, he was "a sharp-eyed little man,

Brigadier General Jerome J. Waters, commander of the Field Artillery Training Center (FATC) in Kunming, watches with two Chinese officers as instructors demonstrate the firing of a 75mm howitzer. ***National Archives via Samuel Hui***

tough, incisive, one of the most forceful and capable generals in China; a ruthless commander of great drive."[11]

Stilwell issued orders for the activation of the first of the training schools—the Field Artillery Training Center (FATC)—in January 1943. Brigadier General Jerome J. Waters assumed command. Waters was a decorated veteran of the First World War whom Dorn described as "thin, sharp, and active."[12] He decided to fashion the school in Kunming after the U.S. Army Field Artillery School at Fort Sill, Oklahoma, with instructors and school troops teaching modern methods of fire. He needed ranges, classrooms, offices, and living facilities. He encountered immediate resistance. Long Yun—Governor of Yunnan Province and political rival and constant thorn-in-the-side to the generalissimo—obstructed progress. The only buildings he was willing to part with had been damaged in bombing raids, so Waters hired local workers to put things into shape. During construction, a local Chinese airfield station master arrested one of Waters' subforemen. The contractor told Waters that the station master was "squeezing" them, insisting all materials be purchased from him at exorbitant prices. "As soon as I learned about this 'shakedown,'" reported Waters, "I informed the station master in no uncertain terms that building operations would continue without interference from him even if it became necessary for armed American personnel to guard the contractor's men." Waters reported the issue to Stilwell, who reported it to the Chinese. A Chinese colonel later phoned Waters and told him, "The station master was being removed for his stupidity." Trouble continued with the station master's replacement. The new man tried tapping into the school's electricity for his personal use and blew out the entire system.[13]

When the school finally opened, Waters' staff included twenty-three Chinese interpreters, fifty-six American officers, and twelve Chinese officers. Of the twelve Chinese, Waters retained only two; he considered the others incompetent and demanded replacements. The 71st Army Artillery Battalion provided forty officers and 348 men as school troops. Most were undernourished and in need of immediate medical attention. The 2nd Battalion of the 2nd Army Field Artillery arrived for the first class of instruction on April 13. They were in better physical condition than the 71st troops, but sent only eighty-seven officers for training, rather than the three hundred the school was designed for. The battalion depended heavily on animal transport due to motor vehicle and fuel shortages in China. Their pack animals were in bad shape. They were afraid they would lose the animals and their handlers if they allowed them out to graze. Waters reported a major obstacle to training was the apathy of the battalion commander. He pressed for his relief and progress resumed with his dismissal. The Chinese struggled with what the Americans saw as basic practices, such as camouflaging pieces and using artillery in mass, instead of singly. According to Waters, another challenge was: "Boys unable to read or write would appear for instruction and training as artillery officers. As they would 'lose face' if sent back to their outfits, the instructors made the best of a bad situation and gave them practical instruction, which in many cases qualified them for non-commissioned, if not commissioned officers' papers."

Typical of the units arriving at the training center, the 53rd Army Field Artillery Battalion reported after marching over four thousand miles from Manchuria. The entire march took more than fifteen months and included several battles along the way. They arrived with thirty-five officers, 593 enlisted men, four Chinese 75-millimeter pack howitzers, one 75-millimeter Krupp pack howitzer, eighty-three mules, and fourteen horses. Their clothes were in tatters. On their feet they wore only straw sandals or cloth slippers. Ninety percent suffered from scabies or vitamin deficiencies, fifteen percent from trachoma or other eye diseases, and thirty-four were unfit for duty due to malnutrition. The FATC hospital treated the sick. Throughout the course of training, the CEF added five hundred recruits to the battalion, but 250 deserted and one hundred died or were lost to unknown causes. The training center eventually equipped fifteen artillery battalions with a total of 994 officers and 2,725 enlisted men. They issued each battalion twelve 75-millimeter howitzers and twelve 7.62-millimeter Bren Guns, plus necessary equipment and supplies.[14]

Colonel Thomas S. Arms received a directive from Stilwell to establish the Infantry Training Center on March 12, 1943. Arms was in the 7th Division at Fort Ord, California, when Stilwell was the commander there in 1941. Dorn described him as "a big, raw-boned, homely guy from Maryland's eastern shore ... a fine, hard-working officer."[15] The course he put together included training in tactics, first aid, medical evacuation, and care of animals, as well as the effective use and maintenance of American weapons, signals equipment, and engineering equipment. Arms was officially the vice-commandant in charge of training. A Chinese colleague controlled discipline and administration. He set up shop in the former Airplane Factory One outside of Kunming. General Chen attended the opening ceremonies on April 4. Like the Artillery Center,

Chinese troops depended on horses and mules for transportation, but would not graze them for fear they would run off or their handlers would desert. *National Archives via Samuel Hui*

Chinese troops reassemble a 75mm pack howitzer at the Field Artillery Training Center. *National Archives via Samuel Hui*

Arms' school troops were in poor condition. Seventy percent had trachoma, scabies, colds, or intestinal disease. Ten of them died within the first three weeks of the school opening.[16]

Colonel Walter S. Wood—commander of the American liaison teams attached to the CEF's XIth Army Group—was not impressed with the training center. "The school had all the outward aspects of a school," he wrote. "It had adequate buildings. It had ample training areas. It had a rifle and machine gun range." However, despite "an elaborate training schedule," Wood claimed "it did not teach. No one fired on the ranges. No one maneuvered on the training areas. Haphazard lectures or, to be more accurate, speeches were the order of the day. When the school was inspected by visitors there was a series of 'set pieces' which were put on to convey the idea of scheduled and progressive training." In Wood's opinion, the Chinese leadership seemed to think, "so long as the opening ceremony went well, the student body remained in attendance and the graduation ceremony and banquet went smoothly, then the school was a success." The unfortunate fact was that Arms' immediate concern was the physical well being of his students, rather than their training. Officers and officer candidates arrived in poor health. Students only received two meals a day until Arms insisted on three. He had to pick his battles with the Chinese brass and he saw the survival of the student body as the most important one. For their part, the Chinese never sent more officers than five-eighths of the school's capacity and often sent officer candidates rather than acting line officers.[17] Brigadier General Theodore F. Wessels replaced Arms and took command of the Infantry Training Center on January 1, 1944. He built on what Arms started and did his best to improve the training regimen.

Dorn was frustrated: "Not only did the students report in inadequate numbers, but hundreds reported sick, lame, and halt, many having traveled on foot from great distances with little food to sustain them on the way and no medical care. Many would first have to go to the hospital for days and weeks before being in condition to report for classes." Ironically, despite the poor medical service in the Chinese Army, which Dorn described as "a tragic farce," there was no medical training school. Four American field hospitals eventually deployed to the front to attend to battle casualties. Chinese medical personnel usually amounted to a few poorly trained field medics. The majority of Chinese soldiers suffered from various maladies associated with malnutrition or poor hygiene. Each soldier was allotted only twenty-eight ounces of rice and one-quarter of an ounce of salt per day, plus the equivalent of three American cents to buy other items. YFOS doctors did try to teach them basic field hygiene techniques and also inoculated a good many against smallpox, typhoid, typhus, and cholera.[18]

Training progressed, but Dorn reported that by mid-March, the Chinese had still not established the promised command structure, nor marshaled troops for the promised divisions, which were still 185,255 men short of full strength. It was a frustrating problem in a country teeming with manpower. Of the eleven armies on hand or expected, only five were even good by Chinese standards. When Stilwell was in Washington in April, he complained to Roosevelt that "the Chinese show an increasing tendency to neglect their obligation of furnishing the manpower which we are to equip and train." He warned that if the Chinese continued to demur, America would not achieve its goals in the Far East and efforts in the theater "will cause some damage, but it will not be vital to the war effort."

Captain George E. Noll instructs a group of Chinese officers in various infantry weapons at the Infantry Training Center in Kunming. ***National Archives via Samuel Hui***

When Stilwell had brought the issue to Chiang's attention, the generalissimo promised action and apparently issued orders on March 23 to concentrate forces in Yunnan. A week later, the situation remained unchanged. Stilwell sent a radio message to T.V. Song, reminding him that without Chinese manpower, American supplies and weapons would be wasted. It was as close as he could come to threatening a withdrawal of American support. He ardently believed in a quid-pro-quo approach with the Chinese. Though Roosevelt still disagreed, the president's frustration was mounting.

On August 7, Dorn told Stilwell that the Chinese were still falling short in several key areas: the CEF had not been reorganized; troops and artillery assigned to the CEF had still not arrived in Yunnan; the training schools outside Kunming were not being utilized at capacity; supply preparations were completely lacking; and General Chen was absent from Yunnan while attending to operations in his war area in the critical Yangzi gorges, which guarded the approaches to Chongqing.[19] Dorn wrote to He Yingqin, asking for a resolution to the command problem and for troops to be moved from Sichuan. General He was both the minister of war and chief of staff of the Chinese Army. He was a classmate of Chiang Kai-shek's at the Japanese Military Academy and like Chiang, left in 1911 to join in the revolution against the Qing government. In his late fifties, he had been the minister of war and chief of staff for well over a decade and was one of the most powerful men in China, both because of his association with the generalissimo and because of the political fiefdom he built around himself. In response to Dorn's concerns, he replied that he was not aware of any command problems and that it would be impossible to move troops from Sichuan, because the Nationalist government had little control over the armies in that province. Of course, what Dorn did not know was that the general himself was responsible for much of the friction. He and Chen were rivals for the generalissimo's favor and he feared the increase in Chen's power that would come with the Americans providing training, equipment, and supplies for his troops.

The friction baffled Dorn and many other Americans. Not only were they frustrated by the command situation, but they also wondered how the Nationalists could order in troops from thousands of miles away when the fragile political situation prevented them from using plentiful resources in a neighboring province. The reality was that out of approximately four million men in more than three hundred divisions that supposedly made up the Chinese Army, Chiang controlled only about thirty divisions worth. The rest were commanded by the war area commanders, who were often at odds with the government. At least half of them had fought in open rebellion against the Guomindang in the preceding fifteen years.[20] Chiang knew that Stilwell did not like him. He feared the implications of putting the few troops he could count on in the hands of the Americans. It was possible Stilwell could keep the troops from coming to his aid in the event of a coup or similar situation. Even worse, it was conceivable that Stilwell could use them to support one of Chiang's political opponents. Considering Stilwell's open disdain of the generalissimo, such worries were not mere idle paranoia.[21]

Progress training the CEF was excruciatingly slow, and it seemed as if Dorn and Stilwell had to fight for every point on every issue. By October 1943, Stilwell decided he had done as much as he could. The Y Force divisions were still far under-strength and Stilwell was concerned the men could not sustain "prolonged hardship" and the officers had "no offensive spirit." He left his concerns to Dorn, however, departing for India to personally supervise the advance along the road from Ledo. The first step in the recapture of Burma was about to begin.[22]

Chapter 6: Back to Burma

Stilwell's promise to return to Burma and take back what he lost would not be an easy one to keep. While Frank Dorn attempted to ready the CEF for operations in Yunnan, Stilwell brought his Chinese troops trained at Ramgarh to the front in North Burma. Over rugged mountains and through dense jungles, he hoped to begin the tedious task of clearing the way for a road from Ledo. Many thought it would prove impossible, but Stilwell remained determined. Meanwhile, the British attempted a few limited jabs of their own. The 14th Indian Division advanced into the Akyab Peninsula, only to have the Japanese 55th fight it to a standstill. After weeks of fighting, the British ended up back where they started—minus 2,500 casualties. The only bright spot in an otherwise bleak, stagnant picture was an experiment in guerrilla warfare by an eccentric British brigadier named Orde Wingate. Wingate's ideas were original and daring, and generated new enthusiasm for CBI at the Quadrant Conference in August 1943. It was at this conference that the Allies decided to totally reorganize the theater and built the special task forces that would revolutionize and reinvigorate the war effort.

On February 8, 1943, Orde Wingate's 77th Indian Infantry Brigade crossed the Chindwin River into Central Burma. His intent was not to retake territory, nor go toe-to-toe with the Japanese. Instead, he devised a concept he called "long-range penetration" (LRP), in which he divided the 2,800-man brigade into seven columns, each small enough to remain hidden in the jungle and infiltrate the Japanese front. The columns then spread out to cut supply lines and create chaos in the rear. When pursued by the Japanese, they simply melted back into the jungle. Wingate nicknamed his force the "Chindits," after the poorly-pronounced name of a mythical Burmese beast.[1]

His unconventional campaign was accompanied by an unconventional plan for supply. The columns brought all they could with them on pack mules, but it took weeks to walk to their objectives through the jungle. With no way of maintaining ground lines of communication to isolated guerrilla units, Wingate planned to supply them from the air.[2] He was inspired by the aerial supply of Chinese troops during the retreat from Burma in 1942. It was an emergency measure then, but Wingate turned it into standard procedure. The RAF attached air liaison officers to each of his columns to coordinate the drops. Once behind enemy lines, the Chindits cut the railway to Myitkyina at several points before continuing east across the Irrawaddy River. The RAF liaisons radioed in each column's supply needs and drop zone information. Flying out under cover of darkness, the transports searched for Chindit signal fires. They did not have direct radio contact with Wingate's men.

The Japanese in North Burma were engaged in a punitive expedition against Kachin tribesmen who had been conducting raids with the help of the British at Fort Hertz. When Wingate's men appeared behind their lines, they cancelled the expedition and devoted three divisions to stop the Chindits instead. Initially, many of their troops lacked the equipment, training, and supplies for jungle warfare and suffered heavy losses to Chindit ambushes. However, their heavy reaction forced the brigade to disperse into small groups to return to friendly territory. Some of the groups went north to Fort Hertz, some east to Baoshan, and some west, back to India. Communication with India was poor to begin with, but lacking gasoline for their battery chargers, many of the columns abandoned their radios when they dispersed. The transports could not find them to keep them supplied. Lacking food and ammunition, the jungle and the fighting took its toll. Only 2,182 of the original 2,800 British and Commonwealth soldiers eventually returned to India and few of the survivors were fit for further duty. Given the cost, Wingate did not accomplish much in terms of battlefield gains, but his concept opened new possibilities.[3]

Wingate traveled to Quebec in August 1943 to present his ideas to the Allies at the Quadrant Conference. After outlining his style of guerrilla warfare, he proposed an expanded operation in conjunction with the planned offensive to retake Burma in the fall. He intended to do very much the same thing he had done in February: divide his force into small columns to infiltrate to the enemy rear. This time he would use a division of six brigades, instead of just one. He asked for light aircraft to support his force and provide a method for evacuating casualties. During his first expedition, men too injured or weak to move were simply left behind. Attrition was high in jungle warfare, and he had no way to evacuate his wounded or receive replacements. "We can't carry him because he becomes a burden," he explained. "We have to prop him up against a tree and give him a gun or let him stay there and give him money ... hoping that the natives would take care of him." It was a terrible fate and terrible for morale. Small aircraft able to land in jungle clearings and remove his casualties to safety would help immeasurably. President Roosevelt was impressed by Wingate's daring and imagination and promised support; he asked Army Air Forces Chief of Staff General "Hap" Arnold to make the arrangements. Arnold selected thirty-three-year-old Lieutenant Colonel Philip Cochran and thirty-year-old Lieutenant Colonel John Alison to head the project.

Cochran and Alison were both unique characters with unique backgrounds that, in Arnold's estimation, qualified them to lead an air task force supporting Wingate's guerrillas. Cochran was the inspiration for the hell-for-leather character "Flip Corkin" in Milt Caniff's comic strip *Terry and the Pirates*. During the North Africa campaign, he led a group of thirty-five P-40s off the deck of the aircraft carrier HMS *Archer*. The fighters moved to a forward airbase in Tunisia, where Cochran found himself de facto commander and became known for his ingenuity and flexibility. He worked to take advantage of the Germans' tendency to methodically do the same thing over and over again while making his own small force unpredictable. He recognized the situation required innovation and informality. "We knew what needed to be done and did it in our own way," he explained. Rather than obliterating the Luftwaffe, which was beyond the capability of his small, ill-equipped organization, he learned "to gain air superiority over one isolated battle." Alison was much more quiet and reserved than Cochran, but was an accomplished fighter pilot in his own right. After working in Russia test-flying lend-lease P-40s, he found himself en route to China, assigned to the Army Air Force fighter group that replaced the AVG. Using Chennault's tactics and network of air bases, he became an ace and a squadron commander in less than a year of combat.

Both Cochran and Alison were disappointed when Arnold ordered them to the "side-alley fight" in Burma, rather than the "big show" in Europe. Wingate requested

From left to right: John Alison, Orde Wingate, and Philip Cochran; three men who pioneered special operations warfare with the Chindits and 1st Air Commando Group in Burma. *National Archives*

light aircraft for supply and evacuation. Both Cochran and Alison were fighter pilots, with no experience in such operations. General Arnold thought an expanded air operation would make the Chindits even more effective and would be the perfect opportunity to showcase the growing capabilities and flexibility of American airpower. He told the pair of reluctant fighter pilots to let their imaginations run wild and "steal the show." "The more we thought of it," recounted Cochran, "the more we built and built. Then we figured that we could turn this thing around and make it … a doggone good air combat effort and really be of great assistance to these ground troops. We could be their artillery, we could be their supply, and we could be their air combat forces."[4]

By the time Cochran arrived in India in November 1943, the light aircraft operation had expanded into a full-blown air task force, later designated the 1st Air Commando Group. In addition to four squadrons of small liaison planes, Cochran and Alison brought two fighter squadrons, a medium bomber squadron, and a troop carrier squadron, including both C-47 cargo planes and CG-4 gliders. The gliders were an important innovation. Instead of Wingate's troops pushing deep behind enemy lines on foot, Cochran and Alison proposed to insert them by air. The gliders could land in jungle clearings, unload troops and equipment, and then be "snatched" out again by low-flying transports specially equipped with a hook-and-reel assembly. Wingate planned his second Chindit expedition to begin in March 1944. The Air Commandos arrived in advance to train with the ground troops.

Air support for the operation was much more complicated than it had been coordinating supply drops for the first Chindit campaign. In North Africa and Europe, fighters and medium bombers struck targets behind a "bomb line" that kept them clear of friendly ground troops. In commando jungle warfare there were no front lines, so bomb lines were not particularly useful. In addition, it was difficult to move and employ artillery in the mountainous jungles, so accurate air support was even more crucial. Instead of using large numbers of aircraft against area targets, the Air Commandos planned to use a small number of aircraft against pinpoint targets. The RAF controllers imbedded with the columns provided the necessary coordination via radio, or with cloth panels or smoke shells. Using rockets, low-level bombing, and dive-bombing, fighter-bombers would hit Japanese troops and positions only yards from friendly ground forces.

In addition to the Air Commandos, General Marshall promised to augment Wingate's division with a regiment of three thousand Americans. The War Department put out a call for volunteers. Corporal Warner Katz had just finished a tour of duty on Guadalcanal when he heard about the "dangerous and hazardous" mission. Katz was drafted in June 1941 at the age of twenty-one. He was originally from Germany, but immigrated to the United States after fighting in the Spanish Civil War. He was eager for more action and enthusiastically stepped forward.[5] Another volunteer was Philip Piazza, a lieutenant in the 33rd Infantry Regiment stationed on the island of Trinidad, in the British West Indies. When Piazza reported to Trinidad in 1942, his commander ordered him and three other officers to put together a jungle warfare school. "I'm a city boy from Bridgeport, Connecticut," he complained. "I was never in the jungle in my life!" The colonel looked him straight in the eye. "I'm not *asking* you!" he retorted. It was an order, not a request. Piazza got to work building the school and writing a tactics manual. It was difficult work. "At that time we didn't know much about jungle warfare," he told me. "We didn't know much about fighting period!" The first he heard about the Burma operation was that it was a dangerous mission and there was a strong possibility he would not survive. He did not know what he would be doing or where he would be going. "It seems crazy," he admitted, "but everybody wanted to volunteer. We had no problem getting volunteers."[6]

In all, the War Department recruited one thousand men each from the Caribbean Defense Command and the United States, three hundred experienced jungle fighters from the Southwest Pacific, and seven hundred from the South Pacific.[7] They were told to expect a three-month combat mission followed by three months of recuperation. They began arriving in Bombay at the end of October 1943 and immediately began training in LRP tactics with the Chindits. The official code-name for the unit was "Galahad." Colonel Charles N. Hunter, a West Pont graduate from Cheyenne, Wyoming, took command. He copied the British table of organization and split the regiment into three battalions, each with two combat teams of sixteen officers and 456 enlisted men. Each team had a rifle company, a heavy weapons platoon, a pioneer and demolition platoon, a reconnaissance platoon, a medical detachment, and an air support coordination section.[8]

The Air Commandos and Wingate's second expedition were not the only results of the Quadrant Conference. The Combined Chiefs of Staff totally reorganized the CBI Theater. Lord Louis Mountbatten—second cousin of Elizabeth II, future Queen of England—became Supreme Commander of the newly created Southeast Asia Command (SEAC). The new command was supposed to bring energy to the theater and reduce inner conflict and confusion. Mountbatten was a strong, charismatic leader, and worked to build cooperation and consensus. However, in some respects the new organization made things worse. Stilwell, for example, became deputy commander of SEAC. His battlefield command of the Chinese Ramgarh divisions though, fell under the authority of the British 14th Army commander, Major General William Slim, his subordinate. Thus, he answered to Slim, who in turn answered to him. Furthermore, Chiang Kai-shek still remained Supreme Commander of the China Theater, an area over which SEAC had no authority whatsoever.

The Quadrant Conference did reaffirm the Allied commitment to operations in Burma and Stilwell continued training the Chinese divisions at Ramgarh. To fill in the battered ranks of the units that survived the retreat from Burma, Chiang sent thousands of men over the Hump to India. Luo Chih-tsai, who fled his home in

Major General Sun Liren, commander of the 38th Division, in late April 1944. He made quite a reputation for himself when he rescued the British at Yenangyaung. He would go on to be one of the most successful Chinese generals of the war. *Merrill's Marauders Association*

Hubei Province under the guns of the Japanese air force in 1939, was, by 1943, an eighteen-year-old staff sergeant in the armored corps. He volunteered to go to India, but was too short and too thin—candidates had to be at least five feet, four inches tall and weigh 120 pounds. Few soldiers in the Chinese Army met these requirements though, and they were soon waived. Before long Luo was on his way. At Kunming,

American medics examined the soldiers' health and fitness before they boarded C-47s to join the stream of transports shuttling over the Hump. "It was a damn cold flight for me when we were flying across the Himalayas," Luo remembered. Many of the troops passed out from the lack of oxygen. Some even froze to death. Luo arrived safely at Dinjan in October 1943 and began training at Ramgarh shortly thereafter.[9]

The training program Stilwell implemented stressed infantry-artillery cooperation in jungle warfare and individual and unit tactics up to the battalion level. Naga tribesmen taught jungle craft in follow-on training at Ledo. Stilwell hoped the training would instill self-reliance and initiative in the Chinese troops.[10] The Chinese Army in India—or X Force, as he called it—was composed of two divisions, each with 12,500 men. Major General Liao Yaoxiang commanded the 22nd Division and Major General Sun Liren commanded the 38th. Liao was a graduate of St. Cyr, the premier military academy in France. Brigadier General Haydon L. Boatner, Stilwell's chief of staff and deputy commander of the X Force, thought he was, "a good field soldier, courageous and determined." Frank Dorn remembered that Liao and Stilwell usually spoke to each other in French, "which sounded a bit odd under the circumstances."[11] Sun Liren was a graduate of the Virginia Military Institute. His daring rescue of the British at Yenangyaung in April 1942 was typical of his character. He was a thirty-six-year-old regimental commander during the Battle of Shanghai in 1937. His regiment was cannibalized to reinforce the crumbling 88th Division in the city. Without any troops under his command, he led his staff to the front lines. There he found Chinese soldiers retreating under heavy attack, abandoned by their officers. He took charge and rallied them to face the enemy. The Japanese were surprised at the sudden turn of events and their attack ground to a halt. Sun remained at the front until he was badly wounded and pulled from action.[12] According to Boatner, Sun was "a good field soldier, courageous and determined. Argumentative, insistent on doing things his way; but much concerned over the well-being of his unit. A capable commander." The training at Ramgarh was the second time Sun rebuilt the 38th Division. The Ministry of Finance originally created the division in 1930 as a Tax Police unit to fight smuggling and salt trafficking. It fought valiantly during the Battle of Shanghai, but by the end was down to only two thousand soldiers. Sun took command in Changsha and rebuilt it as the 38th. Under his leadership, a division that had virtually ceased to exist became one of the most competent units in the Chinese Army.

Stilwell knew that most Chinese commanders avoided combat because a loss of troops meant a loss of power and influence. He pushed the Chinese War Ministry to maintain a steady stream of replacements to motivate Sun and Liao to be aggressive. He also assigned American liaison teams to each division, battalion, and regiment. On October 5, he ordered Sun to move the 112th Regiment forward to shield construction of the Ledo Road in the no-man's land of North Burma. Construction had stalled during the summer monsoon, but by the end of November 1943, the road stretched over eighty miles from Ledo.

North Burma was split in two by the six-thousand-foot-tall Kumon Range. To the west of these jungle-covered mountains were the headwaters of the Chindwin River which, flowing north, carved the Hukawng Valley and then turned to follow

A P-40 flies low over Chinese troops of the X Force as they march through the Patkai Hills into North Burma in late 1943. ***National Archives via Samuel Hui***

Staff Sergeant Luo Chih-tsai remembered the training course in the American M3A3 at Ramgarh as short, but intense. Here he stands on the front of an M4A4 Sherman after the Japanese surrender in 1945. ***Courtesy of Samuel Hui***

the India-Burma border to join the Irrawaddy south of Mandalay. To the east of these mountains was the Irrawaddy Valley and Myitkyina. Just south of the Kumon Range and separated from the Hukawng Valley by a ridge called Jambu Bum, was the Mogaung Valley. This narrow corridor ran east to west, connecting the Hukawng Valley with Myitkyina. If Stilwell's forces could advance through this series of valleys to Mytikyina, they could then make use of existing roads that would become functional very soon after the X Force in Burma connected with the Y Force in China.[13]

General Sun's troops marched over the Patkai Hills into the Hukawng Valley and occupied Shingbwiyang without opposition.[14] In the local language, Hukawng Valley means "the valley where demons live." For the Chinese Army, it meant facing the demons of their past. The valley was littered with the bones of their comrades from the disastrous retreat a year and a half earlier. Things were different now. In India, the Chinese troops were fed as much as they could eat. They were paid in cash and given shoes, clothing, and medical care.[15] "We had changed completely," said Xiao Diaocheng, a platoon leader in the 112th Regiment. "We were armed to the teeth with American weapons! We had many heavy machine guns; we had tanks; we had cannons; we had mortars; we had howitzers; and we had anti-tank guns. Wow! We had everything!" The thorough training filled the soldiers with confidence. "The training was tough, very tough," remembered Wang Tingju. "Every morning, we spent two hours doing formation drill, and another two hours on shooting practice and infantry skills. Every afternoon we had field training—creeping, jumping, charging... All were highly demanding physically. Not a single day passed without tough training." Luo Chih-tsai remembered the four-week training course on the M3A3 Stuart light tank as brief but challenging. The first week focused on using the .30-caliber machine gun. They learned how to operate the 37-milimeter main gun during the second week and how to drive during the third. For the fourth and final week, they practiced long distance drives with their tanks in column. Once they completed their training, they picked up new vehicles and equipment in Calcutta and moved to the front.[16]

On October 30, 1943, as the Chinese moved south down the Hukawng Valley, they met unexpected resistance from the Japanese 18th Division at Yupbang Ga. The 18th had fought the British in Malaya and Singapore before participating in the invasion of Burma in 1942. They were experts in jungle warfare and built strong defensive positions blocking the roads and trails.[17] The Chinese found them dug in where the north-flowing Tarung River met the westward-flowing Tanai. The 18th deftly defended against any direct attack or encirclement. The Chinese took heavy casualties and progress stalled. It was only twenty-five days into the campaign, and it appeared as if the demons of the Hukawng Valley were dogging the Chinese Army yet again. The stalemate prompted Stilwell to leave his headquarters in India and take personal command in the field. Sun advanced cautiously and deliberately. Stilwell urged rapidity. Chiang wanted them to stop the advance and establish defensive positions; he was convinced the Japanese were marshaling for a counterattack. He thought Stilwell's tactics were too risky and ordered prudence. Sun was trapped in the middle of a dispute between his direct superior and the leader of his nation. He did his best to navigate the political minefield, but it was Christmas Eve before an envelopment of the Japanese line finally broke the stalemate.[18]

Stilwell knew he could not achieve his goals if progress continued at such an excruciatingly slow pace. He urged the Chinese Expeditionary Force in Yunnan to cross the Salween to relieve the pressure on his forces. He also requested the American regiment be transferred from Wingate's control to his command. He and Wingate had sparred for some time over Galahad. Stilwell was upset that the only American ground troops in the theater were not under his command. Furthermore, he disagreed with the concept of LRP. He thought he could better use the troops in short envelopments in advance of a general offensive, leapfrogging around the Japanese

Brigadier General Frank Merrill, map in hand, evaluating the Marauders' position. Merrill suffered a mild heart attack during Stilwell's walkout from Burma. Nevertheless, Stilwell appointed him commander of the 5307th Composite Unit (Provisional) in place of Frank Hunter, the original commander. *Merrill's Marauders Association*

flank while the Chinese attacked the front.[19] The outcome was probably inevitable. Stilwell was deputy commander of SEAC and Wingate only a division commander. On January 8, 1944, Stilwell learned that Mountbatten officially transferred Galahad to his command. He immediately replaced Colonel Hunter with Brigadier General Frank Merrill. Hunter was an experienced infantry officer. Merrill's background was as a cavalry officer and language expert. It was becoming typical of Stilwell to keep his top staff within the small clique of men that walked out of Burma with him in 1942, even though Merrill suffered a heart attack during that walkout. The regiment was officially designated the 5307th Composite Unit (Provisional), but *Time-Life* correspondent James Shepley dubbed them "Merrill's Marauders" and the name stuck.[20] Colonel Hunter was second in command. Lieutenant Colonel William L. Osborne commanded 1st Battalion; Lieutenant Colonel George A. McGee, Jr., commanded 2nd Battalion; and Lieutenant Colonel Charles E. Beach commanded 3rd Battalion. They would be the spearhead for Stilwell's advance into Burma.[21]

7

Behind the Lines

In February 1944, Merrill's Marauders arrived in North Burma to give impetus to the Chinese advance. Their daring leapfrogs behind enemy lines would surprise the Japanese, but their lack of heavy equipment and small numbers left them vulnerable to determined counterattacks. Even with their arrival, no one in the Allied command could say with conviction that Stilwell would reach his goal of Myitkyina before the summer monsoon. Meanwhile, the failed British offensive in the Arakan, the Wingate expedition in central Burma, and guerrilla raids by Kachin tribesmen in North Burma prompted the Japanese to reorganize. Lieutenant General Shozo Kawabe stood up the new Burma Area Army, under which the 15th Army—with its 33rd, 18th, and 56th divisions—was now responsible for North Burma and western Yunnan. General Mutaguchi moved up from the 18th Division to command the 15th Army. He was a strong proponent of invading India and his new post gave renewed energy to that idea. The Japanese began planning for a new offensive at a conference in Rangoon in June 1943.[1]

Stilwell met his American troops in the Pangsau Pass as they marched over the Patkai Hills into North Burma. Phil Piazza remembered talking with the general in the pass. Though he was a controversial figure, many of Stilwell's men appreciated his straightforward attitude and found him down-to-earth and relatable. He always wore a steel helmet or an old campaign hat and never wore medals or insignia. Pouring through photo archives of the North Burma campaign, one finds Stilwell in many of them. Not in the center, not the subject nor conspicuous, but off to the side or in the background. One of Piazza's men walked up while he was talking to Stilwell. "Things must be pretty rough over in the States when they send an old SOB like you over here to fight!" the soldier exclaimed, not recognizing the old general. Piazza was embarrassed, but Stilwell chuckled and told him not to worry about it.[2]

The Marauders began arriving at the front on February 19, 1942. Stilwell immediately ordered them to set up a roadblock behind enemy lines at Walawbum, ninety miles southeast of Ledo and only fourteen miles north of Jambu Bum—the ridge that marked the south end of the Hukawng Valley. They set out into the jungle with only what they and their pack mules could carry. Piazza was the leader of one of 2nd Battalion's heavy weapons platoons. "The heaviest equipment we could carry were machine guns and mortars," he recounted. "In other words, we couldn't carry artillery." The platoon had thirty-seven horses and mules. "I used the animals to carry our heavy weapons and our ammunition," said Piazza, "but the men carried very heavy packs."[3] What they lacked in firepower, they made up for in mobility. The Marauders quickly moved into position: 2nd Battalion blocked the road entering Walawbum from the west; 3rd Battalion blocked the road to Shaduzup to the south; and 1st Battalion patrolled to the north.[4] As the lead scout in one of 3rd Battalion's reconnaissance platoons, Warner Katz was the first to encounter the enemy. On February 25, he was walking through tall elephant grass, "dreaming of New York," when he suddenly saw a Japanese soldier ten yards in front of him. He quickly brought up his rifle and shot the man. A machine gun opened fire. Katz hit the ground, taking cover in a shallow

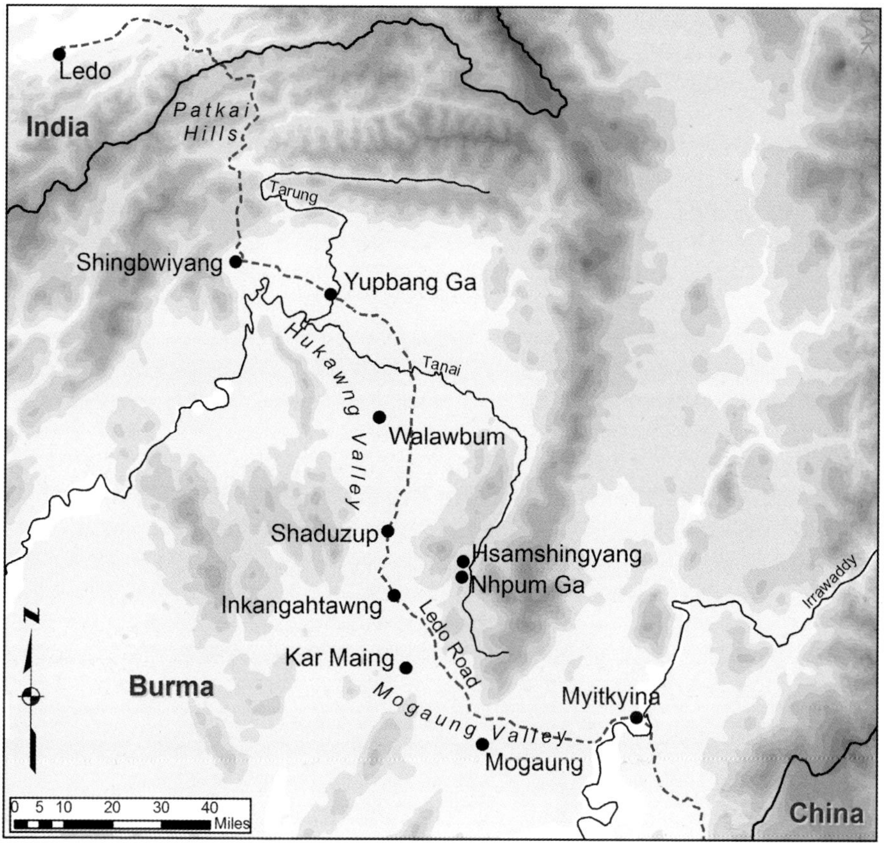

Operations in North Burma

depression. A bullet ricocheted in front of him and grazed his nose and left cheek. His was the first kill and the first injury. Bob Landis, from 2nd Battalion, was the unit's first loss.[5]

Herbert Clofine was a radio operator in one of 2nd Battalion's reconnaissance platoons. He carried a sixty-pound SCR300 radio on his back in addition to his combat gear. While the bulk of the unit was digging in at the roadblock, Clofine came across some telephone lines. He was with Sergeant Roy Matsumoto, one of the battalion's four Japanese interpreters. Matsumoto was a Nisei, meaning he was born a U.S. citizen to immigrant parents. He spent nine years of his childhood living with his grandparents in Hiroshima, but returned to America for high school. Though the United States government sent over one hundred thousand Japanese-Americans to internment camps during the war, Matsumoto decided he wanted to serve his country. He proved invaluable to the Marauders. At Walawbum, he tapped into the phone lines and intercepted Japanese communications. He passed the information to Clofine, who radioed it to the battalion commander, Lieutenant Colonel McGee. The information enabled the Marauders to call in an airstrike on an enemy ammunition dump.[6]

Stilwell (right), wearing his iconic campaign hat, watches as tanks of the 1st Provisional Tank Group move toward the front near Shaduzup, Burma, in April 1944. ***National Archives via Samuel Hui***

The Japanese were confused by the sudden appearance of American troops behind their front lines; they were caught between an American roadblock and the Chinese advance. On March 6, Sun Liren sent the Chinese-American 1st Provisional Tank Group into Maingkwan to help the 22nd Division break through. The Japanese pulled back. The tank group was a joint Chinese-American unit commanded by an American, Colonel Rothwell Brown, with a Chinese deputy, Colonel Chao Chen-yu. The six battalions of Chinese were integrated with a single company of Americans. Staff Sergeant Luo Chih-tsai drove a Stuart light tank in the 1st Battalion. He thought highly of Colonel Brown, whom he remembered as "very patient with the Chinese tank crews." It was tough going through the jungle; the tanks were restricted to narrow roads. Nevertheless, the unit soon proved its worth. After driving through Maingkwan, the group's Sherman and Stuart tanks charged into Walawbum, right into the headquarters of the 18th Division. The tankers opened fire, killing over one hundred enemy troops.[7] Lieutenant General Shinichi Tanaka, the division commander, could not reinforce Walawbum without weakening the impending invasion of India. He decided to make a fighting withdrawal toward Kar Maing.

Matsumoto was still listening to the Japanese communications when the order to withdraw came through. The Marauders' 2nd Battalion was low on supplies, and it sounded like the bulk of the Japanese forces would retreat through their area. Thanks to this intelligence, McGee decided to abandon his roadblock and join 3rd Battalion to the south. The Japanese withdrew, yielding the rest of the Hukawng Valley to the

Corporal Warner Katz of New York City was a German-born veteran of Guadalcanal. He was the first Marauder to encounter the enemy. A long scar marks where the Japanese machine gun bullet creased his cheek and nostril. *Merrill's Marauders Association*

Allies. The combination of a Marauder roadblock in the rear and the Chinese infantry and tanks at the front delivered precisely the kind of decisive advance Stilwell had in mind.

The Chinese 22nd Division continued into the Mogaung Valley and Stilwell sent the Marauders on another mission behind enemy lines. This time, he divided the regiment and sent 1st Battalion to cut the Kar Maing Road near Shaduzup, in the Mogaung Valley, twenty miles south of Walawbum and five miles south of the Jambu Bum ridge. He sent 2nd and 3rd Battalions to cut the road at Inkangahtawng, a jungle clearing fourteen miles further south and only fifteen miles north of Kar Maing. Lieutenant Colonel Osborne led his men in a successful envelopment; 1st Battalion's road block at Shaduzup allowed the 22nd Division to advance south from Walawbum.[8] The 2nd and 3rd Battalions did not fare as well. General Tanaka had orders to hold Kar Maing at all costs and was determined to fix and fight the Marauders north of the town. He sent thousands of soldiers to attack 2nd Battalion's road block at dawn on March 24. "We knew that we were going to get hit at dawn because all night long we heard the Japanese coming up the road," remembered Phil Piazza. "They were good soldiers in some respects, but they were always very noisy."[9] The Americans stressed the value of silence when operating behind enemy lines. They quietly listened as the Japanese unloaded from their trucks, banging the tailgates and "jabbering away."

Just as they suspected, the enemy attacked at dawn, hitting 2nd Battalion with no fewer than eighteen banzai charges throughout the day. It was a fierce and bloody battle. Lieutenant Colonel McGee began a phased withdrawal, leapfrogging his units back to avoid being overrun. Piazza directed his heavy weapons, devastating the enemy every time they charged. "I had bodies piled up so high in front of my machine guns that I had to get out and kick the bodies away so we could fire," he recalled. At one point, he was outside the perimeter, directing his mortars when he was hit by a Japanese machine gun. "I still have two machine gun bullets in my head," he told me sixty-five years later. "Stay back! I'll crawl to you!" he yelled to his men before they could leave the safety of their positions to rescue him. He pulled himself toward them, but then shrapnel from a 90-millimeter mortar hit his leg. Corporal Harry Fosshine jumped out and dragged him the rest of the way to the perimeter. They bandaged his wounds as best they could and carried him to the rear on a stretcher.[10]

2nd Battalion was badly outnumbered and the Chinese were advancing too slowly. They could no longer hold the roadblock. On March 26, McGee ordered them to withdraw east into the mountains. In the midst of the battle, it was impossible to evacuate Phil Piazza. His men carried him on a stretcher for two days and then propped him up on horseback for five more. "I didn't even have time to have the medics take care of me," he said. "We had to do just first aid." The trek was grueling. "You have to have experienced it to understand how serious the situation was," he told me again and again during our interview. I believed him.[11]

While the Marauders fought at Inkangahtawng, events elsewhere in Burma threatened to isolate Stilwell's forces and disrupt his advance. On February 4, 1944, the Japanese 55th Division attacked the British in the Arakan. The Burma Area Army meant for the attack to distract the British and occupy their reserves while they prepared for a major offensive aimed at Imphal and Kohima. Were this major offensive to succeed, it would give the Japanese a foothold in India, cut off Stilwell's forces in North Burma, and threaten the airlift bases supplying China. In the Arakan, the Japanese used their typical tactics that worked so well in 1942: infiltrating the front lines and surrounding the British. This time, General Slim ordered his troops to stand their ground. He used airplanes to supply his forces and attack Japanese lines of supply. The tactic worked brilliantly and went into effect on a much larger scale when the Japanese advanced on

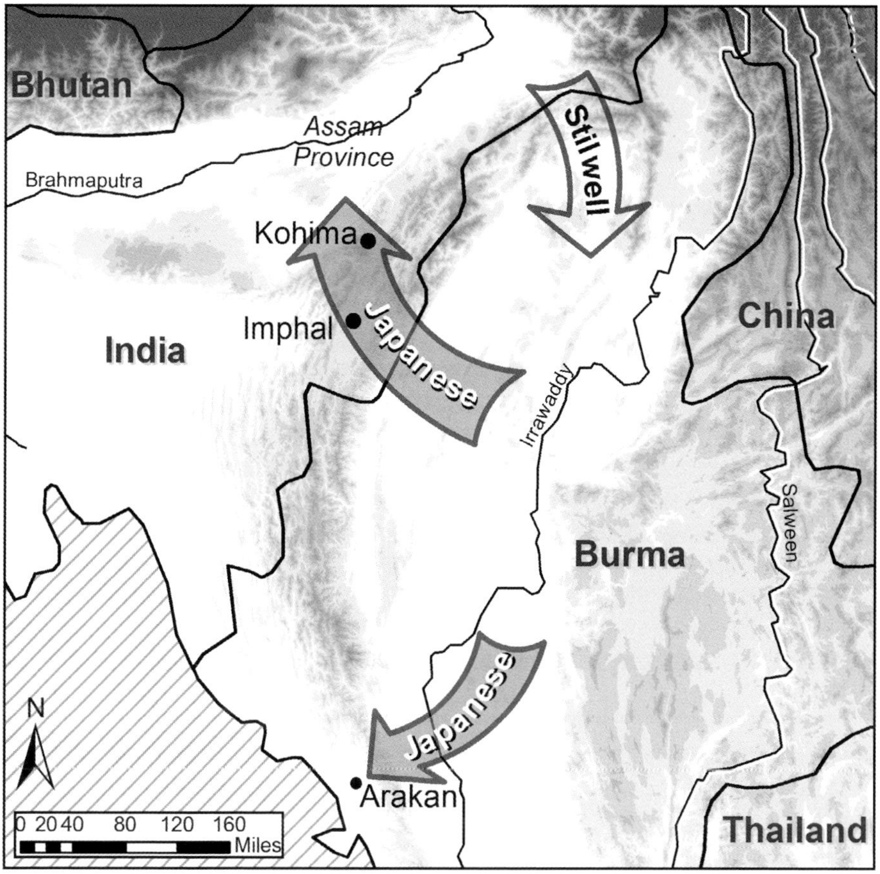

Operation U-Go

A 10th Air Force C-47 drops supplies to Merrill's Marauders in North Burma. *Merrill's Marauders Association*

Imphal and Kohima on March 8, surrounding both of those garrisons with 155,000 troops. The situation was critical for all parties. Air interdiction left Japanese supplies dangerously low, while air supply barely sustained the besieged British garrisons. The Chindits helped; the Air Commandos landed over nine thousand of them in Central Burma by March 11. They began sowing destruction in and amongst the Japanese supply lines. Their campaign helped limit the offensive into India and protected Stilwell's southern flank as he continued his advance.

The Marauders' 2nd Battalion withdrew from the road block at Inkangahtawng on March 26. Merrill ordered them to establish a defensive position in the mountains twelve miles to the northeast at Nhpum Ga, a village of four or five huts on a steep hill overlooking the Tanai River, 2,800 feet above sea level. A captured map showed that a reinforced Japanese battalion was planning to outflank the Chinese by moving north up the Tanai into the Hukawng Valley. The Marauders were ordered to hold the hill and stop the attack. Merrill directed 3rd Battalion to Hsamshingyang—a further five miles north—to hold a field for supply drops and liaison planes. McGee's men arrived on March 28 and prepared as best they could while skirmishing with the leading enemy patrols. At dawn on the thirtieth, the Japanese attacked 2nd Battalion in full force, beginning a savage battle for the position.[12]

Because the Marauders trained with Wingate's LRP brigades, they had an air support officer imbedded with each battalion. The Air Commandos did not support the Marauders—Cochran was ordered to support Wingate and Wingate only—but the Marauders began applying the same system of air support to other units arriving in theater. The 27th Troop Carrier Squadron arrived in India in December 1943 and immediately began air drop missions into Burma. The squadron was part of Arnold's promise for an increase of four hundred transport planes to SEAC. Mountbatten requested more transports because of the supply operations in the Arakan, at Imphal and Kohima, and with the Chindits.[13] For close air support, the 80th and 311th fighter groups both began flying missions from Assam in the fall of 1943. The 80th was equipped with P-40s, the 311th with P-51As and A-36s.

The A-36 was a variant of the P-51; a hasty conversion from fighter to dive-bomber. According to Bill Creech, a pilot with the 311th Group's 528th Squadron, the A-36 "was a real work horse. Her flight characteristics were very similar to the P-51A." Designers augmented the Mustang's four wing guns with two additional .50-caliber machine guns mounted underneath the engine and synchronized to fire through the propeller. Dive brakes on the top and bottom of each wing made it capable of vertical dives. The 1,325-horsepower Allison engine achieved optimum performance at three thousand feet above sea level.[14] According to Creech, the modifications were not effective. "Her big deficiency was the altitude limitation of her engine," he said. "The 'critical altitude' [altitude above which rated power is not available] was only three thousand feet. So, down low she was a 'goin' Jessie,' but altitude performance was poor." Hank Snow, another pilot with the 528th, complained that when using the dive brakes, "one would come out and one wouldn't and they'd . . . corkscrew you into the ground. So we had them wired off so we couldn't use them."[15] If that were not trouble enough, Creech reported "the two synchronized nose guns weren't much help. They had poor cooling and all too often after a strafing pass, they would 'cook off' an unsynchronized round and put a hole through the prop."[16] The A-36s and early-model P-51s still made excellent

Robert Austin, a pilot with the 529th Fighter Squadron, stands in front of his P-51A at an airbase in Assam, India. *Courtesy of Robert Austin*

A P-51A of the 311th Fighter Group over Assam in 1944. The P-51 was fast and agile, but a single bullet in the radiator or coolant lines could cripple it. *Courtesy of Dr. Rose*

attack aircraft, though their vulnerability to ground fire was a notable weakness. Robert Austin, a pilot with the 529th, reported: "When you get down to it, [when flying] any aircraft with a liquid-cooled engine . . . and you get a bullet in the radiator, or in the coolant line, it's not *if* you're going to bail out, it's *when*."[17] The Army Air Forces Proving Ground at Eglin Field, Florida, recommended the A-36 be used as a minimum-altitude fighter-bomber rather than a dive-bomber. The 311th gradually replaced its A-36s with P-51As and eventually, Merlin-engine-equipped P-51Bs.[18]

The 311th worked with the Marauders to bomb and strafe the Japanese around Nhpum Ga. According to Creech: "Our job was to ensure that Merrill's Marauders and all the Army types on the ground could always look up and see a flight of A-36s ready to provide support."[19] Over a period of sixteen days, the 528th Fighter Squadron flew 440 sorties. Weather permitting, a new flight arrived overhead every hour. They identified themselves as "Dragonfly Flight" when they radioed the ground parties.[20] According to Piazza: "Everything was close in, man-to-man, eye-to-eye, so they dropped the stuff right on top of us." Fighter-bomber support "was the one thing we did have. . . . They never got the credit that they really deserved. Our operation could never have succeeded without support from them."[21] Though there were incidents of friendly fire, they were surprisingly rare considering the conditions. Creech recalled that sometimes, when the opposing forces were too close together, the air control parties would "ask us to 'make the next pass dry' so his troops could run over and toss hand grenades into the Jap positions while they had their heads down."[22] In addition to bombs and rockets, the 311th began dropping 325-pound depth charges. The depth charges had more concussive force and less shrapnel than bombs, clearing out the jungle to give the Marauders clear fields of fire. "The blast cleaned out the foliage, blew the Japs up out of their dug outs," wrote one Marauder. "We shot them while they were in the air."[23]

The enemy closed in on three sides of Nhpum Ga. Fighting seesawed along 2nd Battalion's perimeter. On March 30, the Japanese pushed the battalion's pioneer and demolition platoon up the ridge, capturing their only water hole. The next day, the Americans discovered they were completely surrounded. 2nd Battalion had depended on a narrow mountain trail connecting it with 3rd Battalion to the north, but now air drops were their only source of supply. They were running dangerously short of water. Phil Piazza was able to reach Hsamshingyang before the Japanese cut the trail. On the thirty-first, a liaison plane evacuated him to Maingkwan, where he boarded a C-47 bound for the 20th General Hospital in Ledo. He spent the next year and a half in various hospitals recovering. His mother received three different telegrams: the first reported he was killed in action. The second stated he was not killed, just wounded, but was missing. The third finally got it right.[24] Frank Merrill continued to command the battle from 3rd Battalion's position, but he also had to be flown back to India on the thirty-first due to heart trouble. Colonel Hunter took charge. His efforts to relieve 2nd Battalion met with overwhelming enemy resistance. According to Hunter, these were Galahad's "darkest days."[25]

The situation became desperate. During a heavy attack on April 4, the Japanese briefly penetrated 2nd Battalion's perimeter. 3rd Battalion, reinforced by fifty-five Kachin guerillas, kept pressure on the Japanese. The Kachins were a minority ethnic group native to North Burma. Before the war, the British cultivated good relations with them by protecting them from the majority Burmans in the south. The Kachins hated the Japanese. When the Japanese came and the British left, they lost their protection. Operatives from the Office of Strategic Services (OSS)—a forerunner to the CIA—mobilized the Kachins into guerrilla bands to raid and ambush behind enemy lines. At first, the Marauders did not know what to make of them, but their knowledge of the terrain and utter savagery in battle quickly overcame any doubts.[26] With their help, 3rd Battalion began to make some headway.

On the night of the fourth, Roy Matsumoto snuck outside the perimeter. He overheard Japanese troops talking about an attack at dawn. When he got back, he warned his comrades. They pulled back their lines and booby trapped the empty foxholes. The next morning, the enemy attacked on schedule. They expected to surprise the Americans, but they met an overwhelming wall of fire. Many of them ducked into the empty foxholes for cover and tripped the booby traps. Matsumoto preempted the relief of a supporting battalion by yelling "charge!" at the top of his lungs in Japanese. The other Marauders were amazed: Matsumoto was standing, fully exposed, shouting commands in Japanese and firing madly with his carbine at any enemy troops that exposed themselves.[27] It was remarkable that he survived. Meanwhile, Chinese troops relieved 1st Battalion at Shaduzup and Lieutenant Colonel Osborne quickly ordered his men east to help at Nhpum Ga. On April 7—Good Friday—they maneuvered south of the position and cut the Japanese supply lines. The next day, a combined force of 1st Battalion, 3rd Battalion, and Kachin guerillas broke through the encirclement. On the morning of the ninth—Easter Sunday—the Marauders woke up to find the Japanese had completely withdrawn.

In the course of the battle, the unit lost fifty-seven dead and 302 wounded; 379 were evacuated by air because of wounds or sickness.[28] It was a hard-fought victory. The Americans were exhausted. The hilltop was covered with the bodies of dead pack animals and enemy soldiers. Flies swarmed over the carnage. During the battle there was no place for the mules or horses to hide. Most were cut down by shrapnel and stray bullets. 2nd Battalion exhumed their dead from shallow graves and moved them to a cemetery on the hill. Thirty bamboo crosses stood in mute testimony to their sacrifice. The soldiers used flamethrowers and shovels to burn and bury the dead pack animals and enemy soldiers.[29] Merrill wrote the 528th to thank them for "a superb and accurate support mission ... you rang the bell with every bomb with terrific results ...

Lieutenant Colonel Charles Beach greets Lieutenant Colonel George McGee at Hsamshingyang, Burma, after the siege of Nhpum Ga was lifted on April 9, 1944. ***Merrill's Marauders Association***

Galahad is most pleased with support." Stilwell downplayed the intensity of the battle. He still needed the Marauders for the tough campaign ahead. He could not afford for them to be exhausted. In his diary he wrote: "Galahad is OK. Hard fight at Nhpum. Cleaned out Japs and hooked up. No worry there."[30]

After the fighting at Nhpum Ga, the Marauders tried to recover while the Chinese continued inching toward Kar Maing. On April 22, 1944, Lieutenant Colonel John Habecker—a West Point graduate and a senior pilot from the 311th—assumed the duties of air officer at Stilwell's forward headquarters. Despite the system used by the Chindits and Marauders, the X Force still had no method of air-ground coordination. Instead of pinpointing targets for close-in bombing and strafing, the Chinese designated vast areas as targets and were unreliable reading maps. They rarely reported the results of an attack to supporting aircraft.[31] "On one mission," reported Habecker, "I saw seven of our Chinese tanks burning. The smoke rose through the heavy jungle covering the melee. There was no way we in the air could help those on the ground. We did not have the communication we had with the Marauders."[32] General Boatner decided to make air-ground coordination a priority.[33] He allowed Habecker to arrange a series of training exercises with Chinese tanks and artillery.

Habecker complained that "Stilwell's staff had no knowledge of the capabilities of air support." On one occasion, air support stopped when the weather closed in over the mountains between Burma and Assam. Boatner asked why the pilots could not simply fly into Burma and bail out if they could not make it back. "What if you were a Lt Col and a General suggested this?" Habecker lamented. He did the best he could and continued trying to improve communication and coordination. He arranged air support for a tank maneuver against the Japanese front lines. The tanks were from Colonel Brown's 1st Provisional Tank Group. As they advanced, the Japanese countered with heavy mortar fire. Fighter-bombers roared into action, attacking the mortars and strafing the ditches alongside the roadway as the tanks moved forward. It was a stunning success. Colonel Brown told Habecker that his men "got so enthused with the support you guys were giving they wanted to continue to Mandalay." A few successful engagements did not yet equate to a functioning system of air support, however. There was still a lot of work to be done and Habecker was "pretty much operating alone."[34] In the meantime, the general advance continued at a snail's pace. The British were besieged at Imphal and Kohima. The Japanese still held Kar Maing. The Marauders were victorious at Nhpum Ga, but exhausted. It would take a miracle for Stilwell to reach Myitkyina before the summer monsoon. As the spring of 1944 wore on, it became increasingly important for the Chinese Expeditionary Force to cross the Salween River, even as Chiang became more reluctant to allow it to do so.

8

Across the Salween

In December 1943, Stilwell returned to China after attending yet another Allied conference, this time in Cairo. He dropped by Y Force Operations Staff Headquarters in Kunming to visit with Frank Dorn, recently promoted to brigadier general. The conference had not gone well from his perspective. It was the first Allied conference Chiang attended personally. Though the generalissimo agreed *in principle* to Stilwell's plans, he also campaigned heavily for operations in China to focus on Chennault's air plan and demanded the Allies reaffirm their promise for an amphibious assault in Burma. Stilwell spoke to Dorn of his ever-increasing frustration with Chiang's demands and delays, and informed him that President Roosevelt was beginning to share his frustration. He claimed the president confidentially told him he regretted there was not a more cooperative, active leader at the helm of Nationalist China. "In the course of this private conversation," Dorn remembered, "General Stilwell instructed me to prepare a workable plan for the assassination of Chiang Kai-shek." Dorn was shocked. "When I asked if I might be informed of the source of the order for this plan, General Stilwell refused to tell me." All he would say was that it "comes from the very top." He told Dorn that while he was not sure whether the assassination would ever be carried out, if it was, it could not point back to any individual or agency associated with the U.S. government. Dorn was dubious, but nevertheless decided the best way would be for the generalissimo's plane to go down over the Hump. The pilots would feign engine trouble and abandon ship. Only the crew would have working parachutes; Chiang would fall to his death in a "tragic accident." It was "about as fool-proof as anything of this kind could be," wrote Dorn. He explained the plan to Stilwell, who agreed that it would probably work.[1]

The plan was never implemented and Dorn never learned the source of the supposed order. There is no evidence Roosevelt told Stilwell to make such preparations. It is possible the general inferred too much from apparently innocent comments, or that he was being proactive, "just in case." What is certain is that Roosevelt's frustration was mounting. On January 14, 1944, he sent a radio to Chiang, asking him to send the Chinese Expeditionary Force into action. Though it was not the first time the president engaged him on the issue, this instance represented a significant shift in his approach. "If the Yunnan forces cannot be employed," he wrote, "it would appear that we should avoid for the present the movement of critical materials to them." He stressed that lines of communication were limited and he wished to "curtail the continuing build-up of stockpiles in India beyond that which will be brought to bear against the enemy." In April 1943, Roosevelt had scoffed at Stilwell's suggestion for a quid-pro-quo approach with the Chinese. Less than a year later, he seemed to have changed his mind. Whether or not he was thinking of ordering an assassination, Chinese inaction was certainly testing the limits of his patience. If Chiang would not send the Y Force into combat, Roosevelt would stop sending it supplies and equipment.

Chiang replied on February 2. He appreciated Roosevelt's eagerness to open the Ledo Road, "a desire which is also my great concern since it is only through the opening of this land route that China may quickly obtain the heavy equipment much needed by her army." He claimed that the Y Force was nearly ready, but he was waiting for the large-scale amphibious operation promised again at the Cairo Conference. "I stand ready to adhere

The Cairo Conference in October 1943 was the only Allied strategy conference to which Chiang Kai-shek was invited. He is sitting on the far left next to President Franklin Roosevelt and Prime Minister Winston Churchill. Madame Chiang is sitting on the far right. Stilwell is standing fourth from the left behind the president. Lord Louis Mountbatten is standing second from the right behind Churchill. ***National Archives***

to this decision," he said, "and hope that we can carry out operations even before November of this year, which date you mentioned as possible and probable for the diverting of the amphibious equipment to Burma." Though Roosevelt and Churchill agreed to the amphibious operation at Cairo, they subsequently cancelled it after conferring with Stalin at Tehran in November. Chiang's response to Roosevelt's impatience and frustration was to remind him of unfulfilled Allied promises. He felt no obligation to hold up his end of the bargain if the Allies failed to hold up theirs.

As Galahad and the X Force advanced into Burma, Stilwell saw a strategic opportunity slipping through his fingers. He believed the Japanese 56th Division on the Salween Front was sending reinforcements to the 18th Division in North Burma. If the Y Force would only move, he believed the Japanese would crumble in the face of simultaneous advances on two fronts. He sent a radio to General Marshall on March 17, 1944, begging for him to put more pressure on Chiang. The president sent another message, but the generalissimo continued to resist. "It may be observed that seven years of war have taxed China's material and military strength to such an extent that to insist upon her doing something beyond her power would be to court disaster," he replied. "The consequences ... would seriously affect not only Yunnan and Sichuan, but also the whole situation in this theater of war." Chiang's own policy was to tactfully refrain from asking more than his war area commanders could or would provide. He asked Roosevelt for the same consideration given the harsh political realities of his situation.

In the spring of 1944, the Guomindang was not only facing the Japanese, but also an anti-government uprising in Xinjiang (also called Chinese Turkestan) and expanding Communist influence in Shanxi. It was perhaps ironic that while Chiang bitterly opposed Western imperialism, he was all too willing to brutally put down uprisings in Tibet and Xinjiang. Were the CEF to fail in Burma, Chiang thought it possible "the Japanese would invade Yunnan and Sichuan, the revolt in Xinjiang and the Communist activities in Shanxi would assume a new aspect in the furtherance of their plan of bolshevizing this country so that our Government would not be in a position to do its part in this global war." President Roosevelt threatened to cut off supplies, but Chiang warned that China might fall out of the war altogether, freeing hundreds of thousands of Japanese troops to fight the Americans in the Pacific. Before Chiang would engage in Burma, he needed some assurance of victory. He would only use the CEF in concert with a major amphibious attack.[2] For his part, Frank Dorn tried to persuade Minister of War and Chinese Army Chief of Staff General He Yingqin to launch the CEF in early March. He pointed out that any delay would put them closer to the beginning of the monsoon season in May, which would "turn the mountain trails and passes into viscous quagmires, the poorly-clad troops would suffer, transport and supply problems would be multiplied and operations seriously hampered." If wrangling at the top had no effect, Dorn could hardly hope for the Chinese to listen to his appeal. The CEF stayed put.[3]

Roosevelt could not believe it. In the White House map room he noted pins representing the Chinese Army in India moving deeper into Burma. On the other side of the map, a mass of pins representing the CEF remained static along the east bank of the Salween River. He could not understand why Chiang would not advance against just one Japanese division when such a great strategic opportunity was at stake. He sent another strongly-worded message on April 3. It was never delivered, but Chiang received word through other channels that the president was serious about ending lend-lease aid to the CEF and that he even threatened to arm Chinese warlords or the Communists instead. The generalissimo grappled with the risks of sending the CEF into action. His divisions were still under strength. Opposing his seventy-two thousand troops of questionable quality were eleven thousand experienced, well-led, and well-entrenched Japanese. The cessation of lend-lease aid, on the other hand, was a grave threat, especially if that aid was diverted to his political enemies. On April 14, he reluctantly approved an offensive.

Stilwell received the news with jubilation, but a new complication emerged. Chennault informed him that the Japanese were about to launch a major offensive in East China. Unless properly reinforced, his air force and the Chinese troops in that part of the country would be unable to stop it. "It is unnecessary to point out that all new military equipment brought into China in the past two years has been assigned to the Chinese Armies on the Salween Front," Chennault warned. "Both equipment and many tens of thousands of troops have actually been borrowed for the Salween Front from the Chinese forces which must meet the enemy offensives in Central and East China." Stilwell was not sure whether the warning was legitimate, or if Chennault was merely trying to manipulate him into canceling the Salween offensive so his air operations would remain the top priority. He told Chennault to curtail his activities in order to build up supply stockpiles and not to report the warning to Chiang. He did not want to give the generalissimo any more excuses to delay the CEF.

As a matter of fact, the Japanese *were* planning an offensive. In January 1944, Imperial General Headquarters ordered their Expeditionary Army to seize a rail corridor through East and Central China and eliminate Chennault's forward airfields. They called it Operation Ichi-go. Over four hundred thousand Japanese troops were involved in the massive undertaking. Phase One began on the night of April 17, 1944, when the Japanese 37th Division crossed the Yellow River and advanced south to secure the Beiping-Hankou

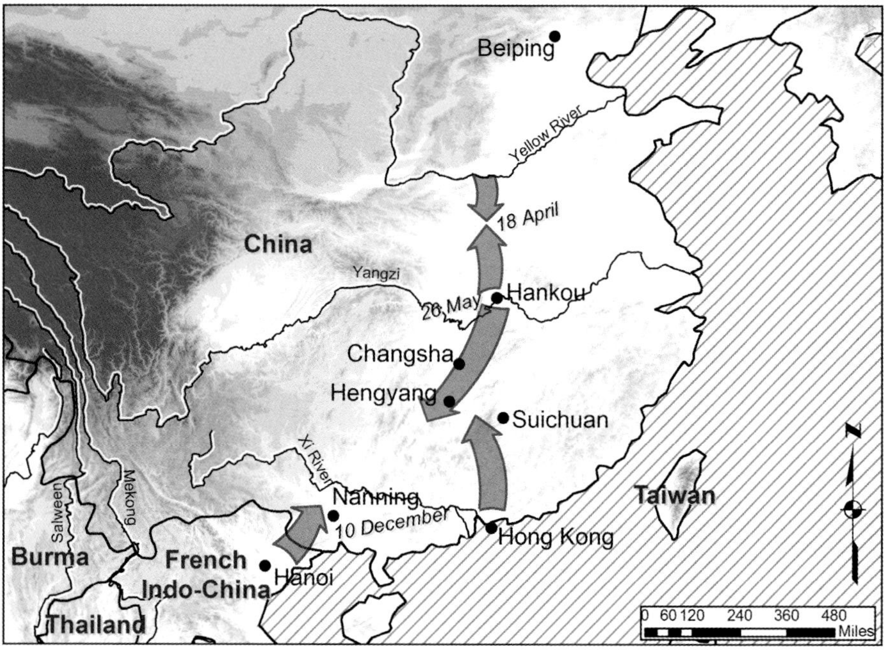

Operation Ichi-Go

railway corridor. For Chennault, the situation could not have been worse. The Japanese used the seasonal bad weather as a screen against airpower. The 14th Air Force received only a fraction of its promised supplies due to the emergencies at Imphal and Kohima diverting precious transports from the Hump. His only hope was to tap into the huge stockpiles of aviation gas and supplies at Chengdu, 170 miles northwest of Chongqing, in Sichuan Province. The problem was, those supplies did not belong to him. Throughout the spring of 1944, the B-29 very-long-range bomber program was coming on-line. General Arnold hoped to launch bombing attacks against mainland Japan from Chinese air bases. He kept control of the project firmly in the hands of the Joint Chiefs of Staff. Chennault could not touch the stockpiles without express permission, nor could he divert the huge bombers from their task of bombing the Japanese steel industry. He radioed Stilwell, asking for him to intercede with the JCS on his behalf. His plea was not well received. Stilwell half-heartedly sent in the request, but would not declare the situation an emergency. The JCS refused to release the stockpiles. "Instructions understood, and exactly what I hoped for," Stilwell wrote to Marshall. "As you know, I have few illusions about power of air against ground troops." Instead of helping Chennault combat the Japanese offensive, Stilwell actually ordered him to make defending the B-29 bases his top priority. Chennault's hands were tied. He had to support a bomber campaign that was not only a drain on his resources, but also could not be used to affect the battle for East China.

Chinese resistance melted away in the face of Ichi-go. On May 27, Phase Two began with an advance south from Hankou toward Changsha. It was the disaster Stilwell predicted in 1943, and he gloated. He believed Chennault and Chiang brought it on themselves:

Chennault's air campaign provoked the response he predicted and Chiang did not listen to his advice about reforming and reorganizing the Chinese Army. In reality, the situation was far more complicated. The Japanese wanted an overland supply route to Southeast Asia free from the harassment of American submarines. Putting an end to Chennault's increasingly effective air campaign was an important, though secondary, objective. Chennault had realized more than anyone what he could accomplish with airpower in China. It allowed him to do something of strategic importance in a theater that otherwise might not have been significant. It was a gamble though. Perhaps he really thought the Chinese could stop an advance. On the other hand, he almost certainly overstated his case in advocating the use of airpower, and it is likely Ichi-go would still have been devastating even had troops and equipment not been diverted to the Salween Front. Almost *half a million* Japanese troops were bearing down on East China. It is controversial as to whether the offensive hurt Japanese efforts elsewhere, as Chennault claimed it would. With over four hundred thousand troops in China, only forty thousand opposed the American landings on Saipan, in the Marianas Islands, on June 15, 1944. It was from this chain of islands that the United States launched its atomic death blow in 1945. However, the Allies had already demonstrated that ships and airplanes counted far more than numbers of soldiers in the Pacific. Even *if* the Japanese could get the troops out to the islands, the American island-hopping campaign would have bypassed tens of thousands of them, leaving them starving and irrelevant.

Chiang's decision to finally launch the CEF thus came at a time when the Japanese were advancing into India and East China, Stilwell's troops were bogged down in North Burma, and the summer monsoon would soon limit air support and greatly complicate things for his troops on the Salween Front.[4] General He set May 11, 1944, as D-Day. The CEF had only three weeks to complete its preparations. Fortunately, in addition to Lu Caiwen's intelligence team, Dorn had organized two long-range infiltration patrols to obtain information on the enemy and terrain west of the Salween. The first patrol included two American officers, one enlisted man, two interpreters, and ten Chinese officers. They crossed into enemy territory in September 1943 wearing civilian clothing. They reconnoitered Japanese defenses, spoke with civilians to collect information and learn the attitude of the population, and made contact with anti-Japanese guerrillas. The first patrol returned to the east bank of the Salween in late November and was followed by another patrol in February 1944. Both reconnaissance expeditions were successful and suffered no casualties.[5]

Since Dorn complained about the command problem the previous summer, Chen Cheng had resigned. He decided He Yingqin's constant meddling undermined his authority. Marshal Wei Lihuang took over command. Wei was short and stocky, with a round, serious face framed by short black hair and a pointed mustache. He came from an upper-middle class family and was well educated and pro-American. He became a general after the Northern Expedition and had considerable experience fighting the Japanese and the Communists. His impressive record earned him the nickname "Hundred Victories Wei," the honorary title of marshal, and the tax revenues from four rich farming counties in Hunan Province for life. According to Dorn, Wei was "dignified, urbane, and humorous ... He and I hit it off right away. Our initial feelings of rapport grew into mutual respect, complete trust, and fondness engendered by true friendship." Wei's chief of staff was Major General Xiao Yisu. "Xiao had a rather rugged look about him," recalled Dorn. He "had lost a thumb while scaling a city wall in one of the anti-Communist campaigns in Jiangxi,

Marshal Wei Lihuang (sitting front and center), known as "Hundred Victories Wei," took charge of the CEF in the fall of 1943. He was aggressive and had an impressive record. Here he visits a forward observation post during the campaign. *National Archives via Samuel Hui*

Major General Xiao Yisu was chief of staff of the CEF under Marshal Wei. Dorn had met him in 1937 and they hit it off immediately. He had a hot temper and bitter hatred of the Japanese. *Hoover Institution*

and was afraid of nothing, be it God, the devil, or Japs." He was "one of the most forceful, capable, and intelligent officers I had ever met." When Dorn first met him in August 1937, Xiao was vigorously fighting the Japanese in Huailai, fifty miles northwest of Beiping. "From our first handshake, an electric current, or something, went through us both," said Dorn. "From that moment, we were not just friends; we were instant-old friends, with the highest mutual respect and trust." Wei, Xiao, and Dorn built what Dorn called "a mutuality—rare in the Far East—of complete frankness, at times even conspiratorial, in our personal and official dealings." Wei established his headquarters at Baoshan, only fifteen miles east of the Salween. Dorn opened a field headquarters for the Y Force Operations Staff there on May 1.[6]

At the beginning of May, Wei's forces included five armies with a total of twelve divisions. These were organized into two army groups: the XIth, commanded by Major General Song Xilian, and the XXth, commanded by Major General Huo Kuizhang. The CEF was still forty percent under-strength and much of it was still not equipped with American weapons. Lend-lease supplied submachine guns, mortars, pack howitzers, and rocket launchers, but the Chinese had to supply their own rifles and light machine guns.[7] Lieutenant Liu Cheng-hua, the infantry officer from Hubei, remembered using the Type 24 "Chiang Kai-shek Rifle," the Chinese version of the German 1933 Mauser. It was a solid, dependable weapon, but since they were built in Chinese factories, individual quality often varied. It could hold five 8-millimeter rounds in an internal magazine loaded by a stripper clip. Liu did not like that it was a bolt-action rifle, unlike the semi-automatic M1 Garand. Over half a million Type 24s were made in ten years of production and it saw service all the way through the Korean War.[8]

Even though the CEF was not up to its full complement of men and equipment, with over seventy thousand troops, it outnumbered the Japanese on the Salween Front by more than six to one. General He established the capture of Longling and Tengchong as the campaign's initial objectives. From there, operations would depend on how the situation developed. Longling was the first major town astride the Burma Road on the west side of the river. The Japanese kept it heavily garrisoned because of trails leading north and south from the Burma Road paralleling the front. Forty miles north of Longling was the walled city of Tengchong, an old trading outpost famous for its jade. Even though it was not on the Burma Road, its capture would be advantageous, not only because it was the northern anchor of the Japanese line, but also because it was connected by a rough trail to Myitkyina, only 124 miles to the west.

Lieutenant General Yuzo Matsuyama commanded the Japanese 56th Division headquartered at Mangshi, twelve miles southwest of Longling. His three regiments were responsible for the Yunnan defensive sector. Before participating in the Burma Campaign, the division fought in the Malayan highlands and captured Kuala Lampur. They were veteran mountain troops. The 148th Regiment garrisoned Tengchong. The 113th garrisoned Songshan, a mountain dominating the Burma Road above the Huitong Bridge site. Elsewhere along the one-hundred-mile front, Matsuyama's division was spread thin, weak from reinforcing units engaged in North Burma. What disadvantages his troops had in numbers though, they made up for in other ways. They enjoyed a better supply situation than any Japanese division in Burma. Supplies traveled by rail through Thailand to Lashio, and thence by truck up the Burma Road and out a well-established trail network. The 56th Division had occupied the Salween Front for two years. In that time they constructed pillboxes, dug trenches, and established artillery positions with prepared fields of fire to defend critical points and mountain passes. They were experienced, they were well-equipped, and they were ready.[9]

The terrain was even more formidable than the enemy. The Salween Front was much more daunting than it appeared on the wall of the White House map room. The Salween River, which the CEF had to cross, raged in an angry torrent through the deep gorge where the Chinese Army and AVG had stopped the Japanese in 1942. The Chinese called the Salween *Nujiang* (怒江), or "Angry River." Along the front it was more than two thousand feet above sea level and seldom more than 150 yards wide, with mountains towering above it on either side. The Chinese destroyed both the Huitong and Huiren bridges over the river during their retreat in 1942. General Xiao told Frank Dorn he did not know of any small boats venturing across the river in recorded history. Dorn conferred with Lieutenant Colonel A.J. Eichenlaub, the YFOS head engineering officer. Despite Xiao's apprehension, Eichenlaub was confident a crossing could be made. He directed his engineers to begin training Chinese troops in the use of small pneumatic rubber boats and rafts on the Mekong River, which follows a roughly parallel north-south course only thirty miles to the east. Both rivers were considered rapid, dangerous, and unnavigable.[10] During the practice, several soldiers and one Chinese officer drowned. Five Japanese shells fired into the practice area killed two soldiers and wounded four more. Crossing the Salween, however, was only the beginning. Once across, Chinese troops had to fight over the Gaoligong Range, a monolithic ridge of steep mountains rising up to twelve thousand feet between the Salween and Shweli river valleys. On the far side of the Gaoligong, the Shweli Valley served as a natural avenue of approach to Tengchong.[11]

With the decision to attack, Dorn shifted YFOS from a training role to supporting operations in the field. General He asked Dorn's organization to assume four key responsibilities for the campaign: first, it was to supervise the ferrying of Chinese troops across the river; second, to coordinate air support; third, to coordinate the American-trained artillery battalions; and fourth, to help Marshal Wei feed and supply the CEF.[12] Dorn agreed and established liaison teams along similar lines to those accompanying the X Force in Burma. Colonel Walter S. Wood commanded the liaison teams attached to the XIth Army Group. Colonel Harry A. Buckley commanded the teams assigned to the XXth. Each Chinese division had a team of approximately twenty-seven officers and men, including a liaison group commander, an administrative officer, intelligence officer, operations officer, logistics officer, signal officer, medical officer, veterinary officer, six infantry officer instructors, tactical air control parties, and enough enlisted personnel to serve as radio operators, assistant instructors, clerks, and medical technicians. Divisions with their own artillery battalions also had four artillery officers and six enlisted men.[13] The advisors went into combat with the Chinese and shared the same hardships as the troops.[14]

The plan of attack Dorn and Wei came up with borrowed heavily from concepts pioneered by the Chindits and Air Commandos in Burma. They would take advantage of the fact that the Japanese depended heavily on fortified positions, but had too few troops to cover the gaps in the rough terrain in between. The CEF would break up into small, highly-mobile combat teams to infiltrate the front lines, cut Japanese lines of supply, and then reduce the surrounded strong points in siege and assault.[15] It was the perfect way to avoid direct confrontation with the more experienced Japanese troops. Wei would wait to drive down the heavily-defended Burma Road until he successfully enveloped it from the north and south. Of course, air drops would be necessary to keep Chinese troops supplied behind enemy lines. Stilwell required that Chennault provide air support for the campaign—a further drain on his resources while he faced the crisis in East China. Though he disagreed with Stilwell's emphasis on the Salween Front, Chennault did believe in supporting the Chinese troops. He thought they were "courageous defensive soldiers," though "they lack offensive firepower." On the Salween Front, his warplanes would compensate for that lack of firepower. "I've found that air can be used as infantry, as machine guns, and as artillery," he once told a reporter. "This is exactly what we've had to do in China."[16]

Chennault presents the Legion of Merit to John C. Kennedy, commander of the 69th Composite Wing. Kennedy established the Forward Echelon at Beiting Field on May 2, 1944, to support the Salween Campaign. *National Archives*

Chennault assigned Colonel John C. Kennedy's 69th Composite Wing to build a task force for the job. On May 2, Kennedy moved his headquarters to Beiting Field, a grass auxiliary strip two miles east of Yunnanyi. The task force he created included the 27th Troop Carrier Squadron—which had been flying air drop missions into Burma since December—and the 19th Liaison Squadron, which arrived in India in April 1944. The 25th Fighter Squadron's P-40s provided close air support, and a detachment of B-25s from the 22nd Bomb Squadron flew heavy support missions. It was an ad hoc organization similar to the 1st Air Commando Group in composition, though necessarily smaller due to the lack of resources in China and not given the status of a special command. There was little point creating special commands in China; Chennault's men were used to operating in small detachments and often made decisions and took initiative without instruction or interference from higher headquarters.

On May 3, 1944, the leading elements of Chinese troops began moving to assembly areas ten miles east of where they would cross the Salween.[17] On the ninth, battalion-sized teams crossed to cover the main landing.[18] At midnight on the early morning of the eleventh, the first wave of Chinese troops pushed out into the river. They crossed in 398 pneumatic rubber boats, on improvised bamboo rafts, and even on empty oil drums lashed together. It was completely dark—a thick overcast obscured the moon. Three reinforced regimental combat teams from the XXth Army Group crossed north of the Burma Road at Menggu Ferry, Shuanghongqiao Ford, and the Huiren Bridge site. Two teams from the XIth Army Group crossed south of the road near Dazhai Ferry. A sixth column advanced toward Kunlong Ferry, ninety miles south of the road at the extreme southern end of the front.[19]

Seventeen YFOS advisors supervised the Chinese engineer companies making the crossing at Menggu Ferry. The current was so powerful it took four engineers paddling for every group of four infantry and their equipment. Apprehension filled the troops as they pushed their rafts out into the darkness. The engineers struggled against the river to bring them across. This was their Rubicon, and crossing it would be their Normandy. None knew whether the landing would be successful, or if Japanese artillery and machine guns would cut them down at the water's edge. The tension was palpable. In fact, General Matsuyama knew of the crossing from troop movements and decoded radio messages. However, he decided to defend the front from his strongpoints atop the Gaoligong Mountains, rather than at the river. He did not believe the Chinese could carry an offensive over the most difficult battlefield terrain of World War II.[20]

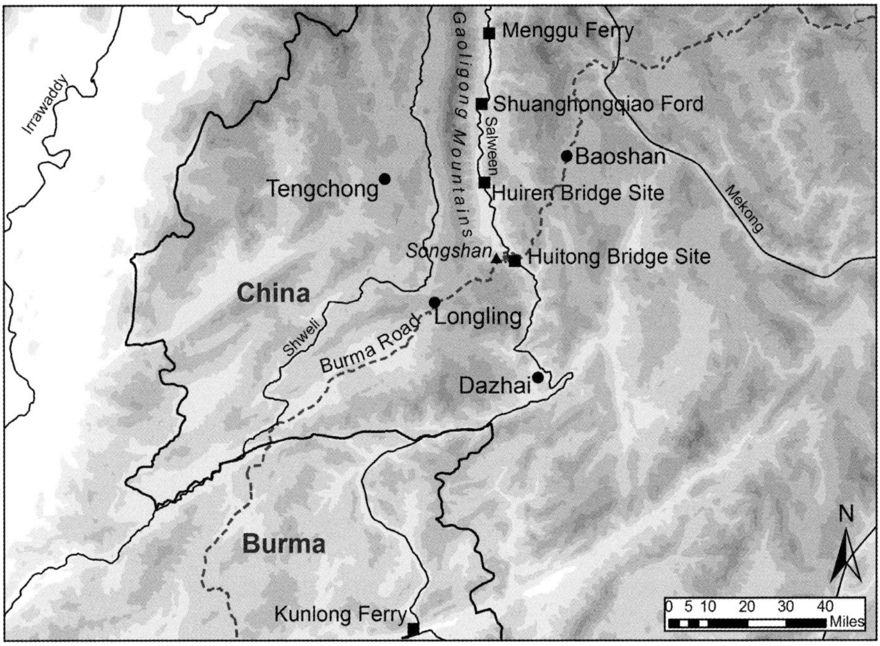

Salween Crossing

The landing forces met no resistance. The Chinese brass was astounded. General Xiao might not have known of any small craft having ever crossed the river before, but in a single night, an armada of rafts crossed and re-crossed, depositing soldiers, horses, and artillery pieces. Despite all the trouble practicing on the Mekong, of the forty thousand troops ferried across the Salween, only one did not make it. Staff Sergeant Deng Chao fell into the river. He did not cry out. Though he could not swim, he did not want to give away the crossing. His sacrifice was the first of many that demonstrated the stoic bravery of the regular Chinese soldier.[21] With firm bridgeheads established, the CEF moved reinforcements across the river *en masse* and began the torturous trek up the Gaoligong Mountains.

Chinese troops crossing the Salween aboard a commandeered ferry. *National Archives via Samuel Hui*

Chinese troops prepare a rubber raft to cross the Salween. On the early morning of May 11, 1944, forty thousand Chinese troops crossed the river using 398 such rafts, in addition to others made of bamboo and empty oil drums. *National Archives via Samuel Hui*

9

The Battle of Myitkyina

Stilwell hoped action on the Salween Front would relieve pressure on his forces in North Burma—he wanted to capture Myitkyina before the onset of the summer monsoon. Myitkyina was a modest town with a population of about seven thousand, nestled in a bend on the west side of the Irrawaddy River. It was historically an important agricultural and trading center and acted as a gateway to North Burma. Its importance to Stilwell was twofold: first, when the Ledo Road engineers finally pushed out of the Mogaung Valley, they could link up with existing roads south from Mytikyina to Bhamo, connecting with the old Burma Road near the China border. Alternatively, once the CEF secured Tengchong, the engineers could push due east from Myitkyina over a rough trail that would cut the distance to Kunming by hundreds of miles. Either option was much simpler than building a road through virgin jungle. The second reason was its location at the southern end of the Hump route. The Japanese used its airfield as a staging base for fighters ranging north to harass transports flying into China. According to Major General William Tunner, who took command of the airlift in 1944: "The Japanese did present a constant threat. They caused us the constant inconvenience of having to fly longer and farther over higher mountains in order to get around their salient pushing up from Rangoon to Myitkyina."[1] If Stilwell's forces captured the town, Tunner's transports could fly a shorter, safer route and increase the tonnage flown into China.[2] In a letter to Winston Churchill justifying the North Burma Campaign, Roosevelt wrote: "Our occupation of Myitkyina will enable us immediately to increase the airlift to China."[3]

With the Japanese still holding Kar Maing and the summer monsoon season rapidly approaching, the capture of Myitkyina seemed a dim prospect. Stilwell's entire campaign—not to mention his reputation—hinged on the capture of that town. He decided on a high-risk operation to seize it before time ran out. On April 21, 1944, he assembled a task force code-named "End Run." The task force would travel over one hundred miles on foot, behind enemy lines, in a surprise attack on the airfield at Pamati, two miles west of Myitkyina. With the field in hand, Stilwell would fly in reinforcements to seize the town. His troops would be isolated, but would in turn cut lines of communication to Mogaung and Kar Maing. Meanwhile, the 38th Division would make an all-out attack on Kar Maing to distract the Japanese and eventually link up with the troops at Myitkyina. It was a bold move and classic Stilwell—a swift flanking movement to win the campaign in a single stroke. Ironically, the plan depended heavily on long-range penetration and airpower—both of which Stilwell's critics attacked him for not using more often. Chindit commander Orde Wingate did not live to see Stilwell adopt his methods; he died in a plane crash on March 24.

Galahad was Stilwell's only unit with the training and experience for End Run. However, after Nphum Ga, there were only 1,400 men fit for combat out of the unit's original three thousand. Stilwell decided to augment the Marauders with Chinese troops from the veteran 22nd Division and the 50th and 30th divisions recently flown from China to reinforce the X Force. He divided the task force into three columns. H Force, commanded by Hunter, consisted of the Marauders' 1st Battalion, the 150th Regiment of the Chinese 50th Division, and a battery of 75-millimeter pack howitzers from the

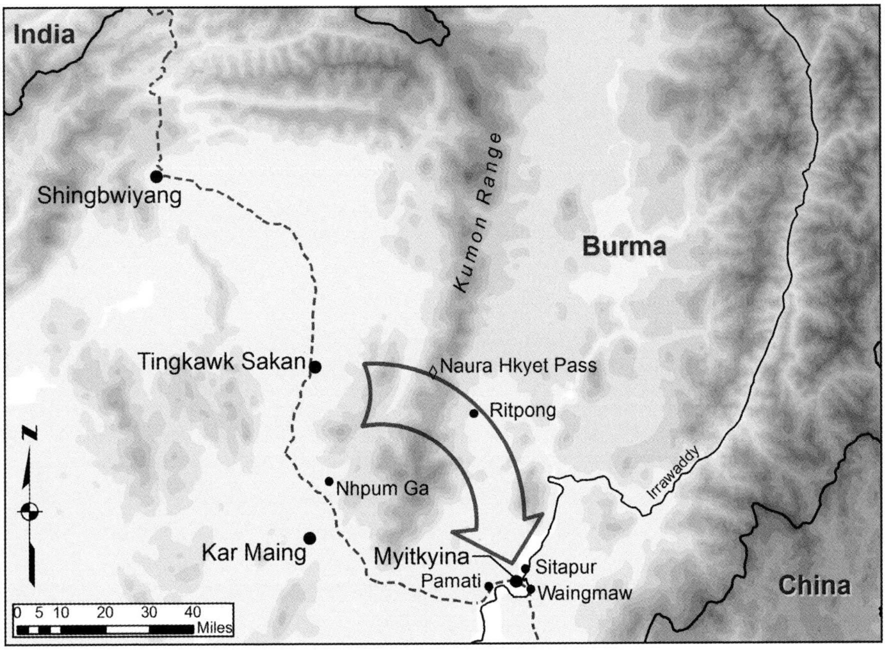

March to Myitkyina

22nd Division. K Force, commanded by Stilwell's operations officer, Colonel Henry L. Kinnison, consisted of the Marauders' 3rd Battalion and the 88th Regiment of the Chinese 30th Division. M Force, commanded by George McGee, consisted of the Marauders' 2nd Battalion and three hundred Kachin guerrillas. Kachin guides led each column and OSS-led guerrillas pushed ahead to forge trails and gather intelligence on Japanese positions. Surgical teams from Dr. Gordon Seagrave's medical unit and the 42nd Portable Surgical Hospital accompanied all three columns.[4] Hunter's force was in the best physical condition and would therefore lead the attack on the airfield.[5]

What Stilwell was asking of his men was monumental. The War Department had indicated it would withdraw Galahad after a three-month combat mission. Merrill told his men that Stilwell promised to relieve them from combat after they seized the airfield. The prospect of relief after one last extraordinary effort energized them. When Stilwell established End Run, the Marauders had been in combat for over two months in terrible conditions and without replacements. Merrill himself had only recently recovered from another heart attack. The men were tired and bitter. They felt Stilwell publicly marginalized their part in the campaign to highlight the successes of his Chinese troops. Exaggerating the effectiveness of the divisions trained at Ramgarh gave him credibility in demanding Chiang institute more military and political reforms. Keeping Americans in the field gave him credibility in asking for Chinese replacements and for support from the British. The Marauders were not particularly interested in the politics of the situation and just wanted the whole business to be over with. They moved out on April 27.[6]

The men of End Run marched through the jungle, stretched out for miles in single-file columns. They worked their way along slick, muddy trails, drenched by rain, depending on aircraft working in under the weather for supply. The first eight days were the worst: they covered a distance of only sixteen miles, though one Marauder commented, "It was a damned sight farther than that by trail." From one thousand feet above sea level, H and K forces climbed the Kumon Range to cross through the Naura Hkyet Pass at over six thousand feet. "The terrain was as much an enemy as the Japanese," remarked Herbert Clofine.[7] Some stretches were so steep the soldiers literally had to crawl on their hands and knees and use their shovels to carve out steps for the pack mules. Twenty of K Force's mules slipped in the mud and fell to their deaths, scattering heavy weapons and equipment down the mountainsides. H Force lost a quarter of its animals. Marching south of the other two columns to protect the right flank, M Force lost half of its mules to falls or exhaustion.[8]

The End Run Task Force marched 112 miles in twenty days. For nearly three weeks they disappeared even from the local theater newspaper, the *CBI Roundup*. It was extraordinary, considering their condition. Despite Stilwell deeming them fit for duty, the Marauders were generally in very poor health. Many of them had dysentery or any number of tropical diseases, and most were malnourished and weary.[9] Colonel Kinnison himself contracted mite typhus, along with 149 of his men. He was evacuated by light aircraft, but died in the hospital. Kinnison's column was the spearhead for the operation; they decimated a Japanese outpost at Ritpong and fought a reinforced battalion to a standstill at Tingkruktawng. During the last days of the march, the columns moved at night for better security. K Force feinted east to draw off the Japanese while Hunter's men made straight for Myitkyina. They reached a heavily forested area near the airfield the night of May 15 and spent the next two days moving into position. Kachin scouts brought back intelligence that only a small military police detachment defended the airfield at Pamati. In Myitkyina itself, they reported over two thousand enemy troops.[10]

Frank Merrill established his headquarters in the jungle north of Myitkyina and promised to be the first man to land on the airfield once it was captured.[11] On May 16, Hunter broke radio silence with the code words "Crossword Puzzle," which meant his men were in position and would attack within twenty-four hours. General Stilwell called his air officer, John Habecker, into his office. He asked if the Air Corps was ready for the attack on Myitkyina and told him the first column of End Run would assault the field the next day. "Frankly, this was the first inkling I had of such an attack," recalled Habecker. "The staff never had meetings, that I can remember, concerning operations, even those with air forces involved." Stilwell's intelligence officer and son, Colonel Joe Stilwell Jr., told Habecker there were only three hundred Japanese troops in Myitkyina and only 750 more in the surrounding area. Colonel Hunter later complained that Stilwell's son never gave him any estimate of the enemy strength and questioned where he got his numbers, which clearly differed from what the Kachin scouts reported. He felt General Stilwell's "impatience with detailed planning" was one reason for the confusing intelligence. "It gradually became obvious," he wrote, "that we were following an artist's sketch rather than architects' blueprints in the campaign."[12]

Habecker knew nothing of Hunter's estimates and thought the Myitkyina operation would go quickly. General John Egan, commander of the 5320th Wing—under which organization fell the 80th and 311th fighter groups—told him to reserve a particular building for his headquarters. He did not want to set up shop in "some bombed-out hut" and used aerial reconnaissance photos to pick out a nice cottage overlooking the

Marauders moving in single file along a jungle trail. The trek to Mytikyina was arduous and the End Run Task Force lost over half its mules to falls or exhaustion. ***Merrill's Marauders Association***

Irrawaddy River on the north side of town. Habecker made a sign which read "RESERVED FOR THE 5320th WING" and put it and a handful of thumbtacks in his pants pocket. Unbeknownst to him, he was destined to "sit on those damn tacks" for a long time.

Air support during the summer monsoon was problematic. Between May and October, North Burma received up to 250 inches of rain. Towering thunderstorms built over the mountains between airbases in Assam and Stilwell's troops in Burma. With no instrument navigation aids, it was often impossible for India-based fighters to provide support in Burma. General Egan's command decided to move units to bases closer to the front as soon as possible. In April, the 88th Fighter Squadron moved to Shingbwiyang, at mile 117 along the Ledo Road in Burma. The 528th moved to Tingkawk Sakan—at mile 164—in May. Elmer Todd, the 528th's engineering officer, led an advanced party to the base on May 14. Tingkawk Sakan was a 3,500-foot crushed gravel strip carved out of the jungle. Hundred-foot-tall trees towered over the field. Todd led his party in clearing underbrush and setting up tents. Nepalese laborers built an operations shack and control tower. Air raid alerts often interrupted the work as Japanese airplanes scoured the area, trying to locate the new field. Todd's crew dug a well for drinking water, but the men had to walk over a mile to bathe in a nearby creek.[13] They turned their boots upside down every morning to shake out snakes and insects. At one point, a small herd of elephants walked through the camp. According to pilot Hank Snow, it was "very

Late April 1944: Colonel Charles Hunter (right) confers with his staff on the final drive to capture Myitkyina. *Merrill's Marauders Association*

primitive. We were there during the monsoon season and had mud up to our ankles."[14] The first group of pilots flew in on May 17 and immediately began flying missions to Myitkyina—only fifteen minutes away by air.

The morning of the seventeenth, a team of Kachin guerrillas blew the road and rail bridges west of Myitkyina to stop any reinforcements coming from the Mogaung Valley. Hunter ordered his men forward. As they swept out of the forested hills and swarmed onto the airfield, he radioed, "We are in the ring."[15] The Chinese troops stormed the airfield while the Americans took a nearby ferry terminal on the Irrawaddy. The attack was a complete surprise: the Japanese were not prepared and gave only minimal resistance. By 1155 hours—less than half an hour after the attack commenced—the airfield was in Allied hands. Hunter thought the attack "went like clockwork, like part of a peacetime maneuver."[16] He broadcast "Cafeteria Lunch," to inform Merrill that he controlled the airfield. His men immediately began clearing logs and empty gasoline drums from the runway. Local villagers from Pamati pitched in and thirty-seven minutes later, Hunter radioed "Merchant of Venice," to indicate the field was ready for the aerial caravan of reinforcements.[17]

As soon as he received word that the airfield was in friendly hands, John Habecker flew out in an L-5 liaison plane. He carried panels to direct gliders landing on the field,

Lieutenant Colonel John Habecker (left) presents one of his men with the Distinguished Flying Cross. Habecker was an experienced pilot with the 311th Fighter Group before serving as air officer on Stilwell's staff. *National Archives*

an SCR 284 radio, and Colonel Manuel Ascencio, assistant to the chief air engineer of Air Service Command. "Swede" Nelson, Habecker's assistant, flew another L-5 with a staff engineer onboard. Habecker thought he would be the first American pilot to land at Myitkyina, but when he flew over, he saw a C-47 already on the field. Four transports from the 2nd Troop Carrier Squadron (TCS) were dropping supplies nearby when they saw Allied troops on the field. The pilots were competing to see who could be the first to land at any of the airfields recently liberated from the enemy. The first troop carrier to land had its hydraulics shot out by Japanese small arms.[18] Much to Habecker's chagrin, within weeks the first pilot to land at Myitkyina was back in the United States on a war bonds tour.

Habecker did not have time to set up the direction panels before the first wave of reinforcements arrived. He watched as ten gliders loaded with engineering equipment descended from every direction. The pilots learned from their intelligence briefing that the field was probably mined. Four of them tried landing perpendicular to the runway and ran into revetments built alongside. In all, eight of the ten gliders crashed. "We had a helluva time extracting the wounded personnel and equipment from the wreckage," said Habecker. Fortunately, there were only three dead and most of the equipment was intact. As the 2nd TCS proved, the gliders were unnecessary. One of the tow planes even landed to evacuate casualties. A steady stream of transports from Assam landed at the field until the weather closed in that evening. "The planes came in promptly," wrote Hunter, "but they brought no ammunition, no food, no General Merrill, only sundry goods and personnel not ordered, not wanted, and not needed." Engineers, a .50-caliber anti-aircraft gun, and a battalion of the Chinese 89th Infantry Regiment unloaded on the field. Hunter thought the anti-aircraft gun "useless" and the additional Chinese troops "had to be disposed someplace where they wouldn't shoot up the troops doing the fighting."[19]

The Japanese shot at the transports as they landed. "A few planes had holes through their tanks and were leaking gas," remembered Habecker. He and Colonel Ascencio watched as a Chinese officer from the 89th Regiment tried to assemble his men. "An enemy sniper was shooting," he recalled. "The sound of his gun was a high-pitched 'snap' like a board breaking." The Chinese ignored the sporadic and inaccurate sniper fire, but then the Japanese began firing a small mortar. The mortar team was firing ranging shots, so the rate of fire was slow, but just as the Chinese got into formation, a mortar burst on either end of their line, both exploding about fifty yards from the troops. A third mortar landed fifty yards in front of the commander. "The commander of the unit got the idea about this time and dismissed the Chinese," said Habecker. "They scattered." "Swede" Nelson flew Ascencio back to Stilwell's headquarters that afternoon. Habecker remained behind to find the air control party attached to H Force. The team was using an old radio frequency and could not contact supporting aircraft. Habecker gave them an updated frequency and helped them set up at the airfield. He also gave them maps made from a photomosaic of the area with a grid overlay. Using the letter and number designations of the grid, ground parties could easily radio target locations to fighter pilots with the same product in their hands.[20]

That night, Colonel Hunter held a staff meeting under a canvas tarpaulin near the field. He told everyone that the other two columns of End Run would arrive either later that night or early the next day, but warned they were in no better condition than his own bedraggled forces. Habecker spent the rainy night in a slit trench. The next day, he had time to fly a short reconnaissance in his L-5 before Stilwell ordered him back to headquarters. When he returned, he reported that everything appeared to be going according to plan. "Little did I know," he admitted in retrospect.

The next morning he learned that Swede was dead. Japanese fighters shot down his L-5 over Myitkyina and destroyed four transports on the field. Despite the danger, Habecker flew back that afternoon, "This time better prepared to stay," he reported. That same afternoon, Stilwell flew in aboard his personal C-47 "Uncle Joe's Chariot" to inspect the progress. "He would have been welcome," said Hunter, "if he had brought food and ammunition, or even an idea of what we were to do next. But he brought only a dozen correspondents anxious to show how brave they were in visiting a combat zone."[21] The seizure of the airfield was the high point of Stilwell's career. He stood there with a steel helmet on his head and a carbine slung over his shoulder. "It seems we are in Myitkyina," he smugly quipped to the correspondents.[22] As he talked to the newsmen on the field, an air control party vectored a flight of fighters onto a target about four hundred meters away. The fighters flew directly over the general on their runs. "I thought this was a beautiful demonstration for the Theater Commander," said Habecker. "But then the shell casings began dropping close to the general so the air liaison team changed the approach direction." Despite what Stilwell told the reporters, the airfield was only the first step in the conquest of Myitkyina—his troops were not yet in the town. He got back in his plane and returned to headquarters. Merrill finally flew in from his jungle command post in an L-5 the next day. As his plane approached the field, he saw Mustangs strafing targets along the river on the east side of the town. He stayed very briefly and provided little direction to Hunter. He suffered another heart attack that afternoon.

Hunter finally got the supplies he needed on the twentieth and ordered two battalions of the Chinese 150th Regiment to move out along the road to Sitapur, just north of Myitkyina. According to Habecker: "Both columns got halfway to town, started shooting at each other and then ran back to the airstrip in disorder. ... Unfortunately they did the same thing the next day."[23] End Run was losing the initiative. Poor weather often prevented air support and reinforcements. The Marauders were under the impression they would be relieved after seizing the airfield and that Chinese troops would take the town. Seventy-five to one hundred of them were evacuated every day due to injury or sickness. More than eighty percent suffered from dysentery.

John Dowling, a correspondent for the *Chicago Sun*, described the chaotic scene: "I no sooner step out of my Piper Cub than a sniper's bullet puts a neat little hole in the wing above my head," he reported. When he visited Colonel Hunter's command post, he found the thirty-nine-year-old West Point graduate "with filthy green baggy pants, mosquito boots, no shirt, three days' beard on a red, dust-caked face and a front tooth missing." He watched as strings of mules crossed the field and transports landed, "raising clouds of red dust against a gray sky that, in the distance, is filled with enormous thunderheads." Bulldozers worked and Chinese troops filed past. "Fighters, Mustangs, roll overhead and are good to see," he wrote. "They peel off and go down into the town of Myitkyina and work it over with cannon and machine guns, and we can see the smoke streaming from their guns as they dive, and then a long time later, we hear the crackle of the shot." The battle raged in all its chaotic glory. "If it sounds confused, that's because it was confused," Dowling surmised.[24]

While the mad scramble continued around the airfield, the Japanese strengthened their position in the town. It was garrisoned by the 114th Regiment, 18th Division. By 1700 on May 17, Colonel Maruyama—commander of the garrison—had brought a full battalion borrowed from the 56th Division on the Salween Front through End Run's porous lines. There were simply not enough Allied troops to seal off the town. Reinforcements trickled in. By the thirty-first, there were 2,500 Japanese troops in Myitkyina—far more than General Stilwell's son estimated. Major General Genzu Mizukami left his post with the 56th Division to command the defense personally. He was committed to fight to the death. His men manned earthworks, networks of trenches, and machine gun nests reminiscent of World War I trench warfare.[25] What Stilwell had hoped would be an easy victory against an unsuspecting enemy was quickly turning into a prolonged siege. He secured the use of the Chindits—under the command of Brigadier W.D.A Lentaigne since Wingate's unfortunate demise—to cut off Japanese reinforcements. Lentaigne moved his troops to cut the road from Bhamo, but they encountered fierce resistance. The situation was critical. Galahad's 2nd Battalion was down to only twelve men. The Chinese 150th Regiment was down to six hundred. According to Philip Piazza: "By the time we reached Myitkyina, we were down from three thousand men to less than two hundred. I would say we had less than 150 and those were in sad shape."[26] John Habecker witnessed Marauders "with their trouser seats split open to permit rapid bowel movement," lined up to depart on any available transport. "Colonel Hunter tried to hold his troops at the field," Habecker recalled, "but some got out anyway. They were so damn tired."[27]

Stilwell flew in to examine the situation on May 25. Hunter met him at the airfield and immediately accused him and General Boatner of discriminating against his Americans in favor of the Chinese. He told Stilwell that morale was low and combat effectiveness nearly nonexistent. He charged that his men received no awards or decorations, no citations, no indication of appreciation whatsoever, and that headquarters denied his officers promotion. He complained that Stilwell underestimated Japanese strength, instead accusing his men of lacking the courage and stamina to get the job done. He reminded the general of his promise to relieve the Americans after they captured the airfield. He recommended that Galahad be disbanded.[28] Stilwell did not take the charges seriously and denied having ever made a promise to relieve the Marauders. He made Boatner the Myitkyina Task Force Commander. He would not withdraw the

Americans because he felt he would not have the moral authority to keep Chinese and British soldiers in the field, particularly the Chindits, who were also only supposed to be employed for a three-month mission. Boatner remembered Stilwell telling him it was important not to "let the impression be created that we were withholding U.S. troops from combat in a sector where as an Allied commander Stilwell was keeping British and Chinese troops in combat." Because Galahad did not have any replacements, Stilwell started sending out any man that could carry a rifle.[29] "That was the first time that we got any replacements," said Piazza.[30]

Stilwell ordered engineers from the 209th and 236th combat engineer battalions to abandon their bulldozers on the Ledo Road, take up a rifle, and go into combat as infantrymen. He sent aircrew trained to man .50-caliber machine guns on bombers to man .30-caliber light machine guns on the ground. He sent troops evacuated for medical issues back into combat. On one occasion, two hundred Galahad troops returned to combat were in such poor condition that ten of them were immediately re-evacuated. Boatner launched reckless attacks that resulted in large numbers of casualties. He told the Americans they were not fighting hard enough. He told the Chinese they were cowards. The men were exhausted. During a Japanese counterattack on May 27, Colonel McGee's men kept falling asleep! An inspector general report found: "the physical deterioration of the unit, after months of arduous jungle combat and culminating in a rapidly growing feeling that hospitalization procedures were not being carried out, resulted about June 1st 1944 in almost complete breakdown of morale."[31]

Stilwell visited Myitkyina again on June 18. He directed the Chindits to take Waingmaw on the east side of the Irrawaddy, but like the Marauders, they were worn out and could not. Boatner told Stilwell that the "U.S. troops are shaky," but Stilwell disagreed. He still believed that only five hundred Japanese defended Myitkyina and blamed Boatner for being a "staff autocrat" that never visited the front. He flew in again on the twenty-third. Hank Snow was in the flight of four Mustangs that escorted him in, "drifting back and forth, in case the Japanese tried to shoot him down. They never did," said Snow, "so we didn't get any action."[32] This time, Boatner told Stilwell, "I don't know what to do and neither does anyone else. The Americans refuse to obey. They will not follow their officers. They will not attack!" Stilwell was enraged and accused Boatner of never going out and investigating for himself. "He's not a commander," he wrote in his diary. "He's just a pompous staff 'orderer,' big director at H.Q. … he does not itch to get down with the troops and sweat it out." On June 25, he replaced Boatner with Brigadier General Theodore F. Wessels from the Y Force Infantry Training Center in Kunming. The official reason for Boatner's relief was that he was suffering a relapse of cerebral malaria. "Luckily," wrote Stilwell, "Can save his face."[33]

Stilwell took Wessels to the front lines that evening to meet with Hunter. The new commander made an immediate good impression. "For the first time we had at Myitkyina a commander with whom we could communicate," Hunter remembered. "He visited every frontline unit, talked to the officers and men, and was receptive to suggestions."[34] Wessels put Hunter in charge of all U.S. troops at Myitkyina and Zhang Denggua, Sun Liren's deputy, in charge of the Chinese.[35] Gradually, morale improved, though the joint Chinese-American task force made gains measured only in yards. They used flame throwers and bazookas to force the Japanese out from one strongpoint after another. John Habecker continued to work with the air control parties, coordinating for fighter-

Colonel McElroy takes off from a dirt airstrip to support the troops at Myitkyina in an 88th Fighter Squadron P-40. The 88th operated two flights out of the Myitkyina airfield beginning on June 21, 1944. Some of their missions were only eight minutes long. *Merrill's Marauders Association*

A C-47 lands at the Myitkyina airfield on May 19, 1944, amongst the wreckage of other transports. By the end of May, the hulks of nine wrecks littered the field. *National Archives via Samuel Hui*

bombers to pound Japanese positions. He personally made thirty-five reconnaissance flights in his L-5, "looking for Japanese troops heading for Myitkyina and sometimes for our own troops."[36] He finally left Myitkyina on June 2 with orders to take command of the 528th Fighter Squadron at Tingkawk Sakan.

During the month of June, the 528th flew 612 bombing and strafing sorties, twenty-two escort sorties, and ninety-seven patrol sorties supporting the siege at Myitkyina, the Chinese at Kar Maing and Mogaung, and the Chindits to the south. Pilots from the 529th and 530th rotated in from India to keep the 528th from complete exhaustion. They later received a Presidential Unit Citation for their work. The 88th Fighter Squadron moved two flights of P-40s to Myitkyina on June 21. Each Warhawk pilot flew up to six sorties a day, sweating heavily in the heat and humidity. Some were only eight minutes long: the pilots would take off, pull up the landing gear, drop their bombs, put down the gear, and land.[37] Weather permitting, they dive-bombed from five thousand feet, holding a forty-five-degree angle and releasing a thousand feet above the ground to keep the bomb within fifteen meters of the target. The 250-pound demolition bombs were usually fused for a tenth-of-a-second delay to penetrate defensive works and contain the blast to a smaller area.[38] According to Habecker: "close air support coordination between the pilots and the ground forces continued to improve." Pilots from the 88th often went to the front lines personally to have the ground troops point out their targets. As the troops' confidence in the pilots grew, they began moving to targets close behind the air attacks.[39] In a letter to the commander of the 88th Fighter Squadron, General Wessels wrote: "The accuracy and effectiveness of dive-bombing ... enemy weapon emplacements close to our forward positions is remarkable." The fighters were frequently able to provide closer support than the artillery. "The ground troops have the utmost confidence in the 88th Fighter Squadron," continued Wessels, "which is proved by their requests for attacks on targets as close as twenty-five yards to the front lines."[40] In stark contrast to American fighter-bomber support, Japanese air action was negligible.[41]

Fighter-bombers relentlessly pounded at Japanese positions while Stilwell's battle-weary troops inched into Myitkyina. Aircraft landed a steady stream of men and equipment at the airfield. By May 26, the hulks of nine wrecked transports littered the field—a testament to the peril. Denial of the Myitkyina airfield to Japanese fighters did help the airlift into China: Hump tonnage rose from just over thirteen thousand tons in May 1944 to over eighteen thousand tons in June and over twenty-five thousand tons in July. The 38th Division finally succeeded in taking Kar Maing on June 16, and with help from the Chindits, took Mogaung on the twenty-sixth. By then, the monsoon rains poured relentlessly over all of North Burma. In such weather, the X Force made slow progress and was far from being able to relieve End Run. As June and July wore on, the battle for Myitkyina ground on with no clear end in sight.[42]

10

Battleground Above the Clouds

On the Salween Front, Marshal Wei Lihuang assigned Major General Huo Kuizhang's XXth Army Group to fight in the area north of the Burma Road. Their ultimate objective was to capture the walled city of Tengchong. Huo's men were elated at their successful, and surprisingly uncontested, crossing of the Salween River. However, as they stood on the west bank in the early morning light of May 11, the Gaoligong Mountains towered ominously overhead. This monolithic range stands as a wall between the Salween and Shweli rivers and made for the highest and most difficult battlefield terrain of World War II. Primitive trails led through high, frozen passes and over peaks up to twelve thousand feet above sea level to battlegrounds literally above the clouds.[1] According to Major Lai Cheng-liang, commander of the Chinese 593rd Regiment, in the steep mountain terrain, "movement is restricted, fields of fire obstructed, maneuver impeded, and logistical support seriously handicapped."[2]

There were four mountain passes north of the Burma Road: Hpimaw, sixty miles to the north; North Zhaigongfang, forty miles to the north; South Zhaigongfang, twenty-five miles to the north; and a pass opposite the Huiren Bridge site, six miles north of the road and twenty-three miles due east of Tengchong. Huo decided to leave

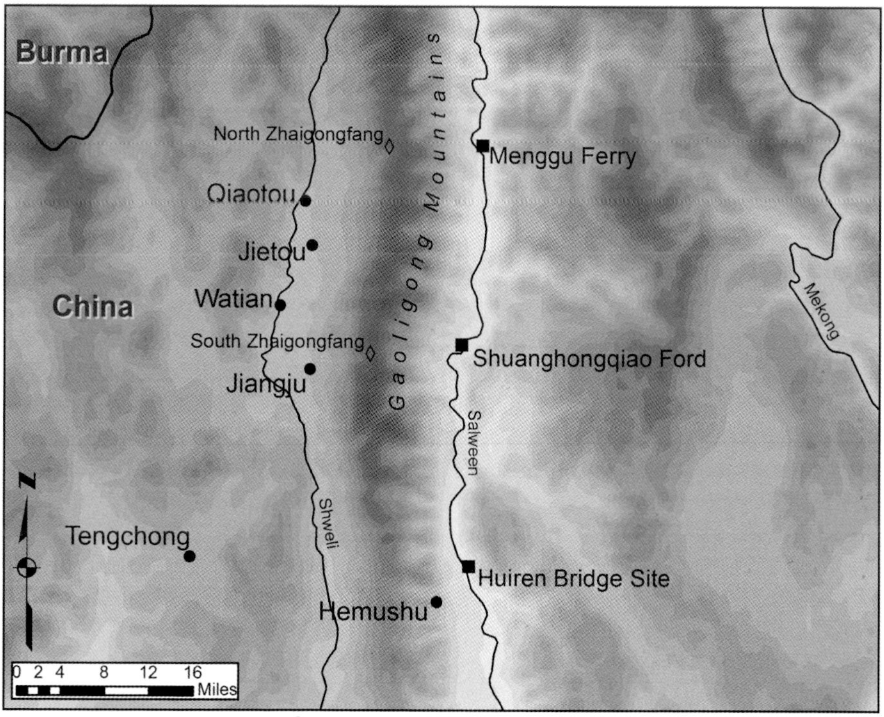

Campaign through the Gaoligong

Hpimaw to the Chinese guerrillas that had harassed the Japanese there since February. He ordered one division of Major General Fang Tian's 54th Army to cross the river at Menggu Ferry and capture the pass at North Zhaigongfang. The other division of the 54th, as well as both divisions of Major General Zhou Fucheng's 53rd Army, crossed at Shuanghongqiao Ford to make the main thrust through the pass at South Zhaigongfang. Both of these passes were over ten thousand feet above sea level. The New 39th Division, on detachment from the XIth Army Group, landed at the Huiren Bridge site. Once the XXth Army Group controlled the Gaoligong passes, its divisions would rendezvous in the Shweli Valley and drive south and west toward Tengchong.[3]

The climb up the Gaoligong was arduous. The peaks were tall and heavily forested. The valleys were hot, damp, and malarial.[4] It took hundreds of thousands of laborers nine months to build the Burma Road over this formidable barrier. Where Huo's troops ascended to the north, there were no roads—just badly worn pack trails. It was more difficult in scope and scale than the End Run Task Force's trek through the Naura Hkyet Pass on its way to Myitkyina. American officers and war correspondents who participated in the difficult campaign over the Owen Stanley Mountains in New Guinea declared the Gaoligong were far worse.[5] Captain Kenneth Scott was a surgeon with one of the U.S. Army portable surgical hospitals accompanying the Chinese troops. He was born to missionary parents serving in North China. When he was called to active duty in 1942, he went to India to train and advise Chinese Army medical officers. In September 1943, he transferred to YFOS headquarters. On the Salween Front, he had "more walking to do than ever before in my life, and over tougher country," he declared. "Going over some of those mountains would make Pikes Peak look like a child's playground." Captain H. Donald Knight, a YFOS advisor assigned to an air control party, wrote: "It is almost impossible to describe the ruggedness of the mountain trails over which all progress must be made." The trails were often too steep to ascend. "Paths must zigzag dizzily in order to give any footing to the marching troops." Captain Scott frequently saw "litter patients climb out and walk up a steep mountain because it was too much for the carriers." He remembered one particular incident when a litter bearer collapsed, exhausted, and the patient got up and switched places with him![6]

Many of the trails followed streambeds which, according to Knight, had "cobbles for footing, so that pack animals slip and slide and must be dragged over spots by the soldiers." The streambeds became rushing torrents in the monsoon. The men did their best to force their way through the freezing waters. "Some trails are covered with black soil which turns to gumbo in the rains, clinging to heavy G.I. shoes," said Knight. "Others are of a slick clay composition." The men would struggle up the slippery slope, making progress, "two-steps-forward-one-step back." The Chinese soldiers sometimes removed their rope sandals to get a better footing with their bare feet.[7] The steep climb and high altitude made the men feel as if their lungs would burst. Knight remembered times when the only way he could continue was to pick out a tree fifty yards up the slope and tell himself, "I'll get that far or die trying." It was not any easier to descend. Men found their knees went numb and their calf muscles quivered and knotted. According to Knight, on the slick clay, any misstep would send a man sliding and stumbling, "gyrating wildly in an attempt to regain balance before he misses a curve and goes over a cliff."[8]

Supplying the Chinese Expeditionary Force in such difficult terrain was challenging to say the least. Every month, the CEF required four million rounds of .303-caliber and

7.62-millimeter ammunition, four hundred thousand rounds of .45-caliber, thirteen thousand rounds of .55-caliber, seventeen thousand rounds of 37-millimeter shells, forty-six thousand rounds of 60-millimeter shells, forty-three thousand rounds of 75-millimeter shells, and almost six thousand rockets, in addition to rations and other supplies. Dorn requisitioned a number of trucks to move supplies from Kunming and Yunnanyi to his forward depots. This upset Chennault, who claimed he needed the trucks to move gasoline and equipment to his squadrons fighting in East China. YFOS engineers worked with the Yunnan-Burma Highway Engineering Administration to improve the Burma Road from Kunming to Baoshan. Because there were no roads for the trucks to ascend the Gaoligong, the CEF used horses, mules, and human porters to carry supplies to the front. The Chinese called these human porters *kuli* (苦力), or coolies, which means "bitter strength." Their lot was bitter indeed, each bent double under the weight of over sixty pounds of ammunition, rice, or other supplies. More than three hundred perished in the climb over the Gaoligong. Tens of thousands of such men and women formed a remarkable human supply chain that was a key instrument in the campaign. It was a means of supply the Japanese did not anticipate, nor fully appreciate. Ten years later, the Viet Minh used a similar system at Dien Bien Phu. Like the Japanese, the French did not anticipate the strength of this human element. YFOS advisors were impressed by the Chinese porters. It was a remarkable effort, but it was not sufficient to keep the tens of thousands of soldiers in the CEF fully supplied.[9]

Horses and mules, however, were hard to come by. Dorn visited the Tibetan horse fairs in northern Yunnan, but they would not take Chinese paper money, nor would they take gold. "The U.S. Army became one of the largest traffickers in opium in order to buy 10,000 animals," he admitted. "We purposely kept no records of such expenditures. But one thing was for sure … the American taxpayers bought a hell of a lot of opium."[10] The horses had trouble ascending the steep, narrow trails. With too few animal handlers, or *mafu's* (马夫), to go around, even the Americans had to learn how to manage the horses and mules carrying their supplies. According to Knight, at first, the "loads were too heavy—a pack animal will only carry from 80 to 120 pounds—and the animals refused to move." Often times, the packs were not properly balanced and would fall off, scattering supplies across the mountainside as they rolled into a crevice or ravine. Enough of these mistakes taught the men to pack the proper amount, balance the load, and use rope ties to keep from losing the packs when they fell.[11]

The arrival of the 27th Troop Carrier Squadron (TCS) at Yunnanyi on May 21 heralded an improvement to the supply situation. The 27th had amassed considerable experience airdropping supplies to the Allied forces in Burma since December, including 148 sorties helping the 1st Air Commando Group insert Wingate's Chindits behind enemy lines. Despite everything in North Burma converging on Myitkyina, the need for air transport on the Salween Front was acute enough to justify transferring the squadron to the 14th Air Force.[12] Though the majority of its operations over Burma were under cover of darkness, all airdrops on the Salween Front would be made in daylight because of the challenging weather and terrain. According to pilot John Welch, the aircrews found the epic view of the Salween and Mekong rivers "breathtaking" on their flight over the Hump to Yunnanyi.[13]

On May 28, the squadron's thirteen C-47s began dropping supplies to the CEF at Target Number 1, alongside the Salween River. Within a month, there were twenty-

Chinese "coolies" carry heavy supplies over difficult terrain. Though not enough to keep the CEF fully supplied, the use of human porters on the Salween Front was an element not fully anticipated or appreciated by the Japanese. ***National Archives***

five numbered targets ranging from north of Tengchong to south of Longling. By the end of July, there were more than fifty. To coordinate the drops, liaison teams used hand-cranked radio sets to relay supply needs and drop zone information to YFOS Headquarters at Baoshan. The headquarters then contacted the troop carrier squadron at Yunnanyi, which in turn briefed the crews. Each round trip was about three and a half hours long. Each crew usually made two trips a day and then handed the plane off to another crew to fly two more This kept a steady stream of transports shuttling between Yunnanyi and the front, with an airplane taking off about every fifteen minutes. Sometimes, the transports delivered supplies faster than the YFOS Air Dropping Detachment could pack them and the aircrews had to pitch in to help them catch up.[14] In June alone, the squadron flew 345 sorties and dropped 588 tons of provisions.[15] The 27th was short on crews and often navigators or bombardiers rode along as copilots. With gasoline critical in China, they flew with only enough gas for the round trip, plus a thirty minute reserve. Lieutenant Robert Binzer arrived in China with the 19th Liaison Squadron, but transferred to the 27th TCS after injuring his back in a flying accident. He commented that while the squadron did not lose any aircraft to fuel exhaustion, the limited fuel was "a great help in sharpening your navigation skills."[16] According to pilot Jack Engle: "we could find Tengchong, Chenanso, Longling, or Baoshan, or any spot on the Shweli, Salween, or Mekong rivers as easily as we could find the corner drug store."[17]

The cargo planes flew as low as possible, usually between twelve and fourteen thousand feet above sea level.[18] The pilots flew without oxygen, as the C-47A had no armor and according to Bob Binzer, if they carried oxygen tanks, "ground fire or a hit from a Zero could spoil your whole day." Later on, when the squadron received C-47Bs with supercharged engines, they reinstalled the oxygen tanks to permit them to fly at

Chinese soldiers load a pack horse with supplies on the Salween Front. Horses and mules could carry from eighty to 120 pounds, but had trouble on the steep, narrow trails. *National Archives*

higher altitudes.[19] According to pilot Bob Jones, the C-47 performed "reasonably good considering the higher elevations we operated in, including narrow valleys."[20] It was stable, easy to load and balance, sturdy, and dependable. The C-46, by contrast, was infamous for its weight and balance having to be arranged precisely with a slide rule and for suffering from numerous technical problems due to it being rushed into service too quickly.[21]

The transport crews had to be careful flying in the weather and terrain. The weather changed frequently and rapidly during the monsoon season. Often, the pilots found themselves picking their way between lines of thunderstorms or flying through violent turbulence. It was dangerous work; during a severe thunderstorm in September 1944, one of the squadron's airplanes slammed into a mountain, killing all six crewmembers on board.[22] As for the terrain, some of the drop zones were in valleys large enough for the transport crews to set up an easy drop pattern. More often, the only place liaison officers could find was the top of a mountain spur or a small mountain meadow.[23] According to Binzer: "there were some drops made to the side of a mountain where the valley was too narrow, and those were most difficult to handle."[24] The transports maintained radio silence, so YFOS air control parties used colored cloth panels arranged in specified patterns to mark the drop zones. Sometimes the Japanese tried to mimic the panels, but they had trouble reproducing the colors.

A downside to aerial supply was its expense. The Services of Supply (SOS) in India estimated it cost $1,909.65 per ton to deliver supplies by parachute. YFOS tried to reduce the cost by using cotton parachutes made in China rather than silk, and by dropping rice free-fall without any parachute at all. Free-fall drops cost only $94.07 per ton.[25] Packers usually double-bagged seventy pounds of rice in two burlap sacks. The transports circled the drop zones between three and five hundred feet above the ground.

"Kickers" piled the bags in front of the open cargo door. They would lie down on their backs, hold onto a bar bolted to the floor, and when they received the drop signal, kick the bags out the door.[26] When the rice hit the ground, the inner bag would break but the outer bag would hold.[27] Using this method, a C-47 could deliver a load of 5,500 pounds of rice in anywhere from three to ten passes, depending on the size and geometry of the drop zone.[28]

Rice was the staple of any diet on the Salween Front and the American advisors ate the same rations as the Chinese. According to G.B. Coverdale, an artillery liaison officer: "It was a fairly common sight to see piles of mildewed rice awaiting to be transported by coolie carry to the troops. The fact that it was mildewed mattered little, as it had to be eaten anyway since there was no replacement, and, as a matter of fact, there never was enough."[29] Each man was allotted two meals a day, with a quarter can of C-rations per meal. Most spread the C-rations over the rice to give it more flavor. When the weather prevented resupply and rations were low, men lived off bamboo shoots and unwary livestock. One American liaison team made steaks from a mountain tiger.[30] Most of the Americans lost fifteen to thirty pounds in the first six weeks of fighting. Almost all of them had diarrhea or suffered some sort of medical disorder. Those who could not continue were evacuated by liaison planes.[31]

Using small airstrips near the front allowed the wounded or deceased to be evacuated in a forty-minute flight, rather than the week or more it took to carry them out on foot. Engineers cleared the first small airstrip near Shuanghongqiao within nine days of crossing the Salween. The 19th Liaison Squadron flew tiny Stinson L-5s, which could operate out of remarkably short fields in challenging terrain—bush planes, essentially. The squadron arrived in China on April 29, 1944, with thirty-two aircraft. Major Richard Day was the commanding officer. The squadron had only fifteen officers and 122 enlisted men. Most of the pilots were enlisted and performed their own maintenance in addition to flying. The squadron established its headquarters at Kunming. Detachments sprang up at Baoshan, Wenshan, and Yunnanyi within the first month of the campaign. The Baoshan detachment was the largest, with two officers and twenty-four enlisted men. Unlike the other squadrons supporting the CEF, the 19th reported directly to YFOS, rather than to the 69th Composite Wing.[32]

In addition to medical evacuation, the liaison planes flew a myriad of other missions, including courier, artillery adjustment, and tactical reconnaissance. Courier missions involved flying up to two hundred pounds of supplies to American liaison teams in the field, including 75-millimeter ammunition, PX rations, food, clothing, and medical supplies. Reconnaissance involved photographing Japanese positions, flying observers over the battlefield, determining the serviceability of roads and trails, and searching for potential locations for new airstrips. Flying low and slow over the battlefield made it easier to spot targets hidden in difficult terrain or concealed by camouflage. This was useful not only for artillery spotting, but also for directing air strikes. Tech Sergeant Matthew Blaszko was with the detachment at Baoshan and flew over one hundred combat missions during his time with the 19th. He remembered directing fighter-bombers from the 14th Air Force in attacks on enemy positions. The L-5 had an HF radio it could use to communicate with other aircraft and the pilot or observer could also carry smoke grenades to mark targets. This wide assortment of missions kept the 19th very busy. Despite poor weather, in June alone the squadron flew twenty-seven

A 27th Troop Carrier Squadron C-47 parachutes supplies to the Chinese Expeditionary Force. Often, the only drop zones available were mountain spurs or meadows. Air control parties marked the drop zones with panels or smoke and the transports made three to ten passes, depending on its size and geometry. *Hoover Institute*

Kickers from the 27th Troop Carrier Squadron push burlap bags of rice out the cargo door of a C-47. Dropping rice by free-fall, instead of by parachute, was much less expensive, though more hazardous for the troops on the ground. *Hoover Institute*

combat courier missions, twenty-one administrative courier missions, nineteen evacuation missions, nine reconnaissance missions, and thirteen training missions, for a total of ninety-four hours and twenty minutes flying time.[33]

The greatest challenge to air support was the weather. Throughout the monsoon, Yunnanyi was often overcast and troop carrier planes had to fly on instruments within minutes of takeoff. The liaison planes did not have sufficient instrumentation and had to work beneath the weather. For days at a time, aircraft were unable to reach friendly troops at the front. From June 3-10, the weather was so terrible that air support was impossible.[34] Initially, the poor weather gave the men on the ground an advantage. The Japanese did not expect them to attack during the monsoon and heavy rains often masked their movements. In the high-altitude mountain passes though, the constant rain turned to sleet, snow, and fog. The cold and damp quickly penetrated the cotton uniforms of the poorly-clad Chinese soldiers. "More of my men were killed by the cold weather rather than the Japanese army," said Yang Chien-chiu, a platoon leader in the 106th Regiment, 36th Division. "I remember that the sun was bright when we were at the bottom of the mountains. As we climbed higher, the weather turned colder." Yang grew up in Sichuan Province and graduated from the Chengdu branch of the Huangpu Academy in October 1943. Eighteen graduates from his class became platoon leaders in the 36th Division. Soon after embarking on their first combat assignment, they all watched as one by one their men collapsed from the cold. "All I could do was encourage them to keep going," said Yang. "If they fell asleep, they would never be able to wake up again. I still dream about them today and cry about it at night because I feel so sorry for them."[35] General Ye Peigao, commander of the 198th Division, also witnessed the death and suffering inflicted by the cold in the high mountain passes. He requested that ten thousand American raincoats be air-dropped to his men to protect them from exposure. The raincoats were not much help on the march. The exertion and humidity made the wearer as wet from sweat as from the rain. The Chinese used them to keep warm and dry at night and usually carried them on their packs in the daytime.[36]

Despite the supply challenges and difficult terrain, the Chinese did not waste any time after crossing the Salween. A battalion on the right flank of the 198th Division made the first attack on North Zhaigongfang in the late afternoon of May 12. Colonel Kurashige, commander of the Japanese 148th Regiment at Tengchong, had moved his 2nd Battalion into the pass in January. The battalion established small patrols to monitor the Salween River, built bunkers and strongpoints from logs and earth, and connected them by networks of trenches. They established artillery positions with prepared fields of fire to cover all approaches. The positions dominated the few trails; they were easy to defend and the Japanese defended them fanatically. Luckily, the initial Chinese attack took them by surprise. By nightfall on the twelfth, the Chinese occupied several pillboxes and trenches.[37]

The men of 2nd Battalion rallied during the night, assembling under cover of darkness for a counterattack at dawn. The inexperienced Chinese troops had not yet learned to consolidate their positions. The fierce counterattack caught them surprised and unprepared and nearly wiped them out. Tao Dagang, commander of the 592nd Regiment, reported that one battalion commander was killed, one wounded, and seven of the nine company commanders were either killed or wounded. Lieutenant Kirk

The 19th Liaison Squadron flew the tiny Stinson L-5 from small airstrips for medical evacuation, combat courier, artillery spotting, and reconnaissance. Using liaison planes, casualties could reach the hospital in minutes instead of days or weeks. *National Archives*

Liaison detachments sprang up at Baoshan, Wenshan, and Yunnanyi within the first month of the campaign. The detachment at Baoshan (pictured here) was the largest, with two officers and twenty-four enlisted men. *National Archives*

Schaible, a liaison officer attached to the 198th, tried to help the Chinese protect their exposed flank; he left cover and was immediately gunned down by rifle fire. Schaible was the first American killed in the Salween Campaign. Chinese reinforcements restored the situation the next day and the Japanese withdrew to positions deep within the pass, biding their time and waiting for reinforcements.[38]

While the bulk of the 198th Division occupied the Japanese in the pass, the 593rd Regiment worked through the difficult terrain to the south to cut off the enemy from behind. There were no trails, only gullies and drainages. "Sometimes weapons were hoisted up by ropes," rembered Lai Cheng-liang, the regiment's commander. On May 15, after a grueling thirty-six hour march that succeeded only because of "the high morale and determination of officers and men alike," the regiment emerged into the Shweli Valley.[39] Two days later it took the village of Qiaotou. A Japanese counterattack recaptured the village on May 28, but the Chinese finally took it and held it on June 4.[40] With their supply lines cut, the Japanese holding the pass began to suffer. The Chinese defeated several columns attempting to relieve them and finally took the pass on June 15. They found only seventy-five bodies in defenses once manned by over three hundred.[41] First Lieutenant Richard Shoemaker, a liaison officer attached to the 54th Army, investigated the positions and reported circumstantial evidence of the Japanese resorting to cannibalism. He reported twelve bodies—seven adjacent to the kitchen—with flesh on the head, hands, and feet showing no sign of decay. "The rest of the body was bare and no flesh whatsoever on the bones," he wrote. The flesh appeared to have been cut off, as "there were no jagged or uneven edges."[42] It was a grotesque testament to the fanatical determination of the enemy; they would rather eat their comrades than surrender to the Chinese.

While the 198th Division attacked North Zhaigongfang, the 36th Division, 54th Army, led the drive on South Zhaigongfang. The Chinese surrounded Japanese outposts at the eastern end of the pass by dusk on May 12. A Japanese counterattack that night pushed them all the way back to the Salween. Major General Zhou Fucheng, commander of the 53rd Army, pushed another regiment across the Salween the next day and attacked the Japanese flank. Zhou's nickname was "Old Board-Back" because he was a strict Manchurian with a ramrod posture. He had the reputation of not yielding an inch to the Japanese. Dorn thought he was "the best of the army commanders on the western front," though he was "temperamental and his feelings are always being hurt."[43] Even Zhou could not restore the shaken confidence of the 36th, which he relegated to a supporting role.[44]

Zhou brought his two divisions—the 116th and 130th—forward to keep steady pressure on South Zhaigongfang. The Chinese advantage in numbers was offset by the strength of the Japanese positions. YFOS advisors encouraged the Chinese to stick to the tactics of infiltrating the front, interdicting supply lines, and then reducing the surrounded strongpoints in siege and assault. However, the Chinese seemed to have entirely abandoned their training, having apparently only cooperated to be polite. Lieutenant Colonel John Stodter was the commander of the liaison teams attached to the 53rd Army. "In view of the enemy's defensive attitude and superior strength," he wrote, "American liaison officers urged the use of a small containing force and a strong encircling movement to cut the trail." Despite this, the Chinese continued to make costly frontal assaults on the Japanese positions. Stodter reported that they often took heavy losses "in suicidal charges by a succession of squads against enemy pillboxes." He noted a lack of teamwork between the assaulting infantry and supporting fire, and that soldiers did not make use of cover. The result was a sickening number of casualties as the men charged up steep mountain slopes into a maelstrom of overlapping fields of machine gun fire. "A general coordinated assault might have overrun the positions by sheer esprit and weight of numbers," he remarked. But platoons advanced piecemeal, sometimes standing idly by while their comrades got mowed down before attempting to attack themselves. "As a demonstration of sheer bravery the attacks were magnificent," wrote Stodter, "but sickeningly wasteful."[45]

Yoshino Taka Kimi was a Japanese field medic stationed in the Gaoligong Mountains. "The Chinese charged our positions in the dark," he remembered. "Rocket flares lit up the sky like day time. Guns were blazing." He could see the shadows of Chinese soldiers as they attacked. "They came after us, one wave after another," he reported. "They got within forty or fifty meters of us. They didn't even pause to carry away their dead." The Japanese machine guns opened up at point-blank range, firing with devastating effect and leaving piles of dead bodies in front of their positions. Some Chinese troops put machine guns on top of the heap, using their dead comrades as cover. "As soon as we shot one gunner, another one took his place," said Yoshino. "Some of them threw down their rifles and fought us with swords and bayonets."[46]

The American advisors were amazed at the bravery, the spirit, and the audacity of the Chinese troops. When one considers they were abducted from their homes and families by conscription officers and then sent to the slaughter by often inexperienced or ineffective leaders on the battlefield, it is truly astonishing. Shen You-chih, the machine gunner conscripted from Henan Province, recounted how his attitude changed throughout his time as a soldier: "When I was conscripted, I felt it was horrible to serve as a private in the Republic of China Army," he said. "However, I began to change my opinion about the war when I began to meet the Japanese face-to-face on the battlefield." Shen first saw combat in the Winter Offensive of 1939 along the border of Henan and Hubei provinces. His unit enjoyed a handful of small victories, but there was no stopping the overwhelming power of the Japanese, with their superior training and equipment. Eventually, Shen and his fellow soldiers went to fight as guerrillas in the mountains between Shanxi and Henan. "With the cooperation of other ROC Army units, we were able to defeat the Japanese thirteen times," he recalled. "During that period of time, we were treated by the local population as heroes for fighting against foreign invaders. I began to be proud of myself and my unit." Shen knew the horrors of conscription and he had no illusions about the competence of his officers, but he began to see the importance of fighting for his people, for China. Despite his unit's success in small actions, the Ichi-go offensive in 1944 forced them to retreat. They marched to Yunnan to reinforce the 71st Army on the Salween Front. The influence of American training, equipment, and values soon became apparent. "Our treatment improved gradually," he said. "We were allowed to have much better food and supplies than when we were in Northern China." Shen's story illustrates the fortitude and grace with which the common soldiers faced death and hardship. As Admiral Chester Nimitz said of the U.S. Marines at Iwo Jima, "Uncommon valor was a common virtue."[47]

Facing overwhelming losses, the Chinese leadership gradually became open to their American teammates. Colonel Buckley, senior liaison officer to the XXth Army Group, thought the lessons learned during the campaign put commanders of all ranks "in the most receptive state of mind as pertains to American-supervised training." Both Americans and Chinese watched "excessive casualties pile up day after day, chiefly as a result of violations of proper tactical and technical procedure," while troops following American training "saw important objectives taken and held, at comparatively small cost." Buckley felt the Chinese "acquired a new respect for the American Liaison Officer who shared with them the dangers and hardships of the campaign, and a new confidence and understanding of the American training methods that proved their correctness in the final test—battle."[48]

The New 39th Division crossed the Salween at the Huiren Bridge site as the southernmost of the three columns north of the Burma road. It began taking fire on the morning of May 11 from the 1st Battalion of the Japanese 113th Regiment. A regimental combat team from the Chinese 115th Regiment reinforced by a battalion from the 116th Regiment crossed nine miles to the north and advanced south to drive them out. By May 17, the 115th had driven them four miles down the trail to the village of Hemushu, only twenty miles from Tengchong. The Japanese soon recovered from the initial assault and in a fierce counterattack, 1st Battalion drove the entire New 39th Division back to the banks of the Salween. The Chinese rallied, and by the twenty-seventh were back within five miles of the village. The battle seesawed until the Japanese withdrew to aid their comrades at South Zhaigongfang. By June 12, the 115th was pushing west from Hemushu into the Shweli Valley. Marshal Wei then ordered the New 39th Division south down the Shweli Valley to assist the XIth Army Group at Songshan.

Chinese reinforcements moving through the pass at South Zhaigongfang linked up with their fellow soldiers moving through North Zhaigongfang in early June. A fierce assault carried Jietou, four miles south of Qiaotou, on June 15. The Japanese withdrew six miles south to Watian, which fell on the twentieth, and then to Jiangju, the western anchor of the pass at South Zhaigongfang, which had been under siege since June 3. Chinese reinforcements poured in from over the Gaoligong, fueling bitter fighting in the villages south and east of Jiangju. On June 22, the Japanese retreated toward Tengchong, leaving the Shweli Valley in the hands of the Chinese. After forty-two days of fighting, the XXth Army Group conquered the Gaoligong, pushed the Japanese from the Shweli Valley, and was poised to attack its primary objective, Tengchong. In the process, General Huo's troops liberated over four thousand square miles of Chinese territory.[49]

11

Failure at Longling

Frank Dorn was impressed by Huo Kuizhang, calling the XXth Army Group commander the "big surprise of the campaign." Before, he had thought Huo was "nothing brilliant," though he appreciated he was dependable and listened to suggestions. Despite initial difficulties and a steep learning curve, the XXth Army Group proved to have good leadership. Dorn thought the 53rd Army commander, General Zhou, was "the best of the army commanders on the western front" and Ye Peigao, commander of the 198th Division, was "one of the better division commanders." Not so with the XIth Army Group. According to Dorn, Song Xilian, the army group commander, was a "professional hero, personally courageous, but a moral coward." At thirty-seven, Song was the youngest army group commander in China.[1] He became rich off the "squeeze" in the two years leading up to the Salween Campaign and played favorites between his military and business associates. Dorn complained that he "makes false reports to cover himself, and militarily does not know what he is doing." To make matters worse, his subordinates were inept and incapable. The commander of the 71st Army, Zhong Bin, was a successful businessman, but according to Dorn, "loses his head in combat." General Wang Lingyun, commander of the 2nd Army, was "a cry baby and not competent."[2] Under the leadership of these men, the XIth Army Group crossed the Salween south of the Burma Road.

Marshal Wei hoped to use the XIth as a left hook to take Longling, the largest town on the road west of the Salween and a conduit for supplies traveling up and down the front. Its seizure would aid immeasurably in the capture of Tengchong and position the CEF to drive down the Burma Road. Longling was only thirty miles from where the Huitong Bridge once crossed the river. Since then, the Japanese 113th Regiment had thoroughly fortified Songshan—"Pine Mountain"—a 6,500-foot peak towering overhead. They turned the mountain into a fortress, with pillboxes, bunkers, and trenches. From Songshan, their artillery could easily harass the bridge site and twenty-seven miles of the road west of the river. Y Force Operations Staff called it the "Gibraltar of the Burma Road."[3]

Rather than risk bogging down in an attack on such a difficult position, the XIth Army Group crossed the river thirty miles to the south. The Japanese had occupied much of the area north and south of the Burma Road, including the villages of Pingda and Xiangda, both of which lay on a trail that intercepted the road west of Longling. If the XIth could drive up this trail, it could attack Longling from the rear and cut off the garrison at Songshan. Two regimental combat teams crossed the river in two columns: one from the 76th Division, 2nd Army, near Dazhai, eleven miles southeast of Pingda; and the other from the 88th Division, 71st Army, seven miles to the northeast. They met little opposition from the Japanese until May 14, when the 76th encountered the first pickets of 1st Battalion, 146th Regiment. Elements of both Chinese columns simultaneously converged on Pingda, brushing aside the enemy patrols and capturing the town on the fifteenth. As in the north, however, they did not consolidate their positions and lost the town to a counterattack on May 23. They suffered the same fate at Xiangda. After securing the town on June 13, a Japanese counterattack the next day forced them to withdraw to the surrounding hills.

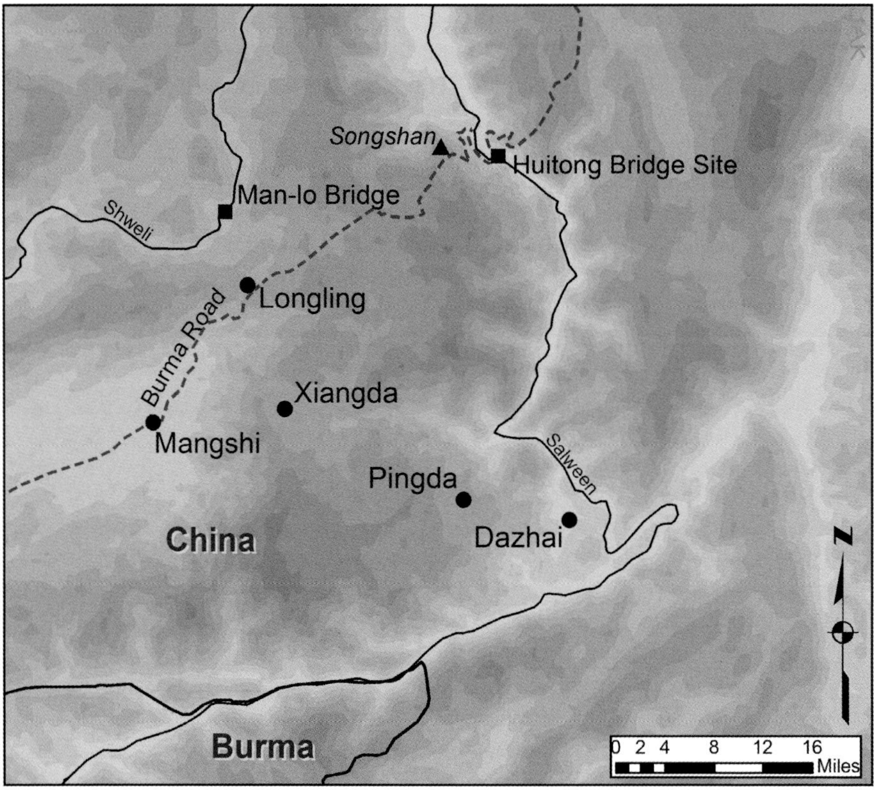

Campaign South of the Road

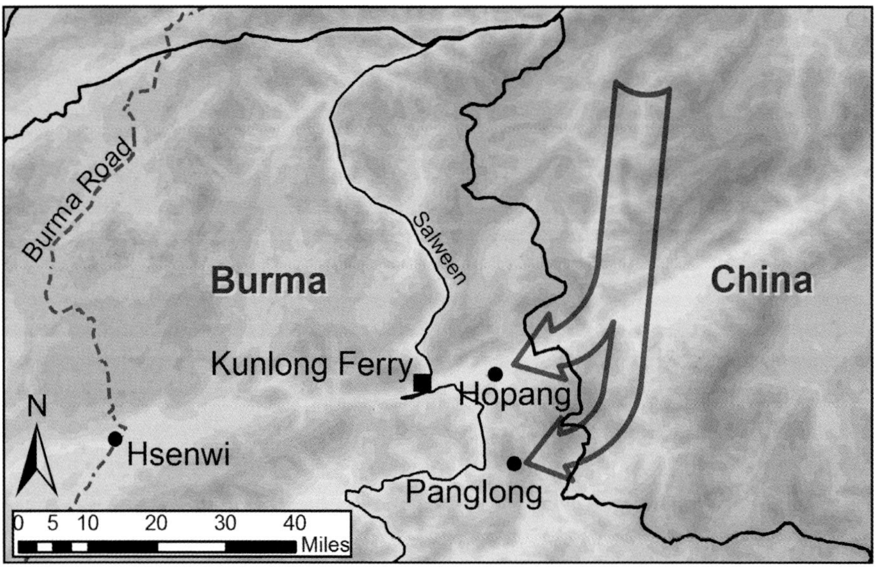

Attack on Kunlong Ferry

The sixth column of the CEF, assigned to cover the left flank, moved out on May 17 for Kunlong Ferry, on the Salween River ninety-five miles south of the Burma Road. A road from Kunlong ran due west to Hsenwi, only thirty miles north of Lashio. The 56th Division stationed three companies of its reconnaissance regiment at the ferry to hold the southern end of the front. Small parties of Japanese soldiers had crossed to the east side of the river, but by May 28, the Chinese cleared them out and occupied Hopang, nine miles east of Kunlong; and Panglong, sixteen miles southeast. With a relatively modest effort, they effectively blocked the Japanese from making a move on their southern flank.

Meanwhile, the Japanese considered holding the Shweli Valley to be absolutely critical and weakened their forces south of the road to reinforce Colonel Kurashige against the XXth Army Group to the north. When Marshal Wei realized this, he pressed to exploit the situation and committed as much of the XIth Army Group to battle as possible. Between May 28 and June 5, twenty thousand troops from the 71st Army crossed the Salween River eight miles south of the Huitong Bridge site, leaving a small force to contain Songshan while pressing toward Longling. The elements of the 71st Army investing Pingda marched north. The 2nd Army left regimental-sized containing forces at Pingda and Xiangda and did likewise. The terrain south of the Burma Road was lower than that over which the XXth Army Group fought in the north. Pingda was only 5,200 feet above sea level. The trail to Longling rarely climbed above seven thousand feet. When the Japanese recaptured Pingda, it was perhaps not the worst thing for the CEF—the town was plagued by malaria and cholera. The small Chinese containing force held in the less disease-ridden mountains above the town. Thus, not only were the Japanese besieged, they were also wracked by disease.

Reinforcements poured across the Salween. The 2nd Army brought its 9th Division across the river on June 1. Eight days later, this division had road blocks across the Burma Road north and south of Mangshi, cutting Longling off from reinforcement. The 71st Army arrived on the outskirts of Longling on June 7 and broke through the outer defenses the next day. General Song personally led an attack on the ninth that captured the west gate and left him in control of three-quarters of the city. Three days later, the Chinese occupied the entire town, save for a pocket of fifty Japanese troops inside the west gate and fifty on the airstrip to the south. Three hundred more fled and Chinese troops pursued them nine miles to the west. By all appearances, all that remained was to mop up the remnants.[4]

As with the columns fighting over the Gaoligong Mountains to the north, the XIth Army Group depended heavily on air support. The 27th TCS struggled through the weather to airdrop supplies. Liaison planes from the 19th continually buzzed over the battlefield. Fighters and bombers from the 25th Fighter Squadron and 22nd Bomb Squadron hit Japanese positions and supply lines. Artillery was important on the Salween Front, but the rugged terrain and lack of roads limited the Chinese to small numbers of 75-millimeter pack howitzers, which they could disassemble and load on mules. The lightly-armed infantry often counted on pinpoint air strikes to soften up targets prior to an advance. Yet air support suffered for a number of reasons. In fact, shortly after the campaign began, Dorn told Chennault he was "not entirely satisfied with the manner in which air support is being given to the Chinese ground armies on the Salween Front." Dorn did not like Chennault, whom he referred to as "an inbred, Louisiana Cajun, the square-jawed enthusiast for his own theories of air power with no background of staff, command, and dull matters like logistics." In turn, Chennault hated Dorn, who on Stilwell's orders had shut down a 14th Air Force "social club" in Kunming. The club was alleged to have been a center of prostitution and black market activities—a "bordello" in Stilwell's words. Dorn shut it down with relish, promptly earning the antipathy of Chennault, who maintained it was nothing more than a harmless club.[5]

Colonel Robert Breitweiser, a 14th Air Force staff officer, travelled to the front in early August to investigate the claims that air support was "less than satisfactory." He found that requests for air action usually came directly from the top leadership of the CEF, rather than from front line commanders or American air control parties. General Xiao Yisu, Wei's chief of staff, made most of the requests at the nightly staff meetings at YFOS headquarters in Baoshan. The Chinese leadership, according to Breitweiser, "fail, understandably, to recognize the needs for accurate target location, ground follow-up of air action, and careful target selection for suitability. They measure the efficacy of air power by its morale effect on their own troops and not by its destructive effect on the troops of the enemy." In short, it was "a policy which subordinates tactical principles to political expediency." He reported that air control parties were "not performing the duties set up for them and their presence in the field is mostly a waste of man power. They should either be backed with sufficient authority to permit their functioning as planned or they should be withdrawn."

Breitweiser also found that the air support process marginalized Colonel Kennedy and the 69th Wing. From General Xiao, requests went directly to General Dorn, who reviewed and approved each one himself. He sent orders to the Air Support Section at Yunnanyi, specifying the type and number of aircraft to be used on each mission, as well as the tactics to be employed. He had good reason to keep close control of the process; the operation was very political. It was important for the Chinese to feel like they were getting enough support from the American planes and to avoid any high-profile mishaps. Dorn also used the implicit threat of a withdrawal of air support as a quid-pro-quo to keep them fighting on the ground. The Air Support Section had little recourse to amend his instructions, and in effect became nothing more than a relay, passing his orders on to the squadrons. According to Breitweiser, it created a system in which "Air support requests go from initiation to completion without being examined objectively by a pilot qualified to pass upon and charged with their feasibility." Consequently, fighter and bomber crews often set out for the front with nothing more than a vague idea of their target or its location. They had no radio contact with air control parties. They only had a set of map coordinates, or sometimes, if they were lucky, they found cloth panels laid out pointing to the target area. William Mitchell was a pilot with the 25th Fighter Squadron and flew over one hundred combat missions in P-40s during his tour of duty in China. "A wooded landscape all flows together when viewed from the air," he reported. "It was difficult to tell which trenches belonged to the Japanese and which to the Chinese. They were so close together that guessing wasn't good enough."

Chennault believed the Chinese would best be served by the contribution of effective air support to a successful campaign, not by manipulating mediocre support for political reasons. Given his limited supplies and resources, he insisted on getting the maximum return for risking his men and machines. He could not afford to have half his missions wasted on targets not appropriate for aircraft, or on attacks not coordinated with or

A Chinese pack artillery regiment moving down the Burma Road to Longling. Note the guns are disassembled and loaded onto mules for transport over rough terrain. ***National Archives via Samuel Hui***

exploited by ground forces. The situation required a flexible system that depended on the knowledge of the air control parties in the field and the professionalism and judgment of the airmen flying the missions. He did not mince words with Dorn: "I thoroughly understand your desire to pass upon each request for air support," he wrote, but "I must warn you against prescribing the type and number of aircraft to be employed and as to the tactics to be employed." He promised he would take personal responsibility for the success of air operations were Colonel Kennedy and his staff trusted and empowered to work without Dorn's interference. "In turn," he warned, "I must make it clear that the responsibility will be entirely yours if you insist upon telling us how to do our job." He told Dorn that he had confidence in the air control parties. "Members of my staff have been in close touch with General Egan and with the methods that have been used with great success in his support of General Stilwell's operations," he wrote. "I am quite certain that General Stilwell relies upon the judgment of his air commander, as to how the support missions will be executed."[6]

Like Stilwell, Dorn did not trust Chennault. However, in this situation, his expertise on the tactical use of airplanes was without question. He was willing to work with Dorn, but it had to be on his terms. The two men never reconciled their personal relationship and Dorn continued to closely monitor air operations, but he left more and more of the details to the 69th Wing. He and his staff worked with the Chinese to give air control parties more authority and freedom of action. Lieutenant Raymond G. Arimond, the 25th Fighter Squadron's communications officer, volunteered to join the controllers near Longling to standardize frequencies and procedures and improve communications between ground and air. From an observation post on a mountainside overlooking Longling, he called down strikes on supply dumps and fortifications. His living conditions were little better than the troops. His observation post had a grass roof that provided little protection from the constant rain. Japanese shells whistled overhead.[7] The cumulative effect of the hard work of Arimond and others, as well as the reforms insisted upon by Chennault, created a system that was amongst the best in the world. Fighter-bombers in Europe struck targets behind a bomb line, where they knew there were no friendly troops. In China, as in Burma, the fighters hit targets only yards from friendly soldiers on the ground.

P-40s typically worked in flights of four. Passing the Salween, the flight leader contacted the air control party for their assigned area. The controllers used terrain features, cloth panels, and smoke shells to talk the pilots onto their targets. "With that kind of help it was fairly easy to deliver the mail," said Mitchell. He remembered one time when the Japanese tried to trick the pilots by firing smoke shells of their own. One of the controllers lost his composure on the radio and shouted, "No! No! Wrong target!"[8] Such instances were rare and good communication prevented too many incidents of friendly fire.

The 25th was stationed at Yunnanyi, 130 miles east of the Salween River. They were originally based at Beiting Field—two miles east of Yunnanyi—but the monsoon weather rendered the grass strip a muddy morass. The Yunnanyi field was an all-weather gravel runway 5,864 feet long and 6,430 feet above sea level.[9] Lieutenant Clifford Long was a pilot with the squadron. He joined the air cadets at the age of seventeen when he was a junior in High School. He went to pilot training when he was eighteen and deployed to China when he was nineteen. By the time he turned twenty, he was on his way home after 104 combat missions. In a *CBI Roundup* article in August 1944, Captain William Livergood, operations officer for the 25th, wrote: "Lest anyone gain the impression that this is an old man's war, please consider this bobby-sox trio, who are doing right well with the old Dragons. They are: Lts Perry L. Endelman, 72 combat missions, Clifford R. Long, 67 combat trips, and William F. Smith, 58 combat missions. And all three are only 19 years old!"[10] Even at the age of eighty-three he managed to keep himself young. When I was working on my last book in 2008, I called and his wife answered the phone. "Cliff will have to call you back," she told me. "He's out riding his bicycle right now." Cliff Long remembered Yunnanyi well. The airfield was surrounded by rice paddies. "I hunted duck all around there in my off hours," he recalled. The squadron had been in China since the fall of 1943. Prior to that, it protected the India side of the Hump route from bases in Assam. They were the "Assam Draggins." Instead of shark teeth on the nose, their P-40s displayed the grinning visage of a dragon. Cliff Long also had the name of his future wife, Shirley, painted on the cowling. Operations in India and China required a great degree of flexibility, but by the spring of 1944, group headquarters felt the squadron needed more discipline. On June 3, 1944, Lieutenant Colonel Henry "Hank" Amen assumed command. Amen was a West Point graduate regarded as a fair man who imparted discipline, but would also protect his officers and men. Long flew on his wing many times and had the highest respect for him.[11]

Clifford Long's P-40N had the mouth of a dragon and the name of his future wife, "Shirley," painted on the nose. The P-40s of the 25th Fighter Squadron were assigned to the Forward Echelon of the 69th Composite Wing to provide close air support for the CEF. ***Courtesy of Clifford Long***

The 25th had the opportunity to re-equip with P-51s early in 1944, but they elected to keep their P-40s. The P-51 was a race horse—fast and nimble, but fragile. As the 311th experienced in Burma, the coolant lines running the length of the underside made it vulnerable to ground fire. The P-40, on the other hand, was a war horse—able to absorb and deliver punishment in equal measure. Its coolant lines were confined to a small area directly beneath the engine and it was more heavily armed and armored. The standard bomb load for the P-40s was a 500-pound bomb slung under the centerline rack or three 250-pound bombs: one on the centerline rack and two under the wings.[12] Later in the campaign they also used napalm and rockets. Like the liaison planes, the fighters lacked adequate instruments to work in the weather. "Unfortunately," said Mitchell, "when weather moved in, the P-40s were of little value to the troops on the ground." Often, one of the fighter pilots would ride along with the 27th TCS on the first airdrop of the day for a firsthand view of the conditions over the target area.[13] The P-40s flew only eight days during the month of June because of bad weather. Still, they managed 160 sorties. Captain Knight, working with an air control party in the Gaoligong Mountains, commented that despite the weather, his team saw many Japanese troops fall victim to 500-pound bombs or .50-caliber machine gun "lead poisoning."[14] By the end of June, there were six air control parties stationed with the Chinese at the front.[15]

The B-25s also flew as often as the weather allowed. The 22nd Bomb Squadron moved to Yangkai, China, from India in January 1944 and flew missions into Indochina, Thailand, and North Burma, in addition to supporting the Salween Campaign.[16] The squadron had old "C" and "D" model B-25s they dubbed "gulls"; "H" models modified to carry a

75-millimeter cannon and four .50-caliber machine guns in the nose dubbed "pigeons"; and a handful of new "J" models, dubbed "jays," of course. The squadron commander, Major Edison Weatherly, intended to establish a detachment of eight aircraft at Yunnanyi, but there was a small hill too close to the southwest end of the runway for a fully-loaded B-25 to clear on takeoff. Just like the P-40s, the weather prevented them from using the grass runway two miles to the east. Until the end of the monsoon season, the B-25s could only use Yunnanyi to refuel on their way back to Yangkai after a mission.[17]

Chapman Hale was a pilot with the 22nd. He ferried one of the squadron's "pigeons" the fifteen thousand miles to China from Columbia, South Carolina, in early 1944. "The B-25 was not suitable for close ground support in the tight mountain valleys," he told me. Not only was the medium bomber not nearly as maneuverable as a P-40, but it used almost three times as much gasoline. "However, when targets such as warehouses and troop housing were identified we readily bombed those targets," he said.[18] The squadron hit bridges and supply depots at Longling, Mangshi, Tengchong, Hsenwi, and other targets, though the weather often interfered.

Hale remembered one mission in particular on June 21, 1944, when the squadron assigned one "gull," four "pigeons," and four "jays" to bomb storage areas in Longling. The nine airplanes flew in three flights of three. Each flight crew usually consisted of a pilot, copilot, bombardier/navigator, flight engineer, radio operator/gunner, and a waist gunner. The first three were usually officers, the last three enlisted. Because of the cannon in the nose, the "H" model did not have a bombardier or copilot—only a single set of controls for a single pilot.[19] Albert M. "Al" Sieck led the second flight on the mission. George Wright was his navigator who, according to Hale, "could always find the target." Hale's crew flew the left wing position and James Brokaw's flew the right. Each plane was loaded with twenty-four 100-pound bombs. The formation took off at 1100 hours from Yangkai, climbing to thirteen thousand feet over a solid deck of clouds. "After takeoff I had a problem," recalled Hale. "It was impossible to engage the artificial horizon gyro." The artificial horizon made it possible to keep the airplane straight and level or change its pitch and roll while flying in the weather. Without it, the pilot could become disoriented in the clouds and lose control. There was no checklist to determine the fitness of the airplane for a mission; Hale had to make the judgment himself. He was anxious to fly, as most of his missions had been cancelled recently due to bad weather. "I made a decision with my 22-year-old 'wisdom,'" he said. "I was not about to abort this mission since I had to wait so long for the opportunity due to the previous bad weather." He reasoned he would not have any trouble, since he was going to be in close formation on Sieck's wing anyhow. "Bill would find the target and we would drop the bombs and return home as I securely hung onto Al's wing," he decided. "A real piece of cake."

The formation let down through broken clouds west of the Mekong, but when they reached the Salween River gorge, they found an overcast layer below the tops of the mountains and in some areas almost to the valley floor. "Not a good sign," Hale noted. Two flights of bombers returned to Yangkai, unable to find a way to the target. Al Sieck found a break in the clouds and led his flight toward Longling along the Burma Road. The overcast kept descending and Al led the formation lower and lower to stay below it. "To my surprise," said Hale, "I saw, at our level and above us, soldiers digging trenches. We were so close that we could see expressions on the faces of the troops." They flew at 180 miles per hour less than five hundred feet above the ground. As they approached Longling, Sieck opened the

A North American B-25H from the 22nd Bomb Squadron on a mission over Mangshi in September 1944. The medium bombers were not suited for close air support, but would readily hit warehouses, bridges, or other such targets. *National Archives*

Chapman Hale, a pilot with the 22nd Bomb Squadron, which supported the campaign from its base at Yangkai with B-25 medium bombers. *Courtesy of the 22nd Bomb Squadron Association.*

bomb bay doors. They were very low. A black wall of a thunderstorm filled the valley beyond the target. Japanese machine gun fire erupted from the ground and stitched three or four bullet holes in each of the airplanes. The B-25s released their bombs on the storage area. According to Hale, the explosions "tossed the ships like a cork." Sieck pulled up into a steep climb and entered the storm. With dismay, Hale realized he had not told him about his malfunctioning gyro. His only chance was to maintain tight formation and stay with him through the weather. "Any deviation to the right or left," thought Hale, and he "would probably hit a cloud-covered mountain." It was "the most desperate time of my life." In the dark storm, he could only just see the shadowy outline of Sieck's ship next to him. "Then came the rain," he recalled, "just bucketsful—with leaking water flying through the cockpit. At times I had zero visibility. I could just make out a dark shape off my right wing. Formation flying under those conditions had to be impossible, but I struggled out of sheer desperation. It was my only option." Finally, the rain eased and visibility improved. When he and Sieck broke out into sunlit skies, Hale breathed a sigh of relief. The formation refueled at Yunnanyi and then returned to Yangkai. Hale remembered the mission as the most traumatic of his life, though "all's well that ends well," he concluded.[20]

Even as air support coordination and procedures improved, the situation on the ground began to deteriorate. General Wang Lingyun, commander of the 2nd Army, was feuding with General Song and against orders withdrew his roadblocks from around Mangshi—even as the rest of the XIth Army Group made gains in Longling and occupied most of the city. The Japanese gathered reinforcements. On June 14, four hundred soldiers of the 113th Regiment departed Tengchong, crossed the Shweli River, and attacked Chinese outposts guarding the approaches to Longling. Two hundred more soldiers followed at dusk, capturing Man-lo Bridge and moving a motorized column across the river. Thus began a fierce counterattack that pushed the 87th Division, 71st Army, three miles from the city. The Chinese still had an overwhelming advantage in numbers. Even though General Song only committed nine of his twenty-one battalions to Longling, he still had approximately ten thousand troops in the vicinity. The Japanese had only 1,500. Nevertheless, on June 16, Song ordered the 88th Division to abandon its positions and retire northeast with the 87th. The retreat turned into a rout. Only a joint mission by twenty-four B-25s from the 22nd and 491st bomb squadrons and intervention by the Honorable 1st Division, 8th Army, stopped Japanese momentum and permitted the Chinese to establish themselves in the mountains and hills around the city. YFOS liaison officers were outraged; they thought the decision to withdraw was nonsensical and inexcusable. General Zhang Shaoxun, commander of the 87th Division, was so ashamed he attempted to commit suicide.[21]

Dorn was infuriated. He wrote to the Chinese Army Chief of Staff, General He Yingqin, to protest Song's actions. "I understand that complete details of the withdrawal from Longling in mid-June have been sent to you by both General Wei and General Xiao," he wrote. "In order to explain the situation to you, I am forced to be unpleasantly blunt." He told the general that Song greatly exaggerated the enemy strength and inflated reports of his own casualties. Despite having more than enough men, he continually "wasted troops by piecemeal commitments and assignment of limited objectives." Dorn praised the leadership of Marshal Wei and told He that "the spirit of the Chinese troops on the Salween Front deserves the very highest praise." Song, on the other hand, was a "stumbling block." He was convinced that as long as Song remained in command of the XIth Army Group, "the campaign to open the land route between India and China is in grave danger of failure."

B-25s from the 22nd Bomb Squadron hit supply warehouses in Longling. Because of its position astride the Burma Road, with trails leading north and south along the front, Longling served as a hub for the 56th Division's supply network. *National Archives*

Dorn, Wei, and Xiao all agreed that Song had to go. "We were a team that worked closely together and almost never failed to see eye to eye," said Dorn. They could do nothing to remove him though, because of his strong political backing.[22] He could not be relieved and he could not be persuaded to attack. Instead, he arrayed his troops around the city and prepared for a lengthy siege. It was a dramatic loss of momentum for the campaign. Any hope of quickly driving down the Burma Road died with the failure at Longling.

12

The Siege of Tengchong

There was no illusion of an easy victory north of the Burma Road as there had been to the south. Longling was ripe for the taking. Tengchong was a fortress. On their way over the Gaoligong Mountains and through the Shweli Valley, the troops of the XXth Army Group encountered many towns and terrain features fortified by trenches, machine gun nests, and improvised wood and earthen bunkers. By the end of June, Chinese soldiers poured into the Tengchong Valley from all sides, surrounding and isolating the Japanese garrison. Nothing they encountered before prepared them for Tengchong.[1] The town of twenty thousand was the largest population center west of the Salween. It was famous since before the days of Marco Polo for its jade markets and trade routes to the west. It was situated in a valley six-and-a-half miles long, north to south, and three miles across, 5,500 feet above sea level. A singular mountain called Laifengshan rose five hundred feet above its southwest corner. What really set Tengchong apart from other towns on the Salween Front though, was the imposing, medieval stone wall surrounding it.

Lieutenant Lu Caiwen, the young intelligence officer who grew up in Tengchong, reported on the Japanese defenses. He was intimately familiar with the city wall. He grew up very close to it and climbed it many times as a child. Each of its faces was almost a mile in length, over thirty feet tall, and twenty feet thick. It was built from compacted earth encased in large volcanic stone blocks. "Perhaps there were not many city walls as strong as Tengchong's stone wall," said Lu. "It was really strong." The wall was well maintained; a remnant of the Ming Dynasty, when more than four thousand cities possessed such fortification.[2] It made the town a neat square in the valley, its four corners pointing like a compass in the cardinal directions. The Yinma River snaked along the northeast wall, flowing into the Daying River at the north corner. The two streams formed a natural moat north of the city. In the center of each of the four sides was a large gate complex. Lu informed his superiors that the Japanese heavily fortified the gates and built pillboxes inside the town, along the outside of the wall, and throughout the valley. They opened embrasures in the wall where they positioned machine guns to cover the approaches and built barriers behind the wall from which they could defend against any efforts to scale it. "It was as one old Chinese saying goes," Lu related, "when one person guards the position, even hundreds of soldiers cannot break through."[3] Colonel Kurashige, who directed the defense of the Gaoligong passes, had 1,850 men from the 148th Regiment at his disposal to defend the city. He turned out the civilian population so they would not be a drain on his resources. He positioned his artillery, along with six hundred men, on Laifengshan. From the eastern slope of the mountain, his guns commanded most of the valley.[4]

General Huo ordered his five divisions to spread out and occupy the heights around Tengchong: the 2nd Reserve Division took up positions to the southwest, the 116th and 130th divisions to the south, the 198th to the east, and the 36th to the north. The Chinese troops used frequent torrential downpours to screen their movements and took many pillboxes and hilltop positions by surprise. Despite the

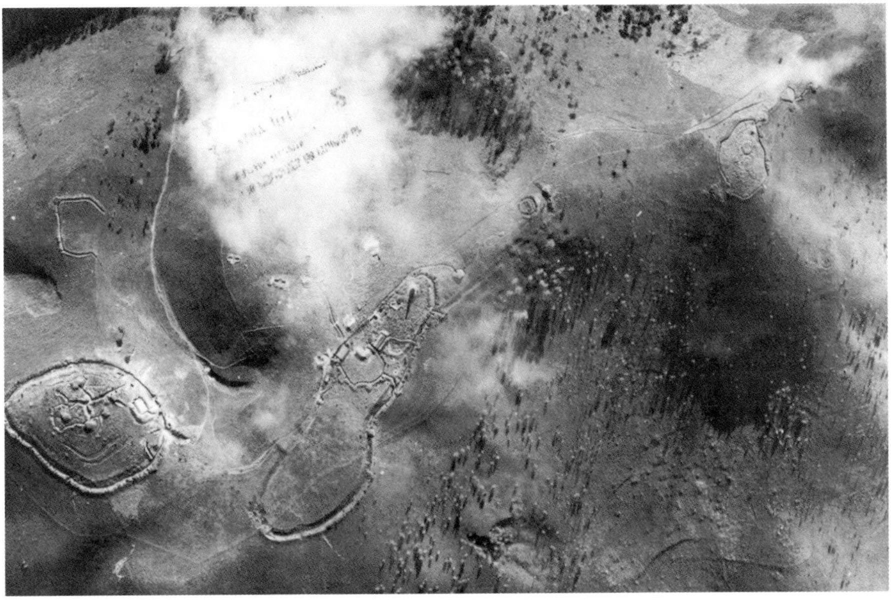

This reconnaissance photo shows the Japanese fortifications atop Laifengshan. Note the multiple bunkers and lines of trenches. The tall white pagoda, which still stands today, is just to the left of center, near the top right boundary of a network of trenches. *National Archives*

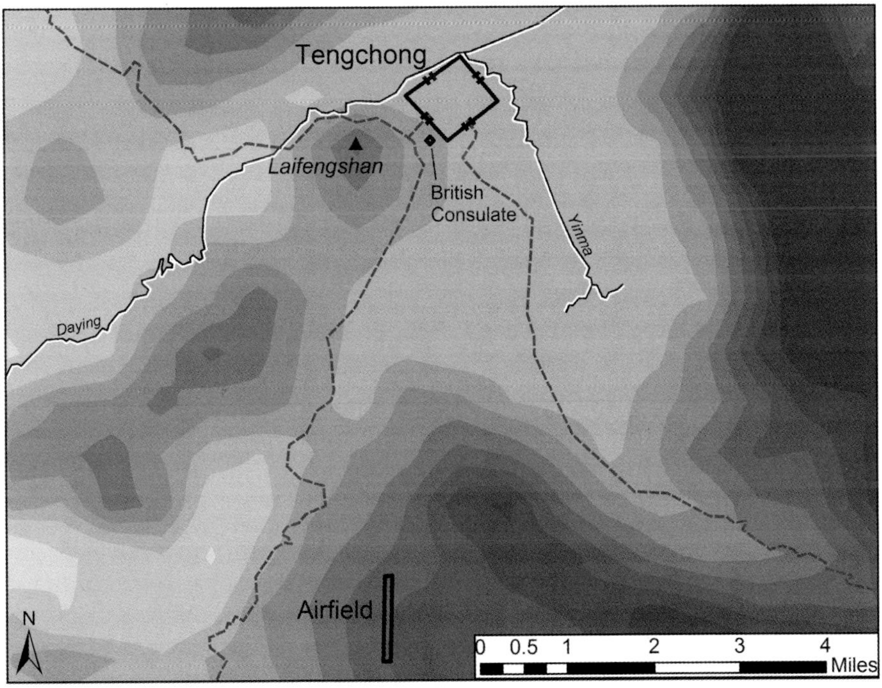

Tengchong

Japanese delaying their advance by demolishing the bridge across the Shweli River, by mid-July, Huo's men had surrounded the town just out of range of Kurashige's artillery. They also seized a small airstrip south of town and linked up with XIth Army Group patrols at Man-lo Bridge, cutting the trail between Tengchong and Longling. The Japanese garrison was completely isolated. Then progress stalled. The CEF's 75-millimeter pack howitzers could not compete with Kurashige's heavy artillery. The Japanese fired volley after volley from Laifengshan to hold them at bay. The eastern slope of the mountain appeared unassailable, but a thorough reconnaissance by Chinese scouts discovered a key weakness: the reverse slope, though steep, was lightly defended and had few pillboxes and no entrenchments. Huo decided an attack supported by American warplanes could wrest the mountain from the Japanese and allow his troops to approach Tengchong.[5]

The attack commenced on July 26. Joining the 25th Fighter Squadron and 22nd Bomb Squadron for the first time on the Salween Front were P-38 Lightnings from the 449th Fighter Squadron. If the P-51 was a nimble race horse and the P-40 a mighty war horse, then the twin-engine P-38 was like a pair of chargers pulling at the reins of an iron chariot. With its speed, heavy firepower, and excellent rate of climb, it was a formidable fighter. Up to this point, the 449th fought the Japanese in East China. However, the situation there had devolved into utter chaos. Japanese troops captured Changsha on June 18 and, after a lengthy, brutal siege, took Hengyang on August 8. A column advancing from Hong Kong in mid-June forced Chennault to evacuate the 449th's base at Suichuan. Since Phase Two of the Ichi-go campaign began in May, the fierce fighting left the squadron battered, damaging or destroying two-thirds of its planes and killing five of its pilots, including Lieutenant Colonel George McMillan, the very popular squadron commander. Chennault assigned what was left of the squadron to Kennedy's 69th Composite Wing and ordered a detachment of eight aircraft to Yunnanyi to support the Salween Campaign.

The squadron rotated pilots between Yunnanyi and their primary base at Chenggong, seventeen miles southeast of Kunming. Many of the P-38 pilots rotating into the detachment were recent replacements: Jerry Doughty, Joe Fodor, and Jim Heitkotter among them. When I interviewed Jim Heitkotter for *The Forgotten Squadron*, I was impressed by his candor and self-effacing humor. After the book was published in 2010, I received a letter from him, inviting me to an air show in Sacramento. The centerpiece of the show was a flying display of four P-38 Lightnings. There were only seven left in the world in flying condition; to see four flying together was a rare sight in the twenty-first century. I decided to go. The show was spectacular: the strange, twin-fuselage fighters winged magnificently overhead. Their upward-directed exhaust made them much quieter than their contemporaries. Their sound was a distinctive, high-pitched, purring whine that grew to a full-bodied roar only when the plane made a knife-edge pass, directing its exhaust straight at the crowd. Besides the excitement of seeing the airplanes, it was truly a pleasure to finally meet Mr. Heitkotter in person. He was of average height and despite his age walked without the aid of a cane. His mind was sharp and his sense of humor undiminished. Before the show he walked up to the lead pilot and asked him if he was ill. "You look awful," he told him. "You should let me take this one." The man laughed. "I bet you would," he retorted.

When Jim Heitkotter arrived in China in the summer of 1944, he was dismayed to find the 449th had no P-38s for him to fly. After the beating the squadron took in East China, there were more pilots than planes. He had to wait for replacement aircraft to arrive and for war-weary men to rotate home. Meanwhile, he and four other replacements went to the 16th Fighter Squadron on the other side of the Chenggong airfield. "Five of us red hot P-38 pilots who came all the way to China to win the war for 'em, and they assigned us to P-40s," he complained. "What a blow to whatever morale we had!" The assignment was short lived. The twin-engine pilots had difficulty adapting to the high-torque, single-engine Warhawks and one of them spun into the ground and died. Those remaining transferred to the troop carrier command, where they served as copilots aboard C-47s for several weeks. "The next big news was very good indeed," remembered Heitkotter. The 449th finally received enough new planes and rotated home enough weary pilots. Heitkotter even got his own airplane. He inherited the *Golden Eagle*, the oldest P-38 in China. The battle-scarred warbird had been the mount of fighter ace Bob Schultz before he rotated home. Heitkotter painted over the faded artwork, but left the six victory flags on the nose.[6]

In command of the squadron after the death of George McMillan was Captain James Bledsoe. Bledsoe had worked with Chennault as a flight instructor for the Chinese Air Force before the United States entered World War II. He was a reserved man, an old China hand with a lot of flying experience. Some of the younger pilots thought he had too much experience. "He thought nothing of flying through a cloud formation with his flight," remembered Jerry Doughty. "Upon breaking out of the cloud cover, he was always on course. We younger troops with little or no weather experience looked like a three ring circus upon breaking into the clear."[7] Some of the young pilots saw Bledsoe as a father figure. Many did not like him. "He came from a transport command and knew little of fighter tactics," said Heitkotter. "His most horrifying demonstration of this came when he had twelve of us stacked in a beautiful echelon right, then went into a right turn. It was extremely lucky that none of us collided in suddenly finding we had nowhere to go."[8]

On July 25, Lieutenant Colonel Amen, commander of the 25th Fighter Squadron, led Captain Bledsoe and Lieutenant Yorkston on a strafing mission to Songshan to introduce the P-38 detachment to fighting on the Salween Front. The next day, they joined in the attack on Laifengshan. At 1200 hours on the twenty-sixth, the first of four waves of fighters arrived overhead. Four P-38s and four P-40s spotted cloth panels southeast of the mountain. From there, air control parties talked them onto several fortified positions. The positions were easy to spot from the air; the Japanese chopped down most of the trees on the mountain to build their bunkers and trenches and to give their artillery clear fields of fire. The P-40s went into action first, dive-bombing and releasing their 500-pound demolition bombs five hundred feet above the ground; all four bombs hit their targets. The P-38s attacked next, each carrying two 500-pound bombs. Four bombs hit, two fell short, and two went long. The Chinese infantry from the 116th and 2nd Reserve divisions advanced quickly in the wake of the air attack, charging up the mountain before the smoke cleared. Their advance demonstrated how much they had learned

Chinese troops hold a pillbox taken from the Japanese during the assault on Laifengshan. Note the log and earthen construction. ***National Archives via Samuel Hui***

in a month and a half of hard fighting on the Salween Front. They advanced as whole regiments, instead of committing small numbers of men piecemeal. They were methodical, calling down mortar and artillery fire on Japanese positions, advancing close behind, and attacking the moment the barrage lifted. After capturing a position, they did not pause to loot from the enemy dead. They used new American lend-lease flamethrowers to great effect, burning the Japanese from their pillboxes.

Late in the afternoon, a flight of four P-38s arrived to dive-bomb positions at the top of the mountain. The Japanese occupied the tall white pagoda at the apex and had their artillery positioned all around it. The Lightnings scored six direct hits on their targets. The Chinese continued the attack and captured the summit by nightfall. Early the next morning, more than three hundred Japanese troops sallied forth from Tengchong to retake the mountain. Again, the Chinese showed how much they had learned. They consolidated their positions, concentrated their forces, and repulsed the counterattack. The Americans believed the name Laifengshan meant "the mountain where the birds come," but it was more specific than that. The *feng* (凤) was a mythical Chinese bird that ruled over all other avians and was often considered synonymous with the phoenix in the West. Thus, Laifengshan meant, "the mountain where the phoenix comes." Indeed, in the ashes of the burning Japanese positions, the Chinese Army proved it had been reborn. The phoenix had returned to the mountain. The victory was particularly meaningful for the 2nd Reserve Division. They fought a desperate guerrilla campaign after

A formation of 22nd Bomb Squadron B-25s hit Tengchong. The bomber pictured is a B-25H modified to carry a 75-millimeter cannon and four .50-caliber machine guns in the nose. ***National Archives***

the Japanese captured Tengchong in 1942. Now, they returned as victors. The American advisors were impressed. Frank Dorn declared the assault on Laifengshan to be the best coordinated attack of the entire campaign. Huo's troops counted 380 Japanese dead for a loss of 1,200 of their own. It was a high price, but it represented a dramatic improvement.[9]

The capture of Laifengshan eliminated the threat of Kurashige's artillery and opened the way for an attack on Tengchong itself, though the Chinese still had to contend with the city wall. General Huo ordered an assault to coincide with the attack on Laifengshan on the twenty-sixth. With the enemy's attention riveted on the mountain, he hoped to gain a foothold in the city. Rockets, mortars, and artillery failed to breach the wall, though. The 22nd Bomb Squadron flew eight missions to Tengchong in July, but the majority of their bombs crashed into the city, hitting barracks, ammo dumps, and supply depots, rather than bringing down the wall. Chapman Hale remembered one such mission. He flew in a three-ship formation of B-25s and commented on how difficult it was to maneuver in the tight terrain: "We went in there and dropped our bombs as best we could," he said, "but I don't think we really got the wall."[10] Chinese soldiers ran bravely forward, despite the fact that the wall still barred their way. They attempted to scale it with bamboo ladders, but the Japanese countered their medieval tactics machine guns. The attack failed.[11]

The XXth Army Group took a week to regroup before its next attempt. Throughout the intervening days, fighters and bombers from the 14th Air Force

B-25s (left) pull up from a low bombing pass on the Tengchong city wall. On August 2, 1944, a flight of six bombers flying at tree-top level hammered five breaches in the southeast wall. *National Archives*

kept steady pressure on Tengchong, striking Japanese strongpoints inside and outside the city. Occasionally, airplanes from the 10th Air Force flew from India and Burma to assist. The Chinese troops continued to attack Japanese positions outside the city and established footholds in many of the small villages abutting the walls. Edward Mark, an armorer from the 25th Fighter Squadron, remembered Wednesday, August 2, as a day that was "clear and hot." The 25th and 449th flew sixty-two sorties to Tengchong that day, carrying sixty-one 500-pound bombs. According to Mark, almost all were delay-fused for skip-bombing.[12] Four P-40s roared up the open end of the valley from the southeast. They flew low, just above the rice paddies, one after another in trail formation. Each had a single 500-pound bomb slung under its belly. A single bomb would do little damage to the wall, so the fighter pilots planned to hurl one after another at the same spot. They hoped the cumulative effect would cause the wall to crumble and give the Chinese troops an open door to the city.

Clifford Long flew the second fighter in the column of four. Each of the bombs had a seven-second delay fuse to allow the low-flying fighters to get out of the way up and over the wall after they released. He watched as the plane in front of him made its run. He was shocked to see the bomb bounce off the volcanic rock, hit the ground, and roll away. Chinese troops waiting in their trenches scrambled frantically to get out of the way. The bomb exploded harmlessly some distance from the wall. The same thing happened to Long's bomb, as well as to those of the fighters behind him.[13] The wall was simply too solid for the bombs to penetrate. Three P-38s, each with two 500-pound bombs, dive-bombed the gate at the center of the southeast wall with only limited effect. Finally, a flight of six B-25s flew in at tree-top level, bombing with 1,000-pounders. Four of the P-40s joined overhead and covered their attack. Flying low in the tight terrain was dangerous, but the bombs hit, hammering five breaches through the southeast wall, the largest just

Chinese troops use bamboo ladders to scale Tengchong's massive stone wall. *National Archives*

over fifteen feet wide.[14] Again, the Chinese infantry charged forward. They laid their ladders upon the rubble and climbed once more unto the breach. Again, the Japanese met them with machine gun fire. By 1500, one company from the 107th Infantry Regiment and one company from the 348th reached the top of the wall just east of the south corner. By dusk, the 198th Division was fighting for an entrance to the north corner. The Japanese defended fiercely, determined to keep them from the city. Yang Chien-chiu, the platoon leader from Sichuan, was shot while climbing the wall. "My forehead was scraped by one of those bullets," he remembered. He took cover behind a statue of Long Yun, governor of Yunnan, having avoided death by only a centimeter. By nightfall on the third, only the battered remains of a single infantry company clung to the southeast wall.[15]

The Chinese fought tenaciously. General Zhang Yuting, commander of the 130th Division, attributed the energy of their attack partly to the presence of three American portable surgical hospitals near the front. His men knew if they were wounded, they would receive excellent medical care. The CEF suffered seventeen thousand battle casualties between the beginning of the campaign and October 1944. YFOS reports indicate that of approximately fifteen thousand patients treated in the American hospitals between April 28 and October 27, including 9,428 battle casualties, only 492 died—an unprecedented five percent mortality rate. What was more, YFOS medical personnel taught the Chinese troops basic health and cleanliness

A Chinese soldier uses a flamethrower on a Japanese position in Tengchong. Chinese troops used American flamethrowers to good effect throughout the campaign in burning the Japanese from their pillboxes, tunnels, and trenches. *National Archives*

Chinese troops from the 346th Regiment, 116th Division, use American rocket launchers and submachine guns to attack strongly-fortified Japanese positions in Tengchong. *National Archives via Samuel Hui*

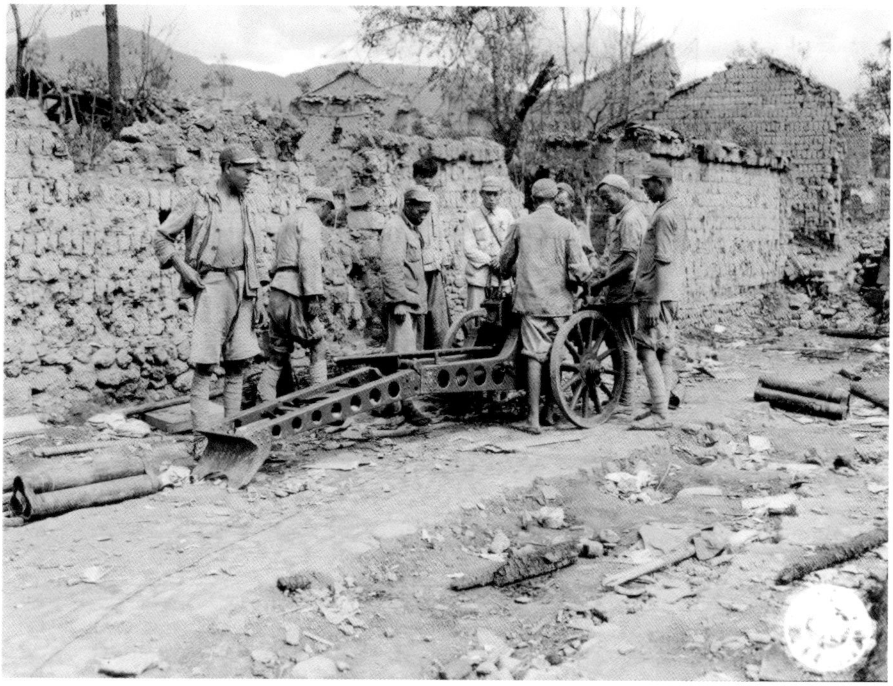

Chinese troops repair a pack howitzer in the streets of Tengchong. During the battle, gun crews disassembled their artillery pieces, carried them over the wall, and then reassembled them to fire point blank Into enemy positions. ***National Archives via Samuel Hui***

practices and inoculated them against smallpox, typhus, typhoid, and cholera. The result was a loss of only two thousand men to sickness. Prior to the Salween Campaign, Chinese commanders resigned themselves to losing as many men to sickness as to battle. Thus backed by American medical support and with American planes overhead, the Chinese troops fought on.[16]

Meanwhile, armorers from the 25th Fighter Squadron acted on an inspired idea. They fashioned twelve-inch long, two-inch diameter steel spikes and welded them to the front of a 500-pound bomb. On August 4, flights of four P-40s flew up the valley only ten feet above the ground. At 250 miles per hour, the southeast wall came up fast. The "walls seemed to rise out of the rice paddies," remembered William Mitchell. Each pilot had to release his bomb and pull up over the wall in one smooth motion. It was risky, but it worked. The first bomb stuck in the wall like a dart and exploded seconds later, sending a geyser of dirt, rock, and flame into the air. The explosion marked the spot for the planes that followed. "The attack was over in minutes," remembered Mitchell, "and the results were much as planned."[17] The fighters hammered two more breaches through the southeast wall. That night, the Japanese drove two companies of the 108th Regiment from the city, inflicting over one hundred casualties. Using the new breaches made by the P-40s though, the 348th Regiment held onto their gains. On the fifth, another flight of P-40s knocked out the north corner of the wall. A flight of five P-38s breached the wall near the west corner. Nine flights of fighters laid down a steady torrent of bullets on the Japanese defenders. Chinese reinforcements finally poured into the city.[18]

Lieutenant Liu Cheng-hua, the infantry officer from Hubei, remembered the fierce fighting around Tengchong. Liu was not assigned to the XXth Army Group. He led his platoon from the 3rd Battalion of the 2nd Regiment, 88th Division, across the Salween and into the bitter fighting around Longling with the rest of the 71st Army. After the Japanese retook the city, Liu's platoon joined a special regiment sent north up the Shweli Valley to cut off the Japanese at Tengchong and assist the XXth Army Group in the siege. Liu painted a vivid picture of the violence of the battle. He remembered several of his men drowning as they tried to cross one of the rivers north of the city. Bullets and shells streaked from the Japanese defenses, hitting all around him. Some of his men were caught in the crossfire as American airplanes strafed enemy positions. "Well, this is war," he said simply, "and shit happened in the war. For this reason we don't blame the Americans. Whenever we saw American planes fly over, we were still very happy about it." In all, thirty of his men lost their lives in the assault. Only seven survived. Shrapnel from a Japanese mortar round hit Liu himself in his back and head. He was evacuated to Baoshan for medical treatment.[19]

It was a brutal siege, but the Chinese Expeditionary Force was finally inside Tengchong. One of the most strangely anachronistic attacks of World War II had somehow succeeded. Chinese soldiers fought a medieval siege while the most modern warplanes roared overhead, pouring destruction into the city much like ancient authors must have imagined fire-breathing dragons laying waste to a castle. Inside the walls, the battle was far from over. What followed was a savage fight for every pillbox and position in the town. The Chinese rooted out the Japanese with flame throwers, bayonets, and hand-to-hand fighting. United Press correspondent Albert Ravendale witnessed the battle firsthand. He described the Chinese soldiers "inching from one battered house to the next within the walled city." The Japanese resistance was legendary, despite weeks of air and artillery bombardment. "The Chinese measure each day's gains in a few yards," wrote Ravendale, "and sometimes fight for days for possession of the wall of a single building in which the Japanese units are holding out." Most of the Japanese fought from deep within bunkers and tunnels dug throughout the city. The only men above ground were those manning pillboxes and other fortifications. Chinese artillerymen disassembled their 75-millimeter guns, carried them over the ruined wall, and reassembled them to fire point-blank into enemy positions. "Frequently the Chinese who attempt to storm forward are mowed down," Ravendale wrote, "but those remaining regroup and storm the Japanese positions again and again."[20] The Chinese displayed terrific courage and took grievous losses. The Japanese were determined to fight to the last man and make them purchase every inch of Tengchong at a dear cost.[21]

13

Aerial Intervention

It came as a surprise to the Japanese garrison at Songshan when the remainder of the 71st Army crossed the Salween in early June to join in the attack on Longling. The Chinese New 28th Division stormed the village of Lameng, four miles west of the river, and captured it on the fourth. The Japanese retreated up the slopes to the prepared defenses of their formidable mountain fortress. The New 28th left behind a small containing force while the Chinese attacked Longling. After the XIth Army Group failed to take the city, General Song shifted his focus back to Songshan. He claimed his forces were not strong enough to take Longling, even though they outnumbered the Japanese by nearly seven to one. The capture of Songshan would allow him to open the Burma Road and move in more men and supplies.

Songshan was no easy objective. The Y Force Operations Staff called it the "Gibraltar of the Burma Road." It was a roughly triangular, multi-peaked mountain that rose to 6,600 feet above sea level. Trees and undergrowth covered its slopes, in some places so thick as to make it impassable even to infantry. From the Huitong Bridge site, the Burma Road ran along the northeast face of this triangular mountain, turned sharply around the northern corner, and then went down along the northwest side before continuing on to Longling. Major Kanemitsu Keijiro commanded its defense with 1,200 troops from the 113th Regiment and a battalion of mountain artillery. His men fortified every village and peak with pillboxes, trenches, and tunnels. Light tanks dug into the mountainside served as fortified artillery positions.[1]

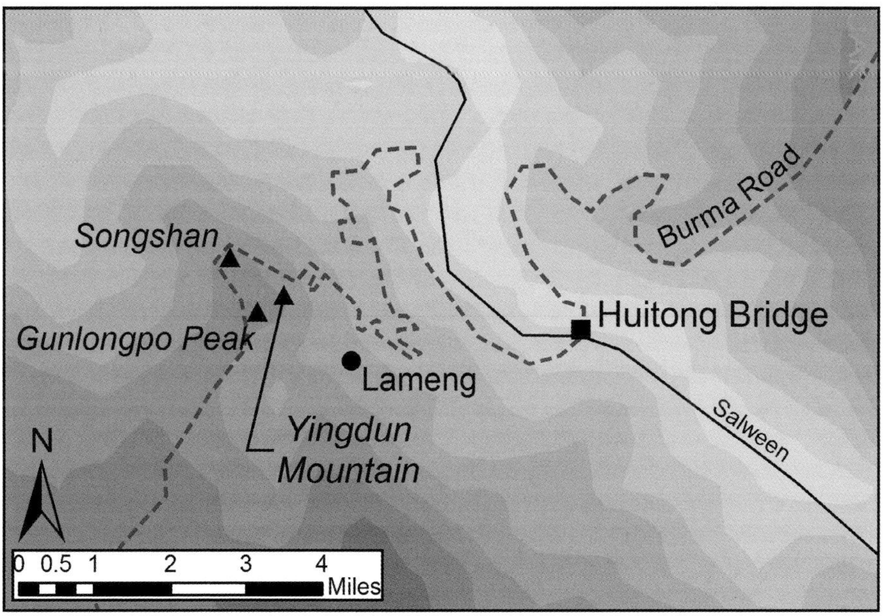

Songshan

The New 39th Division marched south from the Shweli Valley to join the New 28th in a large-scale assault up the steep slopes on June 15. Surprise and bold action led to early successes; within two days, they captured Yingdun Mountain, the peak at the southeast corner of the triangle. They made more progress in those first two days than they would make in the next three weeks. As was often the case elsewhere on the front, the commander of the 71st Army, General Zhong, committed his men in piecemeal attacks. Major Kanemitsu defeated each attack in turn and Chinese progress ground to a halt. The Chinese assembled their heavy artillery, including seven 150-millimeter howitzers, two 75-millimeter howitzers, and two 76-millimeter field guns, on the east bank of the Salween and bombarded the mountain. They even brought an American anti-aircraft battery to the top of Yingdun to fire horizontally at the enemy positions. The Japanese merely retreated inside their tunnels to wait out each barrage and in turn fired their artillery down on the engineers trying to rebuild the Huitong Bridge.[2]

Frank Dorn visited General Zhong at his headquarters near Songshan and was disgusted. Zhong "was not only defeated in his own mind," wrote Dorn, "but would not accept any solution for the dilemma of Songshan." He contrasted the 71st Army's lack of progress and leadership with the XXth Army Group, which "took all except one of the fortified hills around Tengchong in three days."[3] Both Generals Song and Zhong were proving to be frustrating and ineffective. Though he was commander of the CEF, Marshal Wei could not remove them from command because of political considerations. Instead, he decided to bring forward his reserve. The 8th Army marched to western Yunnan from its frontier posts guarding the French Indochina border. Since the beginning of the war, Chiang Kai-shek feared the Japanese would launch an offensive into Yunnan along the Hanoi-Kunming railway. By the middle of 1944, however, it seemed unlikely. The bulk of Japanese troops in northern Indochina were advancing toward Nanning as part of the Ichi-go campaign. After the 8th Army moved west, the 93rd Division, 5th Army remained to defend the lower Mekong Valley at Simao and the 52nd Army and the Yunnan Provincial 1st Army Group guarded the frontier south of Mengzi.[4]

The 8th Army was not as well trained or equipped as the other armies fighting on the Salween Front. Only two-thirds of its officers had been exposed to American training and lend-lease aid supplied only a fraction of its equipment. Dorn thought the commander, General He Shaozhou, a nephew of He Yingqin, "was absolutely worthless as a commander, so utterly hopeless that I recommended that he be relieved." His deputy Li Mi, on the other hand, "was a ball of fire." He was "alert, forceful, intelligent, afraid of nothing, and sharp looking to boot… He was a Catholic and always wore a small gold cross suspended from a chain around his neck. Li was among the very best and we soon became close friends." Unfortunately, of the three division commanders two were terrible. Only Wang Bo from the Honorable 1st Division was "pretty good."[5] One advantage the 8th possessed was that it fell directly under Wei's control and did not have to answer to Song or Zhong. Colonel Carlos G. Spaht commanded the liaison teams attached to it. Its leading elements began arriving at the front in time for the Honorable 1st Division to stave off disaster in the rout at Longling. When the situation stabilized, Wei committed the 8th against Songshan and withdrew the 71st to focus on Longling. On June 27, the 3rd Battalion of the Honorable 1st Division moved forward to replace the New 28th. The transition caused a great deal of chaos and confusion that Major Kanemitsu's men took advantage of to recapture many of the positions they lost

Marshal Wei (center) and his chief artillery officer (right) consult with He Shaozhou (left), commander of the 8th Army, at the top of Yingdun Mountain. *National Archives via Samuel Hui*

Major General Wang Bo (far left), commander of the Honorable 1st Division, and Major General Chow Kai-shing (far right), vice commander, confer with liaison officers Major Delmar Frazier and 1st Lieutenant James Arnold at the 1st Regiment command post on August 30, 1944. *National Archives via Samuel Hui*

in mid-June. The 8th Army—the least trained of any fighting force on the Salween Front—was now responsible for the single most difficult position south of the Burma Road. They spent the next week planning and preparing.[6]

On June 28, Japanese aircraft appeared over the Salween Front for the first time in the campaign. Six Ki-43 Oscars escorted four Tachikawa Ki-36 Type 98 Direct Cooperation Reconnaissance Planes—Allied code name "Ida"—from the 2nd Chutai, 83rd Sentai.[7] The Japanese Army Air Force (JAAF) had been largely preoccupied by operations in Burma, but the rapidly dwindling supplies of the isolated garrison at Songshan led them to attempt an emergency resupply by air. Unlike the Americans, the Japanese did not have much experience conducting air drops and did not have any purpose-built transports with which to carry them out. Each of the Ki-36s carried a bamboo container covered with lacquer-stiffened cloth that could carry up to two thousand bullets or fifty grenades. American anti-aircraft batteries forced them to drop the containers from high altitude and the threat of running into American fighters led them to make the drops hastily to minimize their time over the battlefield. Most of the supplies fell into Chinese hands, including a sizable quantity of feminine products meant for the twenty-four prostitutes with the Songshan garrison. The Japanese brought most of the young women from Korea in 1942. They received no pay, even though they cooked and cleaned and washed the soldiers' clothing. They lived underground during the battle. Fourteen of them did not survive.[8]

The 8th Army was finally ready on July 5. General He felt completely out of his depth and left direction of operations to his deputy, Li Mi. Li was a native of Tengchong and knew the area and the terrain. He also did not shrink from personally leading his men into battle. At 0315 hours, Chinese artillery began bombarding the mountain in preparation for an early morning attack. Two regiments advanced at 0500, reaching the top of Songshan within forty minutes. They took heavy fire from Japanese fortifications on the reverse slope and flanking fire from positions difficult to locate in the surrounding woods and ravines. Though reinforced, Japanese counterattacks pushed the Chinese back to their starting positions by nightfall. The Japanese resistance proved deadly in the daytime, so the 8th planned its next attack at night. This would give them the daylight hours to consolidate their positions and prepare for the inevitable counterattack. On the night of July 7, the 246th Regiment attacked Gunlongpo Peak, at the southwest corner of the triangle. By midnight they held the peak, but a counterattack drove them back, costing them two hundred casualties. YFOS liaison officers reported that the Chinese got confused fighting at night and often shot at each other. They tended to crowd along the easiest paths up the mountain. The Japanese had prepared firing charts that allowed their mortars and artillery to fire from the reverse slope, where they were shielded from Chinese counter-battery fire. Japanese infantry used machine guns to keep heads down and then threw grenades and fired mortars into the masses of Chinese troops.[9]

It took a week for the 8th Army to recover and prepare for another attack. On July 12, they managed to penetrate the Japanese lines, but the attack only carried them fifty yards. They paused again until the twenty-third. This time, they moved their artillery up the mountain to provide direct fire on positions as close as 1,500 yards, sometimes firing at pillboxes only twenty-five feet in front of friendly troops. Three regiments attacked en masse. General Xiong Shouchun, commander of the 103rd Division, personally directed the artillery. The bombardment stripped the top of Songshan of all vegetation and destroyed several Japanese positions. The infantry attack carried almost to the top of Gunlongpo. Major Kanemitsu desperately called for air support to attack the Chinese artillery, which was exposed in the open to facilitate direct fire on his positions. At 1210, sixteen Oscars from the 50th and 204th sentais escorted three Mitsubishi Ki-51 Type 99 Assault Planes—Allied code-name "Sonia"—overhead. The Ki-51s dropped more than twenty parachutes with supplies for the garrison while the Oscars strafed the Chinese artillery and crews. The Chinese opened fire on the parachutes, destroying several. They shot more than ten Japanese soldiers that tried to collect them.[10]

Two Ki-51s escorted by eight Ki-43s from the 50th Sentai appeared again at 1300 on July 26, dropping eighteen parachutes with supplies to the garrison and strafing the Chinese lines. American anti-aircraft batteries put up an intense volley and shot down an Oscar piloted by Corporal Tasuo Koyasu, which crashed in no-man's land.[11] The Chinese continued to advance, but cautiously, making liberal use of their artillery and slowly digging approach trenches, zig-zagging their way up the mountain. They dug until their trenches were only thirty meters from an enemy position. Artillery fire kept the Japanese under cover. As soon as the barrage lifted, the Chinese charged forward, firing into the slits to keep the enemy down, then using rockets, flamethrowers, or pole charges to burn or blow them out.[12] They succeeded in taking Gunlongpo on August 3. This time, the Songshan garrison did not have enough ammunition or supplies to counterattack. Oscars from the 64th Sentai escorted two Ki-51s on another supply drop on the sixth. A C-47 crew returning from their own air drop west of the Salween witnessed half a dozen of the Japanese fighters strafing the Chinese. Two of the fighters pursued the transport, but the pilot escaped by dodging into the clouds. The 64th Sentai had only recently returned to Burma from Indochina, where it had re-equipped with the new Ki-43-III, which boasted a more powerful engine with methanol injection and replaced the .30-caliber machine gun with another .50-cal. The 50th Sentai rotated to Saigon to receive the new Ki-84 Type Four Fighter—Allied code name "Frank"—and the 204th withdrew to Thailand in preparation for a move to the Philippines.[13]

Unfortunately for the Songshan garrison, most of the supplies dropped on the sixth fell into Chinese hands. Increasingly desperate, on the night of the ninth, seven teams of Japanese volunteers raided Chinese supply dumps. They managed to destroy several artillery pieces before making off with as much small arms and ammunition as they could carry. It was a setback for the Chinese, but the 8th Army continued tediously up the mountain nevertheless. The American liaison teams became impatient with the slow progress and were frustrated by mounting losses. American engineers recommended they mine underneath the pillboxes at the top of the remaining peak and blow them up with TNT. Under their supervision, the Chinese dug into the mountainside. General Li Mi himself picked up a shovel and joined in the work. The battle lines were so close that the two tunnels only had to be twenty-two feet long. By August 18, the Chinese reported both complete and began filling them with explosives.[14]

On the morning of the eighteenth, Lieutenant Colonel Hank Amen led a flight of three P-40s in a rocket attack on the former British consulate building near Tengchong. Cliff Long flew Amen's wing. Captain Robert Bell flew second element. The usual fourth P-40 aborted due to maintenance issues, so Bell flew without a wingman. "We took off just at daybreak and it was a beautiful day," remembered Long. Built in 1921, the British

The old British consulate still stands on the southwest side of Tengchong. The Japanese used it as a storehouse and blockhouse during the siege. Hundreds of Chinese troops died trying to capture it. ***Author's Photo***

Hank Amen, Robert Bell, and Cliff Long fired .50-caliber machine guns and 2.75-inch rockets at the old British consulate, but they failed to penetrate the thick volcanic stone walls. ***Author's Photo***

consulate was a singularly impressive building. It was outside the city wall, just west of the south corner. When I visited in 2009, it stood deserted, surrounded by rundown warehouses. Its stone walls were made of blocks about eighteen inches thick, with the north and west sides having an additional three- to four-inch-thick stone façade. The wooden steps and rafters were made of a high-quality, dense, dark hardwood that withstood the ravages of time. In the northwest room, the Japanese dug underneath the foundation, connecting the house to other positions by way of underground tunnels. They used the consulate as a warehouse for food, supplies, and ammunition and turned it into a blockhouse guarding the west side of the city. Wave after wave of Chinese infantry failed to take it. An attack on August 3 left thirty-eight Chinese officers and one hundred soldiers dead or wounded. A major advance on the fourteenth also failed. With any luck, the P-40s could pave the way with their rockets.[15]

Long used a dial in his cockpit to set the rockets to fire one from each tube on each pass. Each plane carried six rockets—three under each wing—in long cylinders the pilots called "bazooka tubes." Amen planned to make three passes, one for each pair of rockets. They attacked in trail formation, approaching the building from the southwest. "The way you fired rockets," explained Long, "you fired your .50-caliber machine guns and as you could see the tracers converge on the target, you pushed the button on top of the control stick to fire the rockets." The machine guns were harmonized to converge at three hundred yards. One by one, the P-40s attacked and rockets streaked into the side of the building. The west wall took the brunt of the attack. Thousands of small pock marks little bigger than a thumb marred the wall where the .50-caliber rounds hit. The rockets left larger craters, the size of a hand, but only a few inches deep. None of the munitions did anything more than superficial damage to the outside of the building. A few rockets streaking through the windows and bursting through the wooden roof managed to hit some of the Japanese inside though. "As soon as we pulled off the target," Long remembered, "the colonel got us in formation and headed southeast away from Tengchong." But Amen was not leading them back to Yunnanyi. Suddenly, Long saw him release his rocket tubes. Bell did likewise. "We were evidently going to get in a dogfight," he realized.

At 0830 hours on August 18, twelve Oscars from the 64th Sentai arrived overhead Songshan. This time, instead of supply parachutes, each Oscar carried two 50-kilogram bombs. Their target was the Huitong Bridge, which American and Chinese engineers were hurrying to rebuild. Though the Chinese operated on the far side of the Salween for months using only air supply, pack animals, and coolies, the Japanese feared what they could accomplish given a dependable ground supply line. Sergeant Toshimi Ikezawa, who eventually became an eleven-victory ace, was one of the pilots selected for the raid. He remembered practicing on a dummy target the exact same size—five meters wide by two hundred meters long—at Maubi airfield, near Rangoon.[16] On the morning of the eighteenth, Major Toyoki Eto, the sentai commander, led the Oscars in a diving attack on the bridge itself. Intense anti-aircraft fire shot down Warrant Officer Kazuo Shake on his run. Ikezawa lined up on the target and released his bombs, but missed. The steep gorge in which "Tex" Hill and the AVG attacked the Japanese ground troops more than two years before made the bridge a challenging target. Not a single bomb hit. The Oscars managed only to injure a company commander from the Transportation

Fighter pilots of the 64th Sentai selected to carry out the attack on the Huitong Bridge. In the front row, from left to right, are Captain Nakamura; Major Toyoki Eto, the sentai commander; and Colonel Kuwazuka. In the back are Sergeant Okada, Corporal Yamazaki, Sergeant Yamamoto, and Sergeant Ikezawa. ***Courtesy of Hiroshi Ichimura.***

Corps and kill two horses. The attack did succeed in scattering most of the laborers putting the finishing touches on the bridge. Major William Moore, the bridge engineer, began seating the final planks himself while one of his junior officers rounded up as many workers as possible. The Japanese fighters departed for Burma.[17]

Hank Amen, Robert Bell, and Cliff Long intercepted them near Longling. In spite of the odds, Amen led his flight in a diving attack on the gaggle of enemy fighters. Long did the best he could as Amen's wingman, watching his six o'clock and firing at any Oscars that attacked him. "The dogfight was very intense for a while," he told me. After three passes he broke away, intending to follow Chennault's maxim and live to fight another day. He was immediately hit by enemy fire. "I didn't see the planes come on me," he said. "I was diving away from the contact." Two Oscars dove in behind him. One of them fired a burst into the right side of his airplane. A bullet zipping through the cockpit shot the goggles off his head. "When he hit me with that burst I could see pieces of the plane falling away," remembered Long. "I put the nose down and pushed the throttle forward more and tried to evade these guys, but almost immediately I got another burst in the same right wing. That burst severed the aileron cable." The plane began to roll violently, corkscrewing toward the ground.

Long began cranking back the canopy to bail out, but the centrifugal force pinned him to the left side of the cockpit. With the stick deflected fully to the left, he managed to stop the rolling and bring the airplane under control. He pulled out of the dive. Looking back, he saw the Oscars peeling away for home. They thought he was dead. Sergeant Ryuzo Yamamoto claimed he shot down one P-51 over the Huitong Bridge. It was his first aerial victory claim of an eventual twelve. Long turned north and began testing the controllability of his damaged fighter. He found it could fly reasonably well between 170 and 200 miles per hour. He could not bail out because as soon as he let go of the stick, the plane began to roll again. The engine was running fine, so he headed for the grass airfield at Baoshan, fifteen miles away. He had no hydraulics to lower the landing gear, so he planned to belly-land at 180 miles per hour.[18]

Baoshan was the only field between Yunnanyi and the front. "It's all mountains," said Long. Besides the Baoshan Valley there was hardly a flat surface. As he flew east, the large valley opened grandly before him. He aimed for the airfield on the western edge, just south of the town. As he approached to land, the propeller struck the ground first, shearing off and careening to the right. The plane ballooned fifty feet into the air. He worked it back down again, but noticed he was rapidly nearing the rice paddies at the end of the runway. Rice paddies in China were usually surrounded by mud walls that served both to contain water and as walkways. The walls were two to three feet tall and almost as hard as cement, making them dangerous for an aircraft making an emergency landing. Without a prop, Cliff Long did not have a second chance to make the runway. "I just pushed the stick forward to dive the plane right into the ground," he said. The right wing caught first and the P-40 cartwheeled out of control. Long lost consciousness. When he awoke, the plane was upright, but totally destroyed around him. Smoke wafted from what was left of the engine in front of him. After some difficulty opening the canopy, he managed to get out. Miraculously, he was uninjured. He threw his parachute on the ground and began pounding it with his fist. "I was physically distressed and looked back at that plane that I had crashed," he said. "I was so mad at myself for doing that to my plane!" Lieutenant Colonel Amen did not give him time to dwell on the crash. An L-5 flew him back to Yunnanyi and he was back on the flying schedule just two days later.[19]

The formation of Oscars returned to the Huitong Bridge that afternoon. Again, they failed to hit their target. As Ikezawa circled to rejoin the formation, he spotted two C-47s returning from drop zones near Tengchong and Longling. Without permission, he broke away to attack. Approaching one of the transports from behind he fired, sending it crashing down into the rugged terrain with the loss of all seven aboard. It was the greatest loss of American life during the campaign. The other transport escaped by diving into the gorge and flying just above the river. Ikezawa noticed American fighters above him. He thought they were P-51s, but in fact it was a flight of four P-40s. He stayed low to avoid the fighters and headed back to Burma.[20]

P-40 pilot Clifford Long was hit by a formation of Oscars over Longling on August 18, 1944. Despite being claimed as shot down, he managed to pilot his crippled fighter to Baoshan for a crash-landing. ***Courtesy of Clifford Long***

Despite the intervention of the Japanese Army Air Force, the battle for Songshan continued. On August 20, the Chinese blew the mines. One contained 2,500 pounds of explosives, the other 3,500. All eyes were on the peak when at 0905, a blast of earth jetted skyward like a volcanic eruption. The explosions left two large craters where there had once been a mountaintop. At least forty-two Japanese soldiers were buried alive. The American engineers had hoped to decisively end the battle, but the few remaining pockets of Japanese resisted fiercely. On September 1, Marshal Wei sent a telegram to the 8th Army: "The remnants of the enemy at Songshan are not many," he told them. "The whole campaign depended on the success at Songshan. There was no excuse, and the Army commander should see to it that all the enemy … be wiped out before the second of the month, regardless of losses." He threatened to court-martial the commander of every regiment and division in the army, as well as the army commander, He Shaozhou. Wei did not care in the slightest that he was the minister of war's nephew. General He earnestly committed his men to the meat grinder. Li Mi grabbed a helmet and rifle and went to the front. He personally led the men in charge after charge. According to Dorn, of all the Chinese generals, "Li Mi was without question the most aggressive, the most capable in combat of all. Though a corps vice commander, he had led combat teams on a number of missions with great success. He was a leader in every sense of the word."[21] The few remaining pillboxes annihilated entire companies. The September 2 deadline passed and the fighting continued. The 8th drew on every source of reinforcement. A steady stream of soldiers marched across the completed Huitong

On August 20, 1944, American engineers detonated six thousand pounds of TNT in the mines underneath Japanese positions on Songshan. At least forty-two Japanese soldiers were buried alive. ***Hoover Institute***

Bridge to the battlefront. For the first time since May 1942, trucks rumbled across the Salween to supply the Chinese at Songshan and Longling. The Japanese commander, Major Kanemitsu, died in the fighting on September 6. At dawn the next day, the remaining Japanese burned their colors and slew their wounded. The full strength of what remained of the 8th Army assaulted the last position and captured it by 1600. The Chinese suffered 7,675 casualties in the battle for Songshan, more than five thousand of which were from the 8th Army. Of the 1,200 Japanese soldiers, ten escaped and nine were captured. The rest were dead.[22]

14

Lightnings Strike Twice

Professor Bi Shixian was only ten years old when the CEF stormed the walls of Tengchong. He lived southwest of the town, near the airfield the XXth Army Group captured in mid-June. The 19th Liaison Squadron wasted no time establishing a detachment there, performing artillery spotting, forward air control, and tactical reconnaissance throughout the siege. Doctor Norman Richard, a surgeon with the 32nd Portable Surgical Hospital at Tengchong, reported that most of his medical supplies were brought in by L-5s.[1] I met Professor Bi during my trip to the area sixty-five years later. He remembered the sergeant pilots of the 19th being very kind to him and the other children. They gave them paper airplanes made from gum wrappers. "They showed us how to make and fly the paper planes," said Bi, laughing fondly.

Though the Japanese Army Air Force was not active over Tengchong in August, the liaison pilots had a few close calls when the fighters intervened at Songshan. Matthew Blaszko was flying nearby when a team on the ground radioed there were "bandits" in the area. "I saw one banking in a direction away from us," he remembered. He flipped his tiny L-5 into a dive. "Needless to say, the deck came up mighty fast and as I pulled back on the stick, the old Gs piled up and the windshield went pop!" Blaszko flew low, dodging trees as he sped back to Baoshan. He made it safely, though with a split windscreen and a passenger who was "hanging on to the crossbars for dear life, his face as white as snow."[2] His was not the only close call. Staff Sergeant Mackiewicz was jumped by an enemy fighter while flying in the Songshan area. He immediately dove toward the American anti-aircraft guns protecting the Huitong Bridge, hoping to lure the Japanese plane into range. The fighter did not follow him. The detachment at Baoshan subsequently restricted flights around Songshan to early morning and late afternoon to avoid Japanese fighters.

On September 3, Captain Hideo Miyabe led a formation of Oscars from the 64th Sentai to Tengchong for the first time. The battle for the city still raged below. Street by street, building by building, inch by agonizing inch, the Chinese pushed the fanatical defenders into the eastern corner of the city. The Japanese were completely cut off. Air supply was their only hope to continue resistance. As the fighters made their drops, they spotted two L-5s over the valley. One of them was flown by Staff Sergeant DeVane. When he saw the Japanese planes, he frantically made for the airfield to the south. He landed, but in his haste to stop, jammed on the brakes and nosed over. He jumped out and ran for cover, sheltering behind a concrete roller as the fighters strafed. The Oscars shot up DeVane's ship, as well as three other L-5s parked next to the field. Two of them went up in flames. Staff Sergeant Paul Hovey was flying the other L-5 over the valley. He made for the hills with at least seven enemy fighters on his tail. Sergeant Ikezawa remembered the light aircraft being a very difficult target because it was so slow and maneuverable. He watched as Hovey made a desperate attempt to crash-land on a hillside. The plane flipped over in the trees. The sergeant-pilot suffered minor back injuries, but managed to escape into the woods while the Japanese strafed the wreck.[3]

The two destroyed and three damaged L-5s at Tengchong, as well as the C-47 shot down by Ikezawa near Songshan in August, added considerable tension to air operations on the Salween Front. "Nerves were on edge," remembered Jack Engle, a pilot with the 27th Troop Carrier Squadron. "It became habitual to keep our heads moving in the cockpit, eyes searching the sky for single-engine aircraft." On each C-47, a crewmember kept watch from the navigator's dome, looking for specks on the horizon. "We had no desire to dogfight a Zero in a C-47," said Engle. "Who does?"[4] The 69th Composite Wing established fighter patrols to protect the drop zones. The patrols cost them bombing and strafing sorties, but the wing could not afford to lose any more L-5s or C-47s. The transport crews still operated under strict radio silence, usually without a close escort, but they often saw friendly fighters patrolling nearby. Bob Binzer remembered once "waving at the P-38 pilot that had come up to ride on my left wing for a bit." If the transports ran into trouble, they broke radio silence with a phrase like "Buicks at Mike Niner." The entire front was plotted on a grid overlay, lettered north to south and numbered west to east. "Buick" was the code-word for enemy fighters and "Mike Niner" described their position.

On September 8, 1944, Binzer was the copilot for Captain William Peters—one of the squadron's most experienced pilots—on an airdrop mission to Longling. The squadron commander requested a fighter escort for the mission because of the recent Japanese activity in the area. The slower C-47 took off from Yunnanyi at 1415. Four P-38s flown by Lieutenants Rea, Heitkotter, Calder, and Forsythe took off twelve minutes later, intending to rendezvous with the transport over Baoshan and escort it to the drop zone. "We arrived at the rendezvous area and started to circle and await the fighters," reported Binzer. At the airfield below them, Air Transport Command C-47s unloaded reinforcements for the CEF. Above them was an overcast layer of clouds at eight thousand feet. After circling for a few minutes, Captain Peters saw what appeared to be a line of thunderstorms to the west. He figured the fighters would not be able to follow them through the storm, so he elected to proceed without them. Binzer helped him prepare the ship for turbulent weather: they put the gear down, reduced speed, lowered their seats, removed their headsets, tightened their seatbelts, and turned on the carburetor heat. "It was the worst storm I had ever been in," remembered Binzer. "The first updraft sent us up way too far to be flying without oxygen. Then suddenly we were in a downdraft, all accompanied with extreme turbulence."

As the transport disappeared into the thunderstorm at 1510 hours, twenty Oscars from the 64th Sentai emerged from the gloomy clouds over Baoshan. Matthew Blaszko was refueling his L-5 when the Japanese fighters appeared over the field. He ran for a drainage ditch as they began strafing the transports and Chinese troops.[5] Toshimi Ikezawa was one of the Oscar pilots. He saw an ATC cargo plane flying nearby, loaded with Chinese soldiers destined for Baoshan. As was becoming his usual practice, he broke formation and attacked. His bullets ripped into the fuselage, killing a Chinese soldier and sending the transport down in flames. Miraculously, the flight crew managed to crash land without suffering any more casualties. Meanwhile, Stuart Rea led the formation of P-38s to the rendezvous over Baoshan. Rea had been with the 449th since the squadron arrived in China in the summer of 1943. Most of the other original pilots had rotated home, leaving him as one of the most experienced men in the squadron. As the four Lightnings approached the valley from the east, "Douglass," the controller at the field, reported they were under attack by at least eleven enemy planes. Flying on Rea's wing, Heitkotter was excited. He had never seen an enemy fighter before. He was

Robert Binzer (right) with one of the 27th Troop Carrier Squadron's C-47s at Yunnanyi. Binzer was the copilot for Captain William Peters on September 8, 1944, and narrowly missed being ambushed by Japanese fighters over Baoshan. *Courtesy of Robert Binzer*

Chinese troops from the 200th Division unload on the Baoshan airstrip on September 30, 1944. *National Archives via Samuel Hui*

Crews refuel an L-5 at Baoshan. Technical Sergeant Matthew Blaszko was refueling his L-5 when the Japanese fighters attacked on September 8, 1944. *National Archives*

A flight of four late-model P-38 Lightnings from the 449th Fighter Squadron on a mission over Southeast Asia. *Courtesy of Michael Bates*

also nervous. He knew they were outnumbered by at least three to one (in fact, they were outnumbered five to one). The Lightnings climbed to just beneath the overcast. According to Heitkotter, as they dove into the melee, "all hell broke loose." Rea opened fire on a Ki-43 flown by Warrant Officer Tadashi Kinoshita. The P-38 Lightning was heavily armed with a 20-millimeter cannon and four .50-caliber machine guns mounted in the nose. With all its firepower concentrated in a four-foot circle, it usually pulverized its target. One of the transport pilots who witnessed the air battle claimed, "When the P-38s fired at a Jap fighter, it looked like the whole nose of the P-38 was spitting fire." Kinoshita's Oscar exploded in flames after Rea's short burst. The Japanese pilot crashed his crippled plane into a C-47 parked on the field, killing himself and destroying the transport. Another Oscar climbed from below to make a pass on Rea, but Tom Calder fired at it and saw pieces flying off the wings and fuselage. The Lightnings zoomed up out of the fight to the base of the clouds and turned around to make another pass.

Some of the Japanese fighters formed a Lufbery Circle: a defensive formation where planes fly in a ring so that each protects the tail of the one in front of it. Rea led the Lightnings slashing straight through the middle. He lined up on two Oscars heading straight for him and fired. One of them pulled up and away, but the other broke laterally. Rea fired a burst into its exposed underside and saw smoke belching from it as it winged over and dove for the ground. As he roared through the swirling mass of airplanes, another Oscar got on his tail and hit him with a burst that knocked out his hydraulics, jammed his right aileron, and stopped his right engine. Heitkotter fired at the attacker and it broke away. Rea departed immediately on one engine to make an emergency landing at Yunnanyi. Heitkotter followed the enemy fighter west, toward the jagged mountains at the edge of the valley. The Oscar suddenly rolled into a split-s less than a thousand feet above the ground. Heitkotter was astonished at its maneuverability. He rolled into a ninety-degree bank, but saw he did not have enough altitude to follow. Looking forward again, he saw he was headed straight for the mountains! He rolled and pulled back hard on the yoke, barely clearing the terrain. Both airplanes climbed as they came around for a head-on pass. "Both of us must have been a little chicken," Heitkotter admitted, "with a little left rudder to avoid a collision, which also aimed our guns aside as there were no hits. We just looked at each other as we passed within fifty feet."

As Heitkotter climbed away from the pass, he noticed the scattered elements of Japanese fighters regrouping as they departed to the south. He lined up behind them to note their heading for the debriefing when he was suddenly struck by an intriguing idea: "I could climb a little into the cloud cover and catch them unseen for a real turkey shoot." He eased into the cloud layer at eight thousand feet. Moments later, he descended again. Much to his chagrin, there were no Japanese fighters in front of him. "My judgment of speed and distance was the basis for a huge disappointment," he reported, "for as I descended out of the clouds I found myself right beside their formation unable to turn into them without colliding." Low on fuel, he turned away and headed back to Yunnanyi. He later found himself wondering about the wisdom of his idea. "My miscalculation might have had me descending into the middle of their formation or perhaps a little in front," he noted. "Then imagine my disappointment!"[6]

Peters and Binzer knew nothing of the dogfight raging behind them, since they removed their headsets to fly through the turbulent storm. The weather was clear over Longling. As they descended to make their drops, the radio operator told them to put their headsets back on and listen to the commotion. "We listened as we flew the drop mission," Binzer recalled, "and realized that had we been circling a little longer we could have been in the middle of that battle. The Japanese fighters had arrived about the same time as our fighter cover." The crew flew ten minutes north to avoid Baoshan on the return leg and landed safely at Yunnanyi. In addition to the ATC transport shot down by Ikezawa, the Japanese fighters destroyed two more on the ground, including the one hit by Kinoshita's crippled Oscar. The fighters also jumped two transports from the 27th TCS returning from air drop missions at the front. The timely intervention by the four P-38s allowed them to escape into the clouds. According to the 27th's records, had it not been for the arrival of the fighters, the total of three destroyed transports and two dead Chinese soldiers "would have been much greater." The detachment of the 19th Liaison Squadron on the field suffered no damage or loss of life. The Japanese focused their attacks on the transports unloading Chinese reinforcements. Nevertheless, Sergeant Blaszko was grateful and said he "would like to thank [the] flight of P-38s that came to our rescue over Baoshan." The 64th Sentai lost only one Oscar in the dogfight, though Rea claimed two. On their return to Burma, however, they encountered the same line of thunderstorms through which Peters and Binzer flew and four of them crash-landed in the rough weather.[7]

The next day, two Oscars made another raid on the airfield near Tengchong. Sergeants Iiames and Crawford were working on one of the damaged L-5s there and were unaware of the attack until the enemy fighters were on top of them. Crawford managed to take cover in a nearby ditch. Kenneth Iiames was standing on a ladder. The Japanese machine-gunned him before he could get to cover, killing him instantly.[8] That same day, inside the city, the Chinese 126th Regiment captured several Japanese soldiers and Chinese collaborators in an underground bunker. One of the collaborators was an interpreter from Taiwan by the name of Bai Bingzhuang. He told his captors the Japanese planned another aerial resupply to the embattled garrison the next morning. The XXth Army Group radioed the information to CEF headquarters at Baoshan, which forwarded it to the Forward Echelon of the 69th Wing at Yunnanyi.[9]

On September 10, two formations of Japanese warplanes winged their way over the Salween Front. Sixteen Ki-43s led by Major Eto, the 64th Sentai commander, escorted two Ki-48 Type 99 Twin-engine Light Bombers—Allied codename "Lily"—to bomb Chinese positions near Longling. Six of the Oscars were loaded with two 50-kilogram bombs each. Captain Fumio Kitazato led the second formation of twelve

Jim Heitkotter was one of the young pilots recently arrived at the 449th Fighter Squadron when it opened its detachment at Yunnanyi. The dogfight over Baoshan was his first encounter with enemy fighters. ***Courtesy of James Heitkotter***

Oscars, which escorted three Lilys to drop supplies to the garrison at Tengchong.[10] As for the Americans, two formations of fighters patrolled the Tengchong area that morning and returned to Yunnanyi before the Japanese arrived. At 1110, four P-38s from the 449th took off to bomb Longling and patrol Tengchong. Three P-40s and one P-51 from the 25th took off at 1245 to escort a supply drop to the same area. When the enemy formation finally arrived at 1320, the Americans were out of sight above the clouds. The Lilys began dropping supplies while the Oscars strafed Chinese positions outside the east gate. Upon spotting the planes below, the P-38s jettisoned their bombs and dove into the enemy formation. Bi Shixian watched from the ground and remembered the fight vividly. The Chinese called the P-38 *shuangshenzi* (双身子), which means "twin bodies," because of its unique double-fuselage design. Bi's eyes brightened and a smile illuminated his time-worn face as he used his hands to mimic the dive-and-zoom tactics the American fighters used against the much more maneuverable Japanese. Lieutenant Russell Robertson shot down and killed the formation leader, Captain Kitazato, and claimed another Oscar as a probable. While the Lightnings occupied the fighters, Lieutenant Colonel Hank Amen led his Warhawks and Mustang against the Lilys, which were unpainted except for the red "meatballs" on their wings. Captain Charles Dundas, a senior pilot from the 27th TCS, was at the controls of the C-47. He made a shallow turn to get out of thc linc of fire and in doing so, witnessed Amen make a diving attack to shoot down one of the Lilys. Captain Bell attacked another, firing a short burst that set its left engine on fire. He ruddered right and shot another burst into the right engine. The bomber-turned-transport dove into the side of Laifengshan and exploded, killing the crew of four. A book co-authored by Bi Shixian colorfully describes the scene of the crash: "To the east lay a head, to the west, a hand. Here were chunks of skin, there, pools of blood. The enemy had planned to come wreak havoc on our army, but they reaped what they had sown."[11] The American fighters shot down all three Lilys. In addition to Captain Kitazato's Oscar, another Ki-43 crash-landed in Japanese-occupied territory. For Bi Shixian, the image of the mighty *shuangshenzi* and the epic dogfight over Tengchong would forever be emblazoned in his memory.

All across the valley, Chinese villagers enthusiastically gathered the medicine, ammunition, and other supplies intended for the Japanese garrison that lay scattered across the countryside. The Chinese captured two surviving crewmen from one of the Lilys. Bi watched as they marched them off to division headquarters. The guards slapped the prisoners in the rear with their rifle stocks to hurry them along the trail. Bi also reported that the third Lily crashed alongside a nearby river. Most of the crew perished, but one of the pilots survived. A local farmer ran to the plane. He opened the door and took the pilot's pistol, watch, and fountain pen. He dragged the survivor from the wreck and brought him to his farmhouse. He fed the man and treated his wounds. He asked him to work for him. The Japanese pilot agreed. He worked the farmer's fields for two weeks until troops from the 198th Division discovered him while passing through the area. They were surprised at the farmer's audacity and took the pilot to a prison camp in Tengchong. He later transferred to Chongqing and the Chinese government repatriated him after the war.[12]

The failed resupply attempt was a heavy blow to the flagging spirits of the Tengchong garrison and the last straw for the Japanese Army Air Force. After September 10, they made only one more aerial attack near the Salween Front—a bombing raid on the night of November 28 that hit a fuel dump at Yunnanyi. There were no casualties. The Chinese knew the end was near for Tengchong when they came across Japanese soldiers that had committed suicide. An officer even surrendered with a small party of men. A large group of about two hundred attempted to break out from the encirclement, dynamiting the east gate and running out into the rice paddies. The Chinese held the area in force and gunned down most of the escapees. Those that made it past the Chinese soldiers encountered hostile civilians. Villagers in the surrounding area used their traditional broadswords to kill at least ten of them as they fled. A relief column from the south could not push past XIth Army Group positions along the Burma Road and in the Shweli Valley.[13] Most of the Japanese troops had gone without food for four days when the Chinese made their final assault on September 14.

One of the officers leading the final assault was Captain Shao Ying-jen, the orphan who fled Tengchong to join the 2nd Reserve Division in 1942. Prior to the battle he served as an assistant to Major Tang Wen-chu, the 5th Regiment's interrogation officer. His job was counterintelligence. He had to ferret out and question suspected traitors and collaborators, particularly from the preservation associations, which had recruited locals to gather intelligence for the Japanese. Shao was valuable in the role of interrogator because he was one of the few 2nd Division officers from Yunnan. Major Tang had a strong Hunan accent and most of the other soldiers were from Hunan, Guangxi, or Sichuan. Still, sometimes Shao had to resort to less-than-savory methods to get the information he needed. In one case, he took into custody a thirty-year-old woman who frequently visited the Chinese camp to sell vegetables. She adamantly denied any involvement with the Japanese. Shao eventually tied her hands with a telephone wire and plugged the other wire into the ground. "We began to operate the telephone to transfer electric shocks through her body," he said. The woman finally confessed and gave them details on who she was working for. They found a map she had sketched of their camp in her pants pocket.

They did not condemn everyone who worked for the Japanese as a traitor. Shao remembered one man he had known before the war. The man's name was Mr. Huang and he owned a bakery in Tengchong. The Japanese demanded he make food for the occupation forces. They threatened to kill his family if he refused. During the fighting, Huang was taken into custody as a suspected traitor. He saw Captain Shao and begged his old acquaintance for help. Shao interviewed several people who attested to Mr. Huang's good character and was able to let him go.

Shao left the dark world of counterintelligence during the Battle of Tengchong. The 2nd Reserve Division lost so many company grade officers in the fighting that it pressed him into service as an infantry officer. He received a lend-lease M1 carbine and entered the town through the southwest wall. He was in the city when the *shuangshenzi* shot down the Japanese fighters on September 10. "I think that was the happiest moment of my life," he remarked. Four days later, he was following Colonel Li Yi—his regimental commander—as they conducted a house-to-house search for the remaining Japanese troops holding out in the east corner of the town. As the colonel crossed Lijia Lane, a burst of fire from a Japanese machine gun caught him in the chest. He was one of the two highest ranking officers killed in the Battle of Tengchong. "He was a brave commander," said Shao mournfully. The Chinese cleared the remaining pockets of resistance that day. Out of almost two thousand Japanese soldiers at the beginning of the siege, only a few escaped and only fifty were captured. The rest fought to the death.[14]

The city was devastated. John Holman—a surgeon from the 32nd Portable Surgical Hospital—found the body of a young child inside a courtyard strewn with debris, apparently a victim of the battle. Doctor Richard reported finding jade "scattered everywhere in the ruins of Tengchong." Albert Ravendale, the United Press correspondent, wrote: "Of Tengchong itself, I found little remained. American bombers, Chinese artillery, and Chinese engineers have blown the great stone wall to bits in places." He stumbled "through the shattered remains of one section of the city" and found shops and homes "collapsed like domino stacks." In the northern corner of the city, only blackened walls remained where American planes had dropped napalm. "The streets where the Chinese drove the enemy out block by block are a maze of trenches and pillboxes," he wrote, "at times constructed from ancient sewers, mud bricks and huge paving slabs torn from the street and from tables taken from the wreckage of homes." The statue of Long Yun, the governor of Yunnan, at the main gate on the southwest wall was missing an arm and a leg. Ravendale was surprised to find Chinese vendors selling sweet meats and wheat cakes in the city even before the battle was over. He reported that some shopkeepers snuck in under shell fire to salvage what they could of their belongings before Chinese soldiers carried it away as booty.[15]

Chinese officers inspect the wreckage of a newly captured section of Tengchong. The battle devastated the city. ***National Archives via Samuel Hui***

A delegation from Tengchong visited Frank Dorn at his field headquarters in Baoshan a few weeks after the final assault. They thanked him for his part in liberating the town and presented him with an embroidered silk scroll to show their appreciation. He took the scroll, but was at a loss for words. The incongruity of being thanked for the utter desolation of the city bothered him. "Liberate!" he finally blurted out. "I destroyed your city! I ruined it completely! How can you thank me?" The leader of the delegation calmly answered, "We thank all of you Americans. Without you we would still be occupied by the dwarf monkey-people. Without you, our own armies would never have destroyed the enemy." Dorn was bewildered. "Imagine!" he wrote. "Thanking me for bringing about the complete destruction of their city, their homes, and their livelihoods."[16] Tengchong *was* devastated, but after more than two years of brutal occupation and fifty-one days of bloody siege, it was finally free. It cost the Chinese Army 8,671 dead, 1,234 of which were officers.[17]

The people returned to their ruined homes and began to rebuild. In the wake of the battle, Captain Shao followed up on reports of Japanese soldiers who escaped. He led a team to find Shirou Mitsuiyama, a Japanese lieutenant who fled with a bag full of puppet government cash. Shao learned he was holed-up in the house of a Chinese civilian by the name of Chiang Kai-tai, whose family he took hostage. Shao's men surrounded the house. Inside, Chiang pleaded with Mitsuiyama and convinced him to let his family go. They left and the Chinese troops went in. It was dark inside. Shao searched the murky rooms with a flashlight. Suddenly, Mitsuiyama sprang out from under a bed and attacked him with a samurai sword. Startled, he reflexively brought up his carbine and shot the lieutenant in the chest. Mitsuiyama fell to the ground, moaning in pain. Shao looked down at him, feeling overwhelmed with hatred. He knew he was not supposed to kill a wounded soldier, but he despised the Japanese with an anger born of bitter pain. They took everything from him. They burned down his house and forced him to flee his hometown. They murdered his friends and neighbors and turned others into traitors he had to hunt down and imprison. He saw his commander, a man he respected and admired, gunned down in the street before his eyes. "Hearing his moan, I gave him one more shot to send him to hell," said Shao. It was the only Japanese soldier he personally killed during the war. He kneeled down and started going through Mitsuiyama's things. He found the useless money. Rummaging through the lieutenant's bag, he pulled out a picture of the man's wife. He was struck at that moment by the cruelty of war. The feeling clashed with, rather than quelled, his hatred for the Japanese, just as the small clue to his enemy's humanity clashed with the inhumanity of the suffering they inflicted on his hometown.[18]

Chinese civilians look over what is left of their homes and property after the battle. Despite the destruction of their town, they were grateful to the Chinese and Americans who liberated them. ***National Archives via Samuel Hui***

15

Crisis in Command

The month of September should have brought a renewed sense of optimism to the Salween Front. The monsoon season was coming to an end. The advent of the dry season brought the promise of better flying weather and better conditions for the troops on the ground. The Battle of Myitkyina ended. As the eventual Allied victory became apparent, Colonel Maruyama withdrew his regiment and General Mizukami committed suicide. Stilwell's troops finally secured the town on August 3. "Thank God," he wrote. "Not a worry in the world this A.M."[1] Songshan fell to the 8th Army on September 7. Tengchong fell to the XXth Army Group on the fourteenth. After failing to affect the course of battle at Songshan or Tengchong, the Japanese Army Air Force withdrew. Many of the fighter sentais in Burma transferred to Thailand and Indochina to defend against raids from U.S. Navy aircraft carriers in the Pacific. Patrols of Chinese and American troops from both the X Force in Burma and the Y Force in China began surveying the Tengchong Cutoff, a rough trail between Tengchong and Myitkyina. On August 27, Major Benjamin F. Thrailkill led a reinforced infantry company of Chinese and Americans on foot from Myitkyina. After a nine-day hike, his party made contact with the Chinese Expeditionary Force in the Kambaiti Pass, thirty-four miles northwest of Tengchong. "China and Burma were linked today on the border," he radioed to headquarters. His men returned safely to Myitkyina eight days later. In the course of their journey, they found the trail to be passable and the area to be populated by natives friendly to the United States, if not the Chinese. They did not encounter a single Japanese soldier.[2]

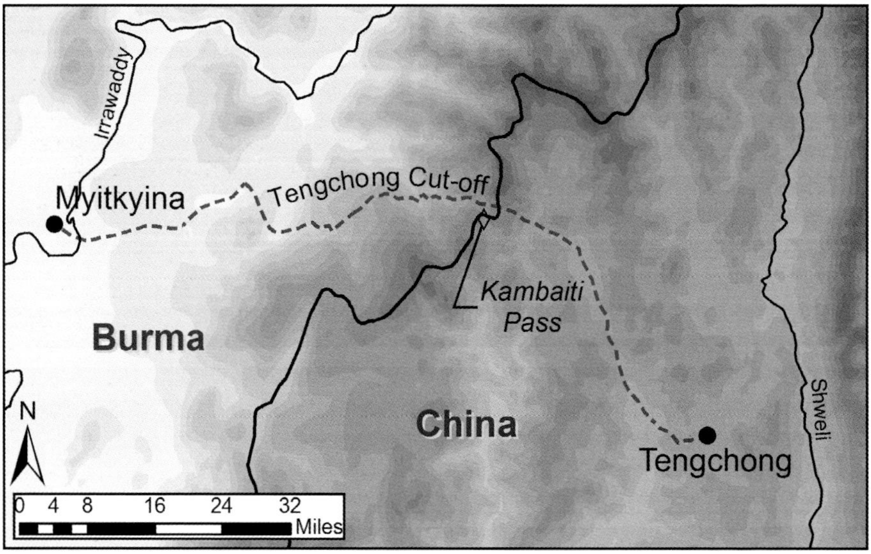

Tengchong Cutoff

Victorious after the grueling battle of Tengchong, Chinese infantry march away to take part in fighting elsewhere on the Salween Front. *National Archives via Samuel Hui*

Major Benjamin F. Thrailkill's expedition to the Kambaiti Pass, September 4, 1944. *National Archives via Samuel Hui*

The only place where there was a distinct lack of progress on the Salween Front was Longling. By mid-August, the XIth Army Group had surrounded the city and secured communications with the XXth Army Group through the Shweli Valley to the north. However, General Song Xilian could not be persuaded to attack. He continued to overestimate the strength of the enemy and told his superiors he needed more men. His inaction left the initiative to the Japanese. The Burma Area Army sent its 2nd Infantry Division, plus one regiment of the 49th Division, north to help the 56th restore its hold on the Burma Road. On August 26, six thousand Japanese troops attacked the Chinese roadblock between Mangshi and Longling. The Chinese fell back. On September 5, the 2nd and 56th divisions began a massive counteroffensive. Twelve thousand soldiers crashed against the Chinese lines north of Longling. The Honorable 1st Division fought stubbornly to hold its ground, but without reinforcements, the situation appeared desperate.

The counterattack at Longling precipitated another crisis in command. Chiang worried the CEF would be dislodged from its gains on the Salween Front and asked for the X Force in Burma to relieve the pressure by advancing toward Bhamo. Stilwell was taking time for his units to rest and refit after the brutal siege at Myitkyina. He told Chiang the situation was not as bad as it seemed. He suggested sending reinforcements from within China—namely the veteran 200th Division, which had fought so valiantly in Burma in 1942. Chiang was outraged. Stilwell's suggestion came at a time when the Japanese had just overrun Lingling, seventy miles southwest of Hengyang, in central China. The Ichi-go campaign continued inexorably toward the key city of Guilin. The tide of Japanese conquest seemed unstoppable. Opening the Burma Road was pointless if there was no Free China for it to supply. When Stilwell still refused to accelerate his campaign, Chiang reluctantly ordered the 200th to the front. Air Transport Command flew the veteran troops aboard C-47s to the airfield at Baoshan. When the 64th Sentai attacked Baoshan on September 8, it was soldiers of the 200th Division they found unloading on the field. From Baoshan, they marched across the Huitong Bridge, past the once-formidable mountain fortress of Songshan, and joined the other Chinese soldiers on the line north of Longling. Within a week, the full strength of the division was battling the Japanese. Despite encouraging progress, General Song sent back grim reports of the enemy's overwhelming strength. On September 15, Chiang threatened that if Stilwell did not move on Bhamo within the week, he would withdraw the CEF to the east bank of the Salween to protect Kunming.

The timing of the crisis could not have been worse for Stilwell. Major General Patrick Hurley had just arrived in China as a special representative for President Roosevelt. He was supposed to negotiate for Stilwell to become commander of all of Chiang's armies. The president was frustrated by the lack of progress in China. He hoped that a strong leader—a leader above the influence of Chinese politics and corruption—could both stem the tide of the Ichi-go campaign *and* open the Burma Road. His choice of Stilwell for this position though, was perplexing. There was obvious friction between him and Chiang. When Vice President Henry Wallace visited China that summer, he recommended Stilwell be recalled. He thought the president should appoint a commander who could win Chiang's confidence. He suggested Major General Albert Wedemeyer, Deputy Chief of Staff at SEAC, a staff officer with less battlefield experience than Stilwell, but more tact and political sense. Nevertheless, on the recommendation of the Joint Chiefs of Staff—namely Stilwell's old friend Marshall—Roosevelt decided to stick with Stilwell.[3]

General Hurley made surprising progress in Chongqing. Chiang agreed "in principle" to the arrangement, but there was considerable work to do ironing out the complications and political difficulties of appointing a foreigner to command the Nationalist Army and sending central government troops into territories only tenuously allied with Chiang. It was not in the intricacies of these negotiations, however, but once again by his own indelicate actions that Stilwell sabotaged the arrangement. After Chiang threatened to withdraw the CEF from the Salween Front, Stilwell sent a frantic message to the president. The generalissimo threatened to undo all the progress made in four months of brutal combat and render meaningless everything he had accomplished in Burma. He pleaded for Roosevelt to intervene. Four days later, he received the president's reply. He thought it was "hot as a fire-cracker" and delivered it to the generalissimo personally.[4]

"After reading the last reports on the situation in China," the letter began, "my Chiefs of Staff and I are convinced that you are faced in the near future with the disaster I have feared." Roosevelt acknowledged that the Y Force "fought with great courage and rendered invaluable assistance to the campaign in North Burma," but asserted that unless reinforced with Chiang's "every capacity," their sacrifice would be in vain. "Furthermore," he continued, "any pause in your attack across the Salween or suggestion of withdrawal is exactly what the Jap has been striving to cause you to do by his operations in eastern China." If the CEF would only continue working with Stilwell and Mountbatten in the re-conquest of Burma, the road to China would open in early 1945 "and the continued resistance of China and maintenance of your control will be assured." Roosevelt appealed to Chiang's desire to maintain his autocratic rule, but he also put forward an ultimatum. The United States and Great Britain were fighting the Axis in Europe and the Pacific. Resources were limited. If Chiang withdrew his forces from the Salween Front, if he did not appoint General Stilwell to unrestricted command of all his forces, he would have to "accept the consequences and assume the personal responsibility" of China being swallowed in political and military disaster. In other words, if Chiang did not submit to his demands, the Allies would write off China and focus instead on fighting the Japanese elsewhere. "I trust that your far-sighted vision, which has guided and inspired your people in this war, will realize the necessity for immediate action," concluded Roosevelt. "In this message I have expressed my thoughts with complete frankness because it appears plainly evident to all of us here that all your and our efforts to save China are to be lost by further delays."[5]

It was the boldest, most threatening letter Chiang ever received from the President of the United States. It was more demanding than Roosevelt had ever been with the Sultan of Morocco. Chiang was stunned. He finished reading and looked up at Stilwell. "I understand," he said quietly. He excused himself. Stilwell was smugly satisfied. He felt vindicated. "The harpoon hit him right in the solar plexus," he gloated.[6] It never crossed his mind that he just sowed the seeds of his own undoing. Patrick Hurley was also shocked by the letter. He believed the only explanation was that Stilwell was trying to get *out* of taking command of the Chinese armies. He thought perhaps Stilwell believed the situation in East China was beyond saving and wanted no part of it. Chiang's shock quickly turned to rage and indignation. On September 22, he ordered a halt to offensive action on the Salween Front until the X Force attacked Bhamo. Two days later, he informed Hurley that Stilwell had to go. He believed the implication of the general personally delivering Roosevelt's letter was that he was Stilwell's subordinate. Appointing such an openly disrespectful man to command his armies might precipitate a full-scale mutiny. He would no longer tolerate the loss of face brought on by the general's disrespect. It was bad enough he had conditions and ultimatums put on his use of lend-lease supplies. Britain and Russia had no such limitations.

Chiang wrote to Roosevelt on September 25 that, while he would still be willing to appoint an American to command China's field armies and air forces, it could not be Stilwell. "It was made manifest to me that General Stilwell had no intention of cooperation with me," he wrote, "but believed that he was in fact being appointed to command me." He asked the president to understand that he could not depend on Stilwell following his direction. He praised his "fine and soldierly qualities," but asserted that he was "unfitted for the vast, complex, and delicate duties which the new command will entail. Almost from the moment of his arrival in China, he showed his disregard for that mutual confidence and respect which are essential to the successful collaboration of allied forces." Chiang reminded the president that he had requested Stilwell's recall the previous October, but the general "solemnly promised that in the future he would unreservedly obey my orders and would give me no further cause for disappointment." Stilwell did not live up to that promise. If he were appointed commander of China's armies, it would cause "grave dissensions" and "do irreparable injury to the vital Chinese-American cooperation." Chiang told Roosevelt he would pledge his support to whatever other officer the president thought capable.

To Hurley, Chiang wrote a memo detailing his issues with Stilwell. First and foremost was that he used "every sort of pressure to induce me to commit additional forces" to Burma. "As I had feared," he asserted, "the Japanese took advantage of the opportunity to launch an offensive." With his best men and equipment in Burma, his forces in China did not stand a chance. "The forces brought to bear by the Japanese in their offensive in east China were six times as great as those confronting General Stilwell in north Burma," he claimed, "and the consequences of defeat were certain to outweigh in China all results of victory in the North Burma campaign. Yet General Stilwell exhibited complete indifference to the outcome in East China." The result was a victory at Myitkyina at the cost of East China. Of course, he left out any mention of the twenty divisions he kept blockading the Communists in North China and refused to use against the Ichi-go campaign. But Stilwell's focus on North Burma and disengagement from events in China made for a compelling argument. He concluded assuring Hurley that if Roosevelt replaced Stilwell with a competent officer, "we can work together to reverse the present trend and achieve a vital contribution to the final victory."[7]

When Stilwell heard about the memos he was outraged. "The Peanut lied about me, and made astounding statements to effect that I was bucking him," he retorted. Chiang's charges, exaggerated or not, stemmed from a lack of confidence. He did not believe in Stilwell. Unlike the year before, there seemed to be no room for reconciliation. Roosevelt did not reply for two weeks. When he finally did, he told the generalissimo that he regretted China's battlefield reversals and deferred to Chiang's judgment when it came to not appointing Stilwell to command his armies. It was, after all, a matter of China's sovereignty. He declined to provide a different officer for the job though, because of how badly the situation had deteriorated. "Old Rubberlegs proceeds to cut my throat and throw me out," wrote Stilwell, caustically referring to Roosevelt by his handicap. "I've done my best, and stood up for American interests," he insisted. "To hell with them."[8]

Roosevelt officially recalled Stilwell on October 18. His deputy, Major General Dan Sultan, took over in his stead.[9] "The axe falls," Stilwell wrote in his diary. "Rubberlegs has quit." He spent the next few days packing and saying his goodbyes. Before he left, Chiang

Stilwell, standing to the right with the CBI Theater patch on his shoulder, addresses a somber group of YFOS officers on his last day in China. Dorn is standing behind him to the far right. ***Hoover Institution***

offered to award him the Order of the Blue Sky and White Sun, the highest decoration a foreigner could receive in China. Stilwell told him to "stick it up his arse." Chiang tried to end things amicably. He said he was very sorry it had come to this. Stilwell had done a great deal for China. It was only because of the differences in their make-ups that he asked for his relief. He implored him to remain a friend of China.[10]

Stilwell departed on October 22, 1944. Patrick Hurley and T.V. Song met him at the Chongqing airfield to say goodbye. He Yingqin pulled up in a touring car and stepped out to give the general a final salute. Stilwell returned the salute, said his farewells, and climbed into the C-47. "What are we waiting for?" he impatiently asked the flight crew. They pulled the door shut and took off.[11] He stopped at Baoshan to meet with Frank Dorn and Wei Lihuang. "I was shocked at the news," said Dorn. Wei told the general he was "deeply grieved." Stilwell had "done more for China than any other individual past, present, or future," and his dismissal was a mistake that would cause irreparable loss. Stilwell asked Dorn if he wanted to return to the United States with him. "I had to say that I could not desert the Americans and Chinese serving with me," he later wrote, "particularly during the unfinished Salween Campaign ... whoever the new commander might be, he'd profoundly need all the experienced hands he could get." Stilwell respected his decision, but told him he would probably come to regret it.[12] He spoke briefly to the staff and then said his goodbyes. It was a poignant moment. Dorn and Stilwell had gone through a lot together. They served together in China before the war. They survived the walkout from Burma in 1942. Now Dorn would continue on without his mentor and friend. Stilwell boarded his airplane and took off to cross the Hump. He asked the pilot to descend over Tengchong along the way and circle the city. Battered, but free, it was the last he saw of China. He said goodbye to his son and staff at Myitkyina before continuing on to India. On October 26, 1944, thirty-two months after assuming command, he departed CBI.[13]

Ironically, the Japanese headquarters in North Burma ordered an end to the counteroffensive at Longling on September 14, the day before Chiang threatened to withdraw across the Salween and Stilwell complained to Roosevelt. On the fifteenth, the 200th Division and the Honorable 1st Division followed the retreating Japanese to reoccupy most of the high ground north and northwest of Longling.[14] The counteroffensive was over before the political firestorm it created even began. The Japanese cited the fall of Tengchong and Songshan, as well as the determined resistance of the Chinese at Longling, as reasons for cancelling the attack. The intervention of the veteran 200th Division was key to holding the Chinese line. Stilwell had been right after all. The situation was not as bad as Chiang thought and the intervention of reinforcements from within China helped stop the Japanese.

Throughout his tenure in the Far East, Stilwell's ideas were usually sound, though sometimes unimaginative and not very collaborative. What created friction was not the content of his ideas, so much as his lack of bedside manner. He was opinionated and stubborn. He had no respect for the generalissmo, nor his position as head of state, and took pleasure in denigrating him amongst his staff. He did not hesitate to use coercion or blackmail to get his way. When General Marshall sent Stilwell to China, he sent a man who was tough, who could survive; his epic walkout in 1942 proved that. Marshall should have sent a man who could act the part of both diplomat and soldier. His decision to send Stilwell, and his unflagging support of his old friend throughout his tenure, was the wrong choice for a difficult situation.

After Stilwell's dismissal, Roosevelt did what he should have done long before. He divided the CBI Theater into two separate commands. Major General Dan Sultan took command of the India-Burma Theater and assumed Stilwell's positions within Southeast Asia Command. Major General Albert Wedemeyer took command of the China Theater. Wedemeyer had more experience as a staff officer than a leader of men. His only direct command of troops was as a platoon leader with the 15th Infantry at Tianjin from 1930 to 1932. He was an expert on the German military, having attended the Kriegsakademie in Berlin before the war, and had little knowledge of the Far East. He had been Chief of the War Plans Division, but was exiled to SEAC in October 1943 because his insistence on a cross-channel invasion of Europe irked the British. It pained him that he was not allowed to participate in the final planning for the invasion he was so influential in conceiving.[15]

His personality was a striking contrast to Stilwell's. He was smooth and controlled, rather than sharp and caustic. He immediately began tending to the precarious military situation and the broken relationship with Chiang. "My overall estimate of American assistance here in the past two years indicates that my predecessor made a botch of the job," he reported in a personal letter. "He spent so much time in the jungles of upper Burma commanding a few battalions and acquiring a great deal of publicity as a great tactician that he neglected sorely the responsibilities inherent in his position as Chief of Staff to the Generalissimo and as Commanding General of American Forces in the China Theater."

Lieutenant General Albert Wedemeyer is greeted by officers of the 14th Air Force upon his arrival at a base in China. After taking command, he immediately began repairing relationships with the Chinese and the 14th Air Force. ***National Archives***

Wedemeyer felt he had to change Stilwell's approach, if not the core of his ideas. In a letter to Marshall on December 10, he wrote: "My approach to the Generalissimo has been friendly, direct, and firm. I believe that he likes and respects me now.... I have been uniformly careful not to take action that conflicts with agreed plans. I have been uniformly careful to massage his ego and place myself in an advisory position so that he will not lose face."[16] He found Chiang frustrating and difficult to work with, as did Stilwell, but he kept it to himself. For his part, Chiang found Wedemeyer trustworthy and capable and listened to his advice. The emphasis on the relationship bore fruit with Chiang, but engendered hatred from Stilwell's former acolytes. Dorn thought Wedemeyer was pompous and rude. "He preaches instead of talking ... an excellent old-style missionary," he wrote. It did not help that Wedemeyer saw loyalty in black-and-white terms. You were either a Wedemeyer man or a Stilwell man. He immediately got along with Chennault's officers, who were definitely *not* Stilwell men. He developed plans that included the 14th Air Force, instead of competing with it. When he very bluntly asked Dorn where his allegiance lay, he answered, "My loyalty would always go to the commanding general, whoever he might be." It was not enough. "He wanted me to join his campaign of belittling and denigrating Stilwell," Dorn wrote. Though he was allowed to remain "the last bastion of Stilwellia" for the time being, his days were numbered.

Though the core of Wedemeyer's ideas differed little from his predecessor, he stressed getting things done "differently," even if it meant only putting a new name and face on an existing practice. Dorn resented this, because it seemed like he was standing on Stilwell's shoulders while claiming any progress as his own.[17] On November 17, Wedemeyer combined the American military training missions in China—including the YFOS—under the umbrella of Chinese Training and Combat Command. He made General Dorn the commander and told him to "carry on" with the Salween Campaign. He began brainstorming ways to stop the Ichi-go offensive and advised the generalissimo on reorganizing the Chinese Army into smaller, more effective units. He advocated using the B-29s in a raid on the Japanese supply base at Hankou. It was too late to save East China, but on December 18, seventy-seven B-29s fire-bombed the city. The massive raid gutted the town and became the prototype for the fire-bombing raids on Japan in the year to come. Considering the volume of supplies the China-based B-29 program used versus the results it achieved, it was probably not worth the cost. The very-long-range bombers only made a two percent dent in the Japanese steel industry. Wedemeyer insisted the Joint Chiefs of Staff remove them from China.[18]

It was a time of transition for China and a time that saw little progress on the Salween Front. Though Chiang was successful in getting Stilwell removed, the corruption revealed in the Guomindang administration necessitated some action on his part. General Chen Cheng took over as minister of war, though He Yingqin remained chief of staff of the army. Unfortunately, few of Chen's ideas for reform made it past his rival's iron-fisted control of the military. Chiang made T.V. Song Premier of the Chinese Republic. Song may have been the generalissimo's brother-in-law, but they were often at odds, and Song's stint as foreign minister was a sort of enforced exile. Appointment of the Harvard-educated businessman to the number two position in China was supposed to signal that Chiang was serious about reform.[19]

On the Salween Front, Wei and Xiao were finally allowed to replace Song Xilian with his deputy, Major General Huang Jie. Huang was another early graduate from the Huangpu Academy when Chiang was commandant and participated in the Northern Expedition in the late-1920s. He met the Japanese in battle for the first time as a division commander during the 1933 Great Wall Campaign. He fought in Shanghai in 1937, but lost Chiang's confidence after suffering a major defeat at Lanfeng in 1938. He would go on to be one of the last Nationalist generals to retreat from the mainland after the Communists took over in 1949.[20] Despite his experience, Huang did not make a good first impression on the Americans. "Not even interested in his troops," Dorn wrote about him. "Rarely spends time with them, spending most of his time in Kunming. Famous as a Mah Jong player, which is about all he does. One of the stupidest and most incompetent of the lot."[21] With General Song finally gone, Huang did in fact leave Kunming to take charge of the XIth Army Group. He consolidated his positions and repaired and reconstituted his forces after the savage counterattack at Longling. Meanwhile, General Sultan resumed the X Force's advance toward Bhamo. The Ichi-go offensive in East China still ground on toward Guilin with no end in sight. Going forward, things would certainly be different without General Joseph W. Stilwell. Like him or not, he had worked hard, pushed his men beyond their limits, and achieved the impossible in Burma. The people he led out in 1942 looked up to him in awe. The men he drove mercilessly to Myitkyina hated his guts. To his successors he left a difficult situation, but not one without hope. He was a controversial figure, and his legacy remains controversial to this day.

16

Interdiction

The Chinese did not get much in the way of close air support during the Japanese counterattack in September. Of the 226 P-40 and P-38 sorties flown during the first half of the month, 190 were dedicated to patrolling for enemy fighters, protecting airdrops, and escorting Air Transport Command C-47s ferrying the 200th Division to Baoshan.[1] When the situation finally stabilized on the ground and the Japanese Army Air Force withdrew from the air, the Warhawks of the 25th Fighter Squadron went back to hammering away at targets in Longling and Mangshi. Meanwhile, the 69th Composite Wing focused its P-38s and B-25s increasingly on long-range interdiction. The 56th Division enjoyed a better supply situation than any Japanese unit in Burma. Trucks and trains travelled across Thailand from Indochina along two main lines of communication: from Bangkok, the Burma-Siam Railroad connected with the Rangoon to Lashio line at Moulmein. Throughout the summer of 1944, three trains a day used this line to carry arms, ammunition, and other provisions into Burma.[2] The other route—Thailand Rail's Northern Line—carried supplies north from Bangkok to Lampang, where they were transferred to trucks following the crude highway system west to Meiktila, Burma. From Moulmein and Meiktila, trucks and trains moved the supplies north to Lashio and thence up the Burma Road to the Salween Front. The United States never declared war on Thailand, though Chennault's planes had attacked Japanese bases in that country since the beginning of the war. America considered it a "reluctant ally," only cooperating with the Japanese to avoid being invaded and occupied. Besides a brief and unsuccessful attack on Indochina in early 1941 and a limited invasion of the Shan States in eastern Burma in 1942, it did not participate as an active belligerent. Instead, it functioned primarily as a conduit for supplies. American airplanes bombed depots, repair yards, and bridges to disrupt the transportation network and often attacked trucks and trains as targets of opportunity.

Characteristic of the 69th Wing's missions in the country was an armed reconnaissance by two P-38s on September 28, 1944. Lieutenants Henry Rogers and Keith Mahon took off from Chenggong at 1145 to look for targets of opportunity between Ban Dara and Lampang. Northbound along the railroad from Ban Dara, they flew just off the deck to stay beneath the low scattered cumulus. They reported strafing a factory at Uttaradit and setting the roof on fire (this was probably an urban market with a large roof). Continuing four miles up the line, they found a large locomotive near Nam Rit. Both pilots hit it with a hail of bullets, causing the boiler to erupt in a huge cloud of steam. They strafed another locomotive at Pang Ton Phueng Station, nine miles further north. Not far from this station, they observed twenty people run into a railway tunnel. The pilots flew low, firing into the tunnel. They flew so low, in fact, they reported seeing tracers come out the other end! They returned to the station and strafed a water tank, twenty-five boxcars, and two possible tanker cars before heading home. Both Lightnings landed safely at Chenggong at 1735. It was all in a day's work for two fighter planes operating alone over Thailand. Hak Hakanson, an American expatriate researching World War II in Thailand, found evidence for this sort of activity at the Ban San Khayom railroad bridge, a World War II-era steel bridge still standing eighteen miles south of

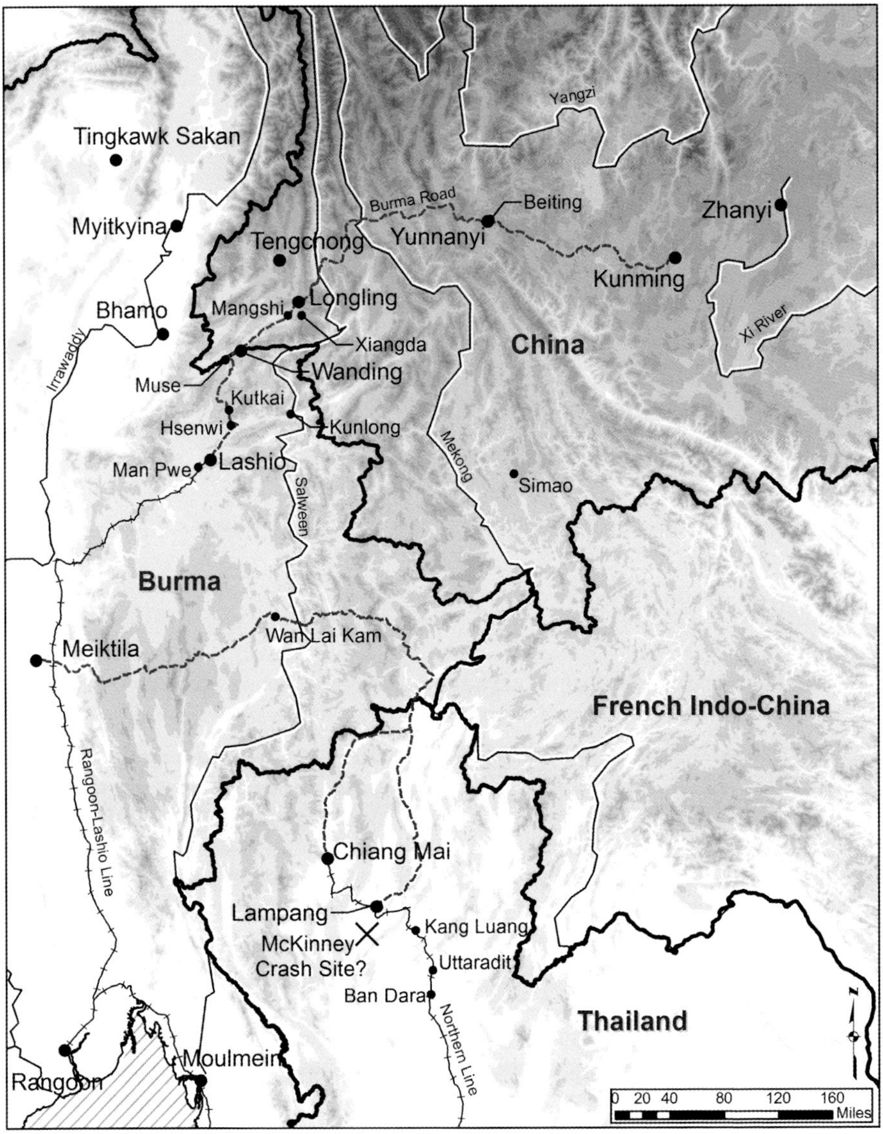

Japanese Lines of Communication

Chiang Mai. Hakanson reported holes through the superstructure that indicate it was hit by 20-millimeter shells, probably from a P-38 strafing north to south at low altitude. The target was probably a train on or approaching the bridge. During the Salween Campaign, the 14th Air Force claimed 108 trains or other motor vehicles destroyed and 130 damaged. It was a seemingly small number compared to other theaters, but the Japanese had very few vehicles supporting their forces in southwest China and attacks by American warplanes forced most of them to operate only at night.[3]

While the airmen had some success trolling for targets of opportunity, most believed bombing bridges was the most decisive way to cut a supply artery.[4] According to Chennault: "Where a bridge had to be blasted, we couldn't afford the European practice of assigning a group of heavy bombers to plaster it from high level with hundreds of tons of bombs."[5] Instead, a single flight of fighters or medium bombers bombed from low altitude; it was dangerous, but accurate. According to P-38 pilot Joe Fodor, "you just aim the damn airplane towards the bridge and let her go." A flight would typically pass the target at high altitude and then descend, turn around, and speed toward it on the deck. "Just before you hopped over," Fodor said, "you dropped your bombs and they would skip into the abutments of the bridge." The bombs had a three- to five-second delay fuse—"not much time to get your ass over the bridge and back down on the deck."[6] The method was effective because most of the bridges in Southeast Asia were made of wood and only lightly defended by small arms or machine guns. The 22nd Bomb Squadron and 449th Fighter Squadron routinely hit bridges at Lashio, Kutkai, Man Pwe, and Kaeng Luang. The 449th in particular earned a reputation for bridge-busting. According to pilot Dick Conway: "we knocked out most of the bridges along the Burma Road in Japanese held areas and down to Mandalay."[7] Between January 1943 and February 1945, the 14th Air Force destroyed thirty-four bridges in the vicinity of the Salween Front and damaged twenty-five. Throughout the war, its airplanes destroyed thirty-four bridges in Thailand and Indochina and damaged fifty-one.[8]

B-25s from the 22nd Bomb Squadron score a direct hit on the Dara Bridge on May 25, 1944, but fail to bring it down because of its sturdy steel and concrete construction. ***National Archives***

One bridge that defied Chennault's economy of force was the railroad bridge at Ban Dara, which had huge concrete piers and a steel superstructure. It became the bane of the 22nd. The squadron first set out for it on May 11, 1944, with six "H" models. Their fighter escort failed to materialize so they returned to base. On May 20, the 22nd and 491st squadrons flew a joint mission to the bridge. It took four hours to fly the almost six hundred miles from Yangkai, China. They encountered low clouds and thunderstorms over the target area and again returned without attacking. Five days later they went out again, this time scoring hits on the ties and rails on the south approach, as well as a direct hit on the south abutment. "The bombs would usually hit those pillars and bounce off," remembered Chapman Hale. "It looked like you knocked the bridge out, but it would still be standing."[9] The bridge became notorious. Missions on September 10, the twenty-third, twenty-fourth, twenty-sixth, and October 25 failed to bring it down, despite several direct hits on the superstructure, piers, and abutments. Contrary to Chennault's usual practice, and much to his chagrin, a flight of B-24 heavy bombers from the 10th Air Force finally brought it down on November 3 with twenty 1,000-pound bombs.[10]

A crucial element in prosecuting the campaign against a vast road and rail network with a relatively small number of aircraft was accurate and up-to-date photographic intelligence. This was particularly important because the lightly-built bridges, though often easy to destroy, were also easy to repair or replace. The Japanese often built as many as three bypass bridges near a crossing, making it difficult to completely stop traffic. The 69th Wing had to keep constant pressure on key choke points to disrupt the network. The 21st Photo Reconnaissance Squadron (PRS) had a flight of F-5s at Kunming. The F-5 was a Lockheed P-38 fighter modified for reconnaissance. Instead of guns in the nose, it carried cameras. It was usually equipped with two 6-inch focal length oblique cameras and either two 12-inch vertical cameras, one 12- and one 6-inch, or one 24-inch. Capable of flying up to forty-four thousand feet at over four hundred miles per hour, it could fly higher and faster than most anything in the JAAF. The flight at Kunming was responsible for the area from Hainan Island, through Indochina, Thailand, Burma, and much of south China. It was an enormous area for one flight to cover. Sometimes, mission planners and aircrews had to use photos that were several months old. Sometimes, they had none at all. The situation improved with the arrival of the 35th PRS.

On June 1, 1944, forty-five officers and 260 enlisted men under the command of Major Albert McChristy disembarked from the HMS *Strathmore* in Bombay Harbor. The ship carrying their aircraft sank en route from the United States, so they waited for replacements through August and finally flew the Hump into China on September 9. The 14th Air Force divided the squadron into four flights and sent each to a different station with four airplanes and four to five pilots. Headquarters was at Zhanyi, eighty miles northeast of Kunming. G Flight, under the command of Captain Lyle Babcock, moved to Yunnanyi on September 16. Lieutenant Russell Dent was the flight operations officer. The other three pilots were Lieutenants Sterling Barrow, Bill Deen, and Frank McKinney. Barrow grew up on the oil fields of south Texas. He left the University of Houston to join the Army Air Forces after Pearl Harbor and met Bill Deen—a fellow Texan—at pilot training. The two of them hit it off and became fast friends. They met Frank McKinney in Oklahoma City, where they attended reconnaissance training

The Lockheed F-5E was a P-38 fighter modified for reconnaissance. It could fly at forty-four thousand feet at over four hundred miles per hour—faster and higher than anything in the Japanese Army Air Force. Here, ground crew service one near a protective revetment at Yunnanyi. It has two 300-gallon drop tanks installed to dramatically increase its range. ***Courtesy of Sterling Barrow***

together at Will Rogers Field in the fall of 1943. The training not only taught them aerial photography, but also stressed high-altitude flying, navigation, and calculating winds aloft. The three lieutenants stuck together on the passage to India from the United States and were happy to be assigned to the same flight at Yunnanyi. Lieutenant Stanley Benham ran the flight's photo lab. Lieutenant Thomas Klausmeyer was in charge of engineering. Lieutenant Art Clark was the intelligence officer, admin officer, censor, and historian. Clark joined the Army after graduating from the University of North Carolina. He was assigned to the 35th after finishing intel school in Harrisburg, Pennsylvania. An avid outdoorsman and "a helluva nice guy," according to Barrow, he sent periodic flight history reports to squadron headquarters, though the flight operated on its own, with little to no direction from the squadron.

G Flight had four F-5Es. They were not pressurized or well heated. The cockpit heater only blasted hot air at the pilot's left boot heel. In addition to a pressure-regulated oxygen mask, the pilot had to wear long johns, boot socks, gloves, a heavy flight suit, and a fur-lined jacket. There was a tube in case he had to relieve himself, "but hell!" exclaimed Barrow, "who could find it in all those clothes!" The F-5 carried an internal load of 446 gallons of fuel. A 300-gallon drop tank under each wing increased it to a total of 1,046 gallons, or approximately ten hours of flight time. Headquarters at 14th Air Force or the 69th Composite Wing called the flight directly on a field phone and gave Lieutenant Clark the targets for each day. He then called the weather section before sitting down with each pilot to go over the target, weather, route, elevation, direction, and timeline. Camera crews installed the appropriate cameras while the pilot changed into his cold weather flying gear. The operations section called in the takeoff time and expected time of return to "Droopy," the controller at Kunming. Every week, 14th Air Force issued a new code sheet so the pilots could query the station for weather conditions. Very few runways in China had instrument approaches in case of bad weather. Yunnanyi had a fifty-watt omnidirectional beacon, but most of the time it did not work and even when it did, the surrounding mountains disrupted the signal. Usually, the pilots had to find a hole in the clouds and fly in at low altitude. The fact that there were few maps of Southeast Asia available hindered navigation. Barrow remembered using French maps made in the 1930s that often had lakes, roads, and other features that simply did not exist. The pilots noted the irregularities and did their best to navigate by time and heading and estimating the winds aloft, all while keeping a watchful eye out for enemy fighters. Somehow, said Barrow, "I never got lost." In addition to photographing targets on the Salween Front and the road and rail networks through Thailand and North Burma, G Flight flew mapping missions using trimetrogon photography to help the 14th Air Force develop better maps for the theater.[11]

Lieutenant Barrow flew G Flight's first mission on September 24—he encountered a solid undercast and returned without pictures. The squadron commander, Major McChristy, and the flight commander, Captain Babcock, also took off. McChristy turned back because of the weather. Babcock had a runaway engine and had to make an emergency landing. When he touched down, the nose gear collapsed and the plane skidded to a stop. Babcock emerged unscathed, but the airplane was a write-off. G Flight was down to three.[12] Bill Deen and Frank McKinney attempted missions on the twenty-sixth. The weather was again unfavorable, but McKinney managed to get photos of Lampang, Thailand. McKinney had wanted to be a fighter pilot and was unhappy with his assignment to a reconnaissance squadron. He hated that the F-5 was unarmed. "Unarmed, alone, and unafraid," was the unofficial mantra of photo reconnaissance, though Barrow said it often became, "unarmed, alone, and scared shitless." On his first mission, McKinney flew everything by the book: He flew at thirty thousand feet. When he saw enemy fighters climbing toward him over Lampang, he turned for home. He yearned for more excitement. On subsequent missions, he often returned with photos taken from twenty thousand feet or lower. He averaged less than twenty-two thousand feet, even when cloud cover did not prevent him from flying higher. Sometimes he flew as low as nineteen thousand feet—well within the reach of Japanese fighters. By way of contrast, Bill Deen tended to fly at twenty-five thousand feet. Sterling Barrow usually flew above twenty-seven thousand and never below twenty-four. Both were concerned about their friend's recklessness and spoke with him about it on a number of occasions.[13]

After McKinney's flight to Thailand, persistent cloud cover prevented further missions for the rest of September. The weather was still a problem throughout October, though the pilots did their best to work through it. Barrow flew to Mangshi and Xiangda on the twelfth, noting large fires visible from twenty-seven thousand feet. The pilots often saw fire and smoke below them, but from high altitude it was impossible to tell if it was related to the war, or if a farmer was merely clearing his fields. Many of the reconnaissance pilots felt disconnected. "You didn't attach a human conflict with what you saw," Barrow told me. He returned to photograph Mangshi again two days later. According to Art Clark, both his missions achieved "excellent results."[14]

Lieutenant Sterling Barrow, one of the young pilots with G Flight, 35th Photo Reconnaissance Squadron, at Beiting Field. Barrow flew by the book and achieved excellent results with his cameras. *Courtesy of Sterling Barrow*

Babcock, Dent, Barrow, Deen, and McKinney rotated through the flying schedule, usually launching one or two sorties a day when the weather allowed. They covered the Burma Road from Mangshi, through Wanding and Muse south to Lashio and west to Bhamo. They took pictures of the highway from Hsenwi to Kunlong Ferry and made photo mosaics of the battlefront. They approached each photo run at an offset, so they could see and identify the target. Once they rolled in to line it up for the cameras, the target disappeared out of sight under the nose. They noted the time, direction, altitude, cloud condition, and counter on the intervalometer, which set the rate of overlap for the photos. G Flight usually knew when to expect each plane back, but the pilots always announced their return by buzzing the field. "We never came back without a buzz job!" exclaimed Barrow.[15] Art Clark always looked forward to it; it meant the pilot was home safe. He got his shot of mission whiskey and Clark debriefed him.[16] As soon as the engines stopped after landing the camera crews pulled the film, processed it, and gave it to the photo interpretation (PI) section. Captain Griffin, the PI officer, made an assessment with the intelligence officer, called headquarters with any pertinent information, and then sent prints aboard the next C-47 to Kunming. Headquarters distributed photos to the squadrons flying strike missions.[17] Clark recalled that if a bridge was out, they would look for a string of barges along the shore. The Japanese would link them together to form a temporary bridge at night, but keep them hidden along the shore in the daytime. This sort of insight helped the 69th Wing keep the Japanese transportation network in shambles.[18]

G Flight found the airfield at Yunnanyi overcrowded with fighters, liaison planes, troop carriers, and Air Transport Command. With the end of the monsoon season, the grass field at Beiting—two miles east—was finally usable. It was five thousand feet long with no lighting. Painted barrels outlined the landing surface. A detachment of eight B-25s from the 22nd Bomb Squadron moved there on October 5. G Flight joined them on the twenty-eighth. There were no revetments. The bombers and reconnaissance ships were spread out and parked in the open. The men moved into tents near the field. They slept on cots and made drawers for their foot lockers with empty .50-caliber ammo cans. Grass rugs covered the dirt floors. There was a generator for electricity, but it could not supply enough power for all the tents, so most of the men turned in early. Barrow remembered a local farm wife supplying his tent with eggs and walnuts in exchange for cigarettes. He and his friends did not smoke.[19]

In addition to their regular missions, the reconnaissance ships sometimes accompanied the fighters or bombers to take pictures before, during, and after a strike. The different squadrons had a friendly rivalry: the recon pilots kidded the bomber crews when their bombs fell into rice paddies instead of hitting the target. "You're whipping the Japanese all right," they told them. "You're starving them to death." It did not make them popular. P-38 pilots from the 449th laughed at the recon pilots as they taxied by, suited up in fur-lined jackets while the fighter pilots sat alert in t-shirts and shorts.[20] Sometimes a flight of four P-38s returned to base, each with one engine shut down and the propeller feathered just to show off to the single-engine P-40 pilots on the field. The P-40 pilots pointed out that while they had half as many engines, they flew three to four times as many missions. According to Cliff Long, the P-38 pilots were "like kids, outside the fence at a ballgame, and could not get in to play."[21] The fighter pilots were "much appreciated" by the transport crews, but according to Bob Binzer, they had little to do with the "truck drivers" on the other side of the field.[22] Despite the rivalries, the men knew they were on the same team and worked hard to carry out each piece of the mission.

On November 20, Bill Deen accompanied eight P-38s in an attack on a wooden bridge near Wan Lai Kam, 120 miles southeast of Lashio on the highway from northern Thailand to Meiktila, Burma. Rather than the usual practice of skip- or dive-bombing with demolition bombs, one of the Lightnings carried two 500-pound incendiary cluster bombs and the other seven each carried two 165-gallon tanks of napalm. The fuel-gel mixture readily adhered to most surfaces and was absolutely deadly. It was normally used against personnel, who died from immolation or asphyxiation when it ignited. The 25th Fighter Squadron used it on Japanese positions in Tengchong and elsewhere on the Salween Front, where it proved useful in burning the enemy out of their tunnels and trenches. The 69th Wing hoped it would be equally useful burning down wooden bridges. The napalm ignited, covering the bridge in flames, but according to Jim Heitkotter, "the constant high humidity there had the timber so saturated they did not ignite." The napalm burned furiously for eight minutes without doing any apparent damage. The P-38 pilots were frustrated. "One 500-pounder would have done it," said Heitkotter. "We had our own brand of snafus you see."[23] The Lightning loaded with incendiaries bombed a group of buildings west of the bridge and the flight strafed targets on both banks. Bill Deen made six to eight photo passes over the bridge before, during, and after the mission at an average altitude of 5,500 feet. He brought back excellent pictures, returning to Yunnanyi with four of the P-38s. The other four landed at Tingkawk Sakan.

Because fuel, ordnance, and ammunition were at a premium in China, the P-38s and B-25s often landed at Tingkawk Sakan after attacking targets in Burma or on the Salween Front. John Habecker and the 528th moved from the field to China after the fall of Myitkyina. The 80th Fighter Group had a squadron of P-47s there. The fighters and bombers from China rearmed and refueled, often flying another mission on the way back to Yunnanyi. They called it "shuttle bombing." It was Chennault's way of getting two missions for the price of one. Because of the tall trees, the strip was particularly difficult for the B-25s. "When flying overhead it looked like a match stick in the jungle," said Chapman Hale. "I remember struggling to get over those two-

On November 20, 1944, Bill Deen accompanied eight P-38s to the highway bridge at Wan Lai Kam, Burma. One of his pictures captured a fighter dropping napalm on the bridge. *National Archives*

Lieutenant Frank McKinney resented being assigned to a reconnaissance squadron and yearned for the excitement of fighters. He routinely flew much lower on his missions than was deemed safe. He disappeared over Thailand on November 5, 1944. *Courtesy of Sterling Barrow*

hundred-foot trees at the end."[24] P-38 pilot Jerry Doughty remembered the runway being "just long enough and wide enough to get a plane up and down. That is, if you held your elbows in." The quarters, mess hall, and latrines were all in tents. "At night, you were lulled to sleep by the wailing of animals," remembered Doughty. "It reminded me of the comic strip *Terry and the Pirates*."[25] Barrow was the only pilot from G Flight to land at the field. Most of the reconnaissance flight's missions ventured too far south to make the detour worthwhile.

G Flight continued their excellent photographic coverage, flying twenty-five missions in October and thirty in November. On November 5, Frank McKinney took off in ship number "811" on another mission to Thailand. This time, he planned to cover Uttaradit, Lampang, Chiang Mai, and the Wan Lai Kam Bridge. Deen and Barrow helped him get ready and saw him off at 1100. It was his fifth combat mission. Barrow had not flown the route before, but he would several times before the end of the campaign. It should have taken approximately five hours, over miles and miles of unpopulated, dense tropical forests. Besides time and heading, the only way to navigate was by the contours of rivers. McKinney never returned. At first, Deen and Barrow thought he must have landed elsewhere, possibly because of weather or a maintenance issue. "We didn't get too concerned about Mac until the other bases within range could be checked," said Barrow. "Bear in mind this was 1944 in China without instantaneous communications." When he left China in May 1945, Barrow still did not know what happened to his friend. McKinney "was one helluva pilot," he said. "I flew formation with him, buzzed with him, and saw him off and back on all his missions." He never gave up on getting into a plane with guns, though. Barrow thought he was probably flying too low and got jumped by enemy fighters. "He was an excellent pilot, but lacked good judgment in my opinion," he said. "One of these days his plane will be found amongst all that dense forest of Southeast Asia." Art Clark thought he probably went down attempting to get through a thunderstorm on his way back to Yunnanyi. Whatever the reason, McKinney was G Flight's first loss. His disappearance haunted his friends. For Barrow, it was made all the worse by the fact that Bill Deen also disappeared. Deen never felt confident flying in the weather. "I don't know if he had any near misses that shook him up or not," commented Barrow. On August 1, 1945, just weeks before the end of the war, he was flying on instruments from Nanning to Zhanyi and reportedly crashed into a mountain.[26]

On November 11—one week after McKinney's disappearance—eight P-38s from the 449th and nine P-51s from the 25th flew an offensive reconnaissance mission to investigate the airfields and railway between Chiang Mai and Ban Dara in the area where McKinney disappeared. The P-51s were brand new. Cliff Long, William Mitchell, Henry Minco, and nine other pilots had just picked up a dozen of them from Calcutta and flew them over the Hump on November 2.[27] The formation departed Yunnanyi at 0920. One of the P-38s turned back shortly after takeoff because of engine trouble, but the rest of the formation continued to Thailand at fifteen thousand feet. Over Chiang Mai, four of the Mustangs dropped down to sweep the airfield and follow the railway at low altitude toward Ban Dara. The other twelve fighters stayed high to cover them. The flight of P-51s damaged a locomotive and strafed a single airplane on the field at Lampang before five Ki-27b Nates (called "Ota" in Thai service) from the Royal Thai Air Force (RTAF) jumped the top cover.

P-38s and P-51s take off on a joint mission. On November 11, 1944, seven Lightnings from the 449th and nine Mustangs from the 25th encountered five Thai Ki-27s over Lampang. All five Thai fighters were destroyed, but Lieutenant Henry Minco was missing in action. ***Courtesy of Bruce Carnachan***

When the JAAF upgraded to the Oscar in 1942, it gave the RTAF many of its obsolete Nates—a small, single-seat fighter with fixed undercarriage. The Ki-27s posed a challenge to the American fighters. According to Joe Fodor: "they were maneuverable as hell, but slow as hell." Pilot Officer Kamrop Bleangkam and Chief Warrant Officer Chuladit Detkanchorn attacked the Lightnings. Captain Dale Desper led his flight of P-38s in a head-on pass. All four of them scored hits on Chuladit's fighter, which erupted in flames; Chuladit bailed out. Dick Conway claimed another Nate as probably destroyed before Kamrop shot out his left engine. Kamrop claimed him as destroyed, but in fact he immediately turned for home and made an emergency landing at an auxiliary field at Simao, only 170 miles from the Thai border. Kamrop then attacked Lieutenant Leonard Flomer from behind, setting his right wingtip gas tank on fire and sending the young pilot into a panic. According to Fodor: "He was holding the mic button down and hollering: 'Somebody get this Jap off my ass!'" Captain Desper came to his rescue, damaging the Thai fighter and forcing it to crash land. He was upset with Flomer for panicking and abandoning good radio discipline. He angrily told him that if he wanted him to, he could stop the burning plane in midair and "I'll get out and piss on it for you!" According to Fodor, he was "madder than hell" because he had to leave the fight to escort Flomer's damaged fighter back to Yunnanyi.

The other three Nates hit the Mustangs. Lieutenant Roger Vadenais was one of the flight leaders. Henry Minco was flying on his wing. He saw the three Nates diving on the formation from above. "Do you see them, Vad?" he radioed. "Got them," Vadenais responded. The small fighters flashed by. Vadenais missed on the first pass, but pulled around and fired again. He saw the propeller break off one of the Nates as his bullets struck home. Minco saw two Thai fighters below him; he broke away from Vadenais and dove to attack. "I've got one trapped in the valley down here!" he called out on the radio. According to Joe Fodor: "That was the last we ever heard of him." His P-51 was the only American loss on the mission. The RTAF lost all five Ki-27s: Flight Lieutenant Chalermkiats made a forced landing after getting hit in the engine. Chief Warrant Officer Nat Thara Kaimuk crashed nine miles from Lampang. Chief Warrant Officer Nat Sunthorn bailed out, but later died from his wounds. After the dogfight over Lampang, the RTAF no longer challenged American fighters over Thailand. Through persistent sweeps of the railroad between the wrecked bridges at Dara and Kaeng Luang, the 14th Air Force effectively put an end to a very important supply route.[28]

Cliff Long was saddened to hear about the loss of Henry Minco. They were good friends, having both trained at Perry, Florida, before deploying to China. Minco was a good pilot, with over seventy combat missions. However, he had no more than twenty hours and no formal training in the P-51. He told Long before the mission he had a premonition of his own death. Later, there was a rumor around the squadron that a missionary found Minco in his parachute—his head severed, possibly in the bailout—and buried him. After the war, a team from the American Graves Registration Service (AGRS) attempted to find the wreck northeast of Lampang. Their report recommended calling off the search because the thick jungle and annual monsoon rains made it hazardous and hopeless. A panel of officers later declared his remains unrecoverable.[29]

As for Frank McKinney, the China Zone of Graves Registration searched his route of flight up to the China border and coordinated with the India-Burma Zone to see if they discovered any remains in their sector. Neither zone found anything that correlated to McKinney. Due to the lack of information, they declared him "KIA-Body unrecoverable" in May 1948. The search did not include any of McKinney's route over Thailand. On May 27, 2012, Captain Sakpinit Promthep from the RTAF Museum e-mailed me that during the relocation of historical documents after a flood, he found a report detailing a plane crash on November 5, 1944. The report said that at 1340, during a heavy rain storm, a twin-engine plane was struck by lightning. Witnesses on the ground heard an explosion and saw the plane catch fire and crash in the jungle near Ban Mae Kua, in Lampang Province. The authorities discovered the plane was a P-38 marked with a white star on a blue disk and the number "811" on the tail. They also found a skull in the wreck.[30] Hak Hakanson visited Ban Mae Kua in March 2014. He spoke with a Buddhist monk there who indicated McKinney's remains were likely cremated and his ashes scattered to the winds in accordance with traditional Buddhist practices. More than sixty years later, Sterling Barrow was relieved but sad to hear the fate of his friend. "I've enjoyed reminiscing about our experiences in China," he said, "but I'd rather be sitting down with Bill Deen and Frank McKinney over a cold one face to face—maybe in another life."[31]

The Final Battle

There was little activity on the ground after the failed Japanese counteroffensive in September 1944. It was only after the resolution of the political crisis and Stilwell's departure from the theater that the CEF finally resumed the offensive. They faced a Japanese division with its supply lines in a shambles and with no hope of reinforcement. Two months of hard fighting would bring them to Wanding, the last bastion of the 56th Division in China. There, they fought the final battle to liberate western Yunnan from the Japanese. At the same time, the X Force in Burma drove toward Bhamo against the tattered remains of the 18th Division. The victory for which Stilwell had worked so hard was shortly at hand, though neither he nor Dorn would be around to see it through to the end.

While the B-25s and P-38s wreaked havoc on Japanese supply lines and the Chinese troops waited out the political crisis, the 25th Fighter Squadron kept heavy pressure on the front. The pilots were frustrated by the lack of progress. While they continued to daily risk their lives in the air, they grew cynical over whether the Chinese would do their part on the ground. They continued to fly their missions in spite of their mounting pessimism though. On October 13, four P-40s attacked the road bridge south of Mangshi with 500-pound bombs. Lieutenant Charles White was the flight leader and Lieutenant Ankris flew his wing. Vadenais led the second element and William Mitchell flew tail-end Charlie. "The flight to Mangshi was routine," remembered Mitchell. "Soon we passed mountain peaks around Longling and started to move down the west side of the Mangshi Valley." Lieutenant White made a sharp turn over the valley and rolled into his dive. Mitchell continued east, waiting his turn as the three fighters in front of him made their runs, one after another. Their bombs all hit around the bridge without causing much damage. Mitchell rolled in: "The welcoming committee was up there on the foothills surrounding the bridge," he reported. At least three anti-aircraft guns put up an intense barrage. The plane shuddered as he released his bomb. "Almost immediately," he said, "I knew I had been hit." He watched the oil pressure drop. It would be only a matter of minutes before he had to bail out and he and the P-40 "would have to part company." He turned north, putting as much distance as possible between himself and the Japanese. He radioed White that he was going to have to bail out, but there was no answer. He took off his microphone, released his safety harness, and took one last look around the cockpit. "I hated to leave that plane!" he lamented. "We had shared some interesting experiences and it had been a very good P-40. But there was no time for sentimentality." He made it about thirteen miles north of Mangshi before his engine quit. He put the fighter into a climbing left turn, rolled back the canopy, and dove out over the side.

He searched frantically for the ripcord as he tumbled through the air. He found it tucked into the harness and pulled, feeling a sharp jerk as the parachute blossomed overhead. "It was unbelievably quiet and peaceful as I drifted down through the clouds," he remembered. He landed on the north bank of the Shweli River. He was not sure whether he was in Chinese- or Japanese-occupied territory. He heard a machine gun firing in the distance and scrambled for cover. Hiding underneath a tree growing out of a steep embankment, he watched for traffic on the river and a nearby trail. A flight of P-40s passed overhead looking for him, but he dared not expose himself for fear of being caught by the Japanese. As night fell, he left cover and walked to a small farmhouse two hundred yards from the river. He had decided to make contact with the Chinese farmer, but as he walked up to the man, a group of ten soldiers suddenly burst out from the woods behind him. He was relieved to discover they were Chinese. "In seconds they were all around me," he recalled. "One was carrying a Thompson submachine gun. He looked at me, patted the gun, and broke into a big laugh. I frankly didn't share the humor." One of the soldiers explained to him in broken English that they had been on patrol nearby, saw him bail out, and thought he was Japanese. They took him to their bivouac and gave him a ration of rice. The next morning, they set out into the mountains, where they handed him off to a Chinese guerrilla. "He was a small man," remembered Mitchell, "lightly built, with a deeply tanned and wrinkled face. He spoke very little as I followed him through the woods." Local guerrilla fighters had proved useful in gathering intelligence and menacing the Japanese during the XXth Army Group's advance to Tengchong. Now they patrolled the trails crisscrossing the frontier, searching for Japanese stragglers retreating to the south. The man Mitchell followed certainly seemed to be familiar with the thick forests, deep ravines, and steep mountains over which they hiked. It took them four days to reach Tengchong. "I had visited the city many times from the air," said Mitchell, "but this was the first time I had seen the city and its wall from the ground. We passed through a big open gate, and I wondered how Marco Polo had made his entry back in the thirteenth century." Mitchell entered the north side of the city and was surprised to see the wall there mostly intact. He did not have time to visit any of the sections he bombed during the siege. The guerrilla brought him to an American liaison team, which paid him for his services. Within minutes, Mitchell caught a ride on an L-5 to Baoshan, and from there, found a C-47 departing for Yunnanyi. Everyone at the squadron was surprised to see him. Nobody had heard anything since he bailed out. The day after his return, the commander ordered him to India for a brief rest before bringing back one of the squadron's new P-51 Mustangs.[1] Mitchell was lucky. Two other pilots from the 25th were killed in action on the Salween Front after taking ground fire: Lieutenant Lewis Earnest on a mission to Tengchong on May 18, and Flight Officer Lincoln Seguin on a mission near Kunlong Ferry on December 18. A third pilot, Lieutenant Benjamin Parker, bailed out after his fighter was hit on a bombing mission near Mangshi on September 26. A Chinese patrol reported he was captured by the Japanese. He did not survive the war. Colonel Masanobu Tsuji—an officer with possible links to the Bataan Death March and other notorious atrocities—allegedly executed him and ate his liver.[2]

While American airplanes maintained steady pressure from the air, neither the Chinese nor the Japanese took initiative on the ground. Following the counteroffensive in September, the XIth Army Group recaptured the high ground around Longling, but did not make an attempt on the town. Finally, on October 29—only three days after Stilwell left the CBI—the Chinese resumed the offensive. Two divisions of the 71st Army attacked Longling from the east while the veteran 200th Division swung around to cut the Burma Road to the west. The 25th Fighter Squadron supported the attack with thirty-two sorties on the twenty-ninth, forty-one on the thirty-first, thirty-four on November 1, twenty-eight on the second, and thirty-seven on the third.

The air control parties at the front directed the pilots to priority targets in the Longling-Mangshi area.

Lieutenant Colonel John Habecker was a new arrival to the 25th. When the 528th moved to China in August, the 14th Air Force decided to make use of Habecker's close air support experience on the Salween Front. He took command of the 25th in October and Hank Amen moved up to a job at group headquarters. On November 1, Habecker led a three-ship of P-40s to attack a gun emplacement on a hill southwest of Longling. The 200th Division advanced within three miles of the city on the first day of the offensive, but the stubborn hill position barred further progress. The situation called for closer air support than usual. Each of the three fighters dive-bombed with a 500-pound demolition bomb at over 300 miles per hour. Habecker's bomb hit close to the emplacement. The second bomb, dropped by Major Albert Criz, hit dead center. Criz was on his second tour in China, having first served with the AVG. The third bomb, dropped by Flight Officer John Duda, also landed close. Only twenty-five yards away, Chinese troops hugged the ground with panels on their backs to identify them to the fighter pilots. After dive-bombing, the three Warhawks each made two strafing passes to cover the troops as they inched forward, sometimes firing only a few feet in front of them. The Japanese broke and ran under the weight of the assault and the Chinese moved in behind them and took the position. Not one of them was killed or injured. Habecker said the very close support was "like trying to thread a needle while passing it at 350 miles an hour." Frank Dorn commended the pilots, saying it was the finest example of air-to-ground support he had ever seen.[3]

By the end of the day on the first, the 200th Division was only two and a half miles west of Longling. The next day, the Honorable 1st Division captured several Japanese strongpoints east of the city and the 36th Division advanced within one mile to the southeast. Shen You-chih, the conscript from Henan, arrived at the Salween Front in time to fight in the final battle for Longling. He remembered the Japanese fighting tenaciously, despite being cut off from supplies and reinforcements. "They defended their positions with strong determination," he said. But while their determination remained strong, they no longer had an overwhelming advantage in firepower. "The Japanese were no longer as invincible as they were during the earlier phase of the war," he observed. He watched as American fighters rained destruction on enemy positions. "The American pilots fought pretty well to protect us from the sky," he said. For the first time in his five years as a soldier, Shen fought for the side with overwhelming strength.[4] Under attack from the east and west and unable to withstand the terrific onslaught from the air, the remaining Japanese withdrew on the night of November 3. The Honorable 1st Division marched into the ruined city at 2300; barely a single building remained intact.[5]

Frank Dorn thought the CEF should capitalize on the victory at Longling by aggressively pursuing the Japanese as they retreated to Mangshi, fourteen miles to the southwest. Instead, the Chinese delayed. Dorn voiced his concern to Wedemeyer, who explained to Chiang that it was necessary to finish the campaign as quickly as possible so the Y Force could shift east to oppose the Ichi-go offensive. Chiang agreed and issued the necessary orders on November 9.[6] With Tengchong secure, Marshal Wei decided to reorganize the CEF. He dissolved the XXth Army Group, assigning the 54th Army to garrison Tengchong and Longling. He ordered the 53rd Army to drive south and

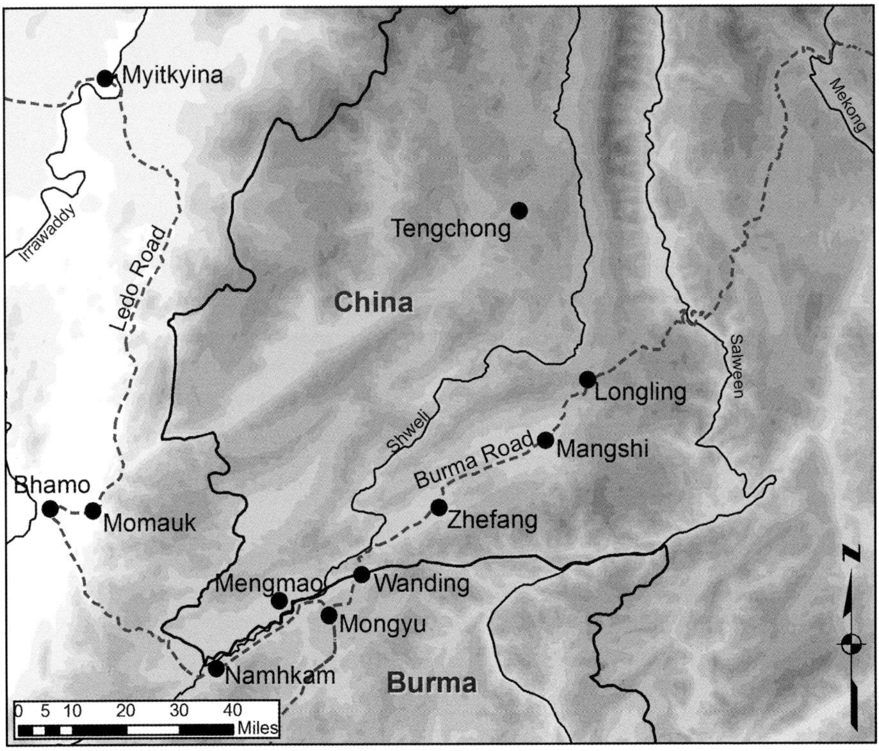

The Final Battle

west along the Shweli River to aid the XIth Army Group in its attack on Mangshi.[7] Six miles north of Longling, the river turns west to parallel the Burma Road all the way to the border. Following the river, the 53rd paralleled the road to the north while the 2nd Army paralleled the road through the mountains to the south. The two armies formed two wings of a double envelopment, while the 71st and 6th armies attacked down the road itself.[8] Facing overwhelming odds and lacking supplies, the Japanese chose to avoid a pitched battle. They demolished what they could and set fire to the rice harvest while delaying the CEF with a rearguard action. The Chinese suffered few casualties as they moved into Mangshi on November 20.[9]

American engineers immediately began clearing mines and booby traps from Mangshi airfield. The field was valuable because instead of air dropping supplies, the 27th Troop Carrier Squadron could land and unload there. It was easier, safer, and considerably less expensive—$49.61 per ton instead of $1,909.65.[10] Jerry Disharoon—a pilot with the 27th—also remembered evacuating wounded Chinese soldiers from the field. There were no litters or seats in the airplane. The crew spread straw on the cabin floor to absorb the blood and laid the injured men side by side. "These were amputees," said Disharoon, "many with gangrene or other wounds that would prevent them from ever returning to the front. The smell was overpowering and after unloading, we pulled out all the plugs from the windows to air out the plane on the way home." The C-47s also flew sections of pipe into the field for the gasoline pipeline that would eventually run from Ledo to Kunming. The sections were so long, they reached all the way from the cabin bulkhead, out the cargo door, to back underneath the tail.[11]

Wei's troops methodically cleaned up pockets of resistance around Mangshi and continued toward Zhefang, the next town on the Burma Road. Using the double envelopment again, they outflanked the small delaying force and occupied the town on December 1. By the end of the year, they were on the threshold of Wanding, on the China-Burma border.[12] Meanwhile, in mid-October, the X Force in Burma—now under the command of Lieutenant General Dan Sultan—advanced in three columns: one toward China down the Myitkyina-Bhamo Road, one south toward the lower Shweli Valley, and one down the railway from Mogaung toward Mandalay. After the battle of Myitkyina, four thousand fresh reinforcements from the United States joined the survivors of Galahad to form the 5332nd Brigade (Provisional), dubbed the Mars Task Force. Brigadier General Thomas Arms organized and trained the brigade, but he was injured in a car accident and passed command to Brigadier General John P. Willey at the end of October. The Chinese Army in India, now five divisions strong, was organized into the New 1st Army under the command of General Sun Liren. The 38th Division led the advance on Bhamo. The Japanese were dug in along the Taping River, fifteen miles north of the town. The Chinese crossed unopposed several miles upstream and outflanked the enemy positions in a sweeping envelopment that brought them out on the Bhamo

Chinese X Force troops fire at Japanese positions in Bhamo with a 105mm howitzer, December 11, 1944. *National Archives via Samuel Hui*

Plain on November 10.[13] From the Taping, the Mytikyina-Bhamo Road runs eleven miles south to Momauk before heading west seven miles to Bhamo. The Chinese encountered heavy resistance at Momauk, but the Japanese were outnumbered and outgunned. On November 14, the survivors retreated to Bhamo, some without rifles or even shoes.[14] The X Force quickly surrounded the city and began making inroads against its defenses. Cut off from supplies and reinforcement, what was left of the 18th Division broke out from the city on the early morning of December 15, retreating toward Namkham. From Bhamo, it was only fifty miles to the Y Force in China.

Marshal Wei waited to attack Wanding until after the X Force advanced past Bhamo. He wanted to make sure it did not bog down in another siege like at Myitkyina. Wedemeyer personally visited Wei's headquarters on December 20 to impress upon him the need to finish the campaign as quickly as possible. While more diplomatic with the generalissimo, Wedemeyer's ignorance of the Far East showed in his dealings with subordinate commanders. He and Dorn found Wei accompanied by a dozen of his staff officers. "After brusquely cutting through the amenities," remembered Dorn, "Wedemeyer launched into a windy, half speech-half lecture ... if Wanding was not taken by a certain date, he would withdraw all American personnel—medical, air, liaison, and supply—from the CEF." Wei was shocked. Wedemeyer put him in a difficult position: To comply with such an order after being confronted in such a direct and aggressive manner, in front of his subordinates no less, would mean a serious loss of face.[15] "Every Chinese in the room turned to look questioningly at me," said Dorn. "There was nothing I could do, except to shake my head." Wei knew with the end of the campaign so near, Wedemeyer could not follow through on his threat. He decided to ignore the order and attack in his own time.[16]

Dorn tried to speak with Wedemeyer about his mishandling of the situation, but the latter resented the criticism and took it very personally. He already disliked Dorn because he felt his negative attitude about Chiang and the Nationalist government was an unfortunate artifact of the Stilwell regime—a stumbling block that had to be removed. The exceptional working relationship Dorn had built with Wei and Xiao did not signify compared to this perceived greater issue. His time was almost up. On December 27, Major General Robert McClure, Wedemeyer's chief of staff, sent Dorn a memo informing him that Wedemeyer was splitting Chinese Training and Combat Command into separate training and combat components. Dorn thought the split was a bad idea, but Wedemeyer's mind was made. He thought Dorn's disagreement with this most recent issue fit into a general trend of insubordination and disloyalty to his command—it was the last straw. On January 6, McClure arrived in Kunming and announced he was taking over Chinese Combat Command. Dorn was to report to Wedemeyer in Chongqing. When he got there, Wedemeyer scolded him for acting too much like an "independent warlord" and ordered him back to the United States. Officially, he reported that Dorn was showing the strain of too many years in combat overseas.[17]

Dorn's fitness report, dated January 25, 1945, reflected the bitterness that had come to characterize so much of the American effort in China. Wedemeyer rated him "excellent" in performance of his duties, physical activity, and physical endurance, but only "superior" in knowledge of his profession. He would not recommend him for command, only "as an assistant." He reported that Dorn was not willing to support the plans of his superiors regardless of personal views and ranked him 499 out of 500 general officers he personally knew—a hurtful exaggeration. At the end he remarked: "This officer is bright, clever, and decisive. He is of questionable loyalty, uncooperative, extremely selfish, of immature judgment, and not dependable." It was a death sentence for Dorn's career. He wrote a rebuttal to the Adjutant General in Washington, claiming Wedemeyer's remarks were "matters of opinion only, and are not based on fact." He asked that reference be made to previous fitness reports that showed his consistent excellence. "Shortly after their arrival in China," Dorn explained, "Generals Wedemeyer and McClure made frequent remarks of a critical and disparaging nature—both as statements and by obvious inference—that many affairs had been run in a careless manner by the former commander and his staff, in general that everything was wrong." In other words, he felt there was a prejudice against anything related to Stilwell from the outset and that he was a victim of that prejudice. When he tried to advise Wedemeyer about how to work effectively with the Chinese, he found his advice and experience unwelcome.

Dorn packed his things and departed in late January. "Leaving China was a great sadness for me," he related. "It had indeed been my second country in which I had many roots." In a farewell letter, Marshal Wei expressed regret at his departure. "The sincere association between us during the past year has always impressed me," he wrote. "We believe it is your deliberate war plan relating to the continued operations along the Salween Front that has helped us lead this conflict to a success." Though Dorn began his service in the Far East linked to the rising star of Joseph Stilwell, when that star fell, he had built enough of his own reputation that he remained to continue the Salween Campaign. Unfortunately, that momentum only carried him just short of the finish line before his star also fell.[18]

On December 24, Wei ordered the 53rd Army to occupy the Shweli Valley to Mengmao, seventeen miles west of Wanding, and to cross the river to cut the Burma Road at Namtao. This would prevent the Japanese from reinforcing Wanding. The 53rd began the Salween Campaign with 20,255 men, twelve 75-millimeter pack howitzers, and twelve 37-millimeter anti-tank guns. After the campaign over the Gaoligong, the siege of Tengchong, and the advance down the Shweli to Zhefang, it was down to only 13,835 men, ten howitzers, and six anti-tank guns, including 1,797 new recruits and 2,453 casualties returned to service. The constant wear and strain of battle had taken its toll. The 116th Division led the advance on Mengmao, pushing back the enemy patrols around the town. On January 3, 1945, Wei finally sent the 2nd Army forward in an attack on the Japanese right flank at Wanding itself. The 9th Division broke through into the city, but the Japanese pushed them back in bitter hand-to-hand fighting. On the fourth, one battalion from each division of the 53rd Army entered Mengmao. Bombing and strafing by several flights of fighters the day before left twenty Japanese soldiers dead and a good portion of the city in ruins. With his right flank secure, Wei ordered one division of the 53rd to cross the Shweli and attack Wanding on the Japanese left. The crossing met a determined counterattack by two Japanese regiments and the attack stalled. The battle for Wanding was at an impasse.[19]

Meanwhile, the X Force in Burma drove up the lower reaches of the Shweli Valley from Namhkam toward Wanding. On January 9, 53rd Army patrols from Mengmao made contact with advanced elements of the 38th Division. On the sixteenth, the X Force occupied Namkham after a brief skirmish with the enemy rearguard. The next day, the Mars Task Force fought its way to the Burma Road between Wanding and Lashio.

Resistance was far less than expected. Most of the Japanese 33rd Army fell back to Mandalay. Only the 56th Division remained to make a final stand at Wanding, while just one regiment of the 49th Division held the junction at Mongyu, where the new Ledo Road would join the old Burma Road into China. With the Mars Task Force cutting the road from Lashio, the 56th Division estimated it could only hold out for one more week.

Tanks from the 1st Provisional Tank Group move into Hsenwi, Burma, on February 24, 1945. *National Archives via Samuel Hui*

On January 10, a flight of six B-25s from the 22nd Bomb Squadron attacked hill positions on the Japanese right flank at Wanding in a rare close support mission. Four of the bombers each carried six 250-pound bombs, while the other two each carried sixteen 100-pounders. The mission was carefully coordinated to avoid friendly casualties. A P-51 escorted the bombers to the target from Yunnanyi. Another fighter pilot flew in the copilot seat of the lead bomber. Both had made several flights to Wanding in the preceding days. Over the target, the escorting Mustang peeled off and marked the Japanese positions with rockets. Jim White was the bombardier on the lead B-25 and sat in the "greenhouse" in the nose. The pilot put the "J" model into a 200-mile-per-hour dive toward the hill. When he got within range, he opened fire with the four .50-caliber machine guns mounted in pods on the outside of the nose. The top turret gunner opened fire with his twin .50-cals and White let loose with the single flex-fifty mounted in the bombardier compartment. "The

A pair of 25th Fighter Squadron P-51Cs join up with a 22nd Bomb Squadron B-25 over Wanding in January 1945. *National Archives*

din was unbelievable," he remarked. "Within seconds, the greenhouse was filled with acrid smoke and the stench of cordite." The pilot dropped the bombs at one hundred feet and pulled up and to the left in a "gut-wrenching" chandelle. White looked back at the target area and saw the second B-25 making its pass. "We saw Jap troops stand and fire at him as he passed overhead," said White. One after another, the bombers attacked. After the sixth bomber made its run, the ships wheeled around to continue strafing. "By now, the remaining Japs were desperate enough that they were sporadically returning our machine gun fire," he observed. Again, his B-25 opened up with its seven forward-firing fifties. An observer sitting in the green house with him asked "what those white balls zipping through the air might be."

"Tracers, old buddy," was White's matter-of-fact reply. "They're shooting back." The observer was shocked. The color drained from his face and he sat down in fearful silence. The attack was devastating; all of the bombs hit the target area. The Chinese reported finding over four hundred bodies when they took the hill several hours later. The attack aided their incremental advance into the city, but it was not decisive.[20]

Colonel Stodter, promoted to command all the liaison teams attached to the XIth Army Group, suggested a surprise attack on the center of the Japanese line. He believed it was weak after reinforcing against attacks on the right and left. He and his teams worked with the Chinese to plan a coordinated air, artillery, and infantry assault. On January 19, he watched from an observation post as they advanced. Artillery, mortars, and machine guns pounded the Japanese positions. As soon as the curtain of fire lifted the infantry attacked, sweeping across the line with grenades and bayonets. The front became a bloody free-for-all. The Japanese tried to rally for a counterattack, but the overwhelming assault left them no room to regroup. On the morning of the twentieth, Xiong Xinmin, vice commander of the 88th Division, sent out patrols to reconnoiter the enemy positions. "Our patrols went right up to their bunkers and discovered there

was no sign of Japanese troops at all," he remembered. "They waved their hands and shouted, 'There aren't any enemy soldiers here!'"[21] Leading elements of the 9th Division found the town of Wanding completely empty—the Japanese had abandoned the city. In stark contrast to their suicide stands elsewhere during the war, in the final battle on the Salween Front, they simply withdrew. In order to avoid an incident with the X Force, Wei ordered the advance to stop at the Burma border. The 53rd Army pulled back into China and waited for Sun Liren's divisions to clear the junction at Mongyu. For seven days, the X Force battled the remnants of the 56th Division as it retreated south from Wanding. On January 27, they mistakenly fired on Y Force soldiers holding at the border. Brigadier General George W. Sliney, sector chief of artillery for the X Force, realized what was happening and threw himself into the line of fire, yelling for them to stop. The troops ceased fire. Sliney, who walked out of Burma with Stilwell in 1942, now walked across the line to greet the Chinese Expeditionary Force. The troops cheered and surged forward to shake his hand. With their bedraggled cotton uniforms, rope sandals, and bolt-action rifles, they made for a great contrast to their X Force comrades with khaki uniforms, leather shoes, and semi-automatic Garands. "While I recognized that the soldiers of the X Force were Chinese like us," said Yang Chien-chiu, the platoon commander from Sichuan, "they had much better equipment than us. Our mules looked like puppies compared to their horses."[22] The X and Y forces mingled freely together, celebrating the momentous occasion. The Salween Campaign was complete. The blockade of China was over.[23]

Colonel John H. Stodter (left) worked with the Chinese to plan a surprise attack on the Japanese center at Wanding on January 19, 1945. Here he watches from an observation post in June 1944 with Frank Dorn, Lieutenant Colonel Frank J. Sherman, and Lieutenant Colonel John Darrah. ***Hoover Institution***

Epilogue: The Open Road

When Colonel Lewis Pick became the chief engineer for the Ledo Road in October 1943, he called his staff together. "I've heard the same story all the way from the States," he told them. "It's always the same. The Ledo Road can't be built. Too much rain, too much mud, too much malaria. From now on we are forgetting this defeatist spirit. The Ledo Road is going to be built. Mud, rain, and malaria be damned!"[1] Thirteen months later, shortly after the X Force captured Bhamo, Pick's engineers connected the Ledo Road to the old Burma Road. To make the project possible, he had to make a number of compromises. Instead of a two-way, all-weather highway as originally planned, it could only accommodate traffic in a single direction and was barely usable during the summer monsoon. Nevertheless, it was an impressive accomplishment. The inaugural convoy departed Ledo on January 12, 1944. It passed through Myitkyina on the fifteenth and arrived at Namhkam a week later. All along the route, soldiers and engineers stopped what they were doing to watch the line of jeeps and trucks drive past. To them, it represented the culmination of an impossible effort. At Namhkam, the convoy stopped to wait for the X Force to finish clearing out the last pockets of Japanese resistance before continuing on to China.

Meanwhile, another convoy crossed into China via the Tengchong Cutoff. While Pick preferred the route through Bhamo, the Chinese worked to improve the trail between Tengchong and Myitkyina. Twenty thousand laborers, many from the recently liberated towns and villages in Tengchong County, worked feverishly to put the road into service. With the help of a small group of American engineers led by Colonel Robert Seedlock, they cleared 145 miles in less than sixty days.[2] Unfortunately, the route's steep grades and sharp curves limited the number and type of vehicles it could accommodate. The small convoy consisted of only jeeps and light trucks under the command of Captain Richard C. Gales. The convoy's chief mechanic, Staff Sergeant Michael Paolucci, had to rebuild two clutches because of the rigorous mountain driving. "At one point," said Gales, "we had to push those vehicles up a mountain by hand. Chinese workmen helped us. We made just 14 miles that day." The convoy encountered landslides and drove through torrential rains. When it arrived at Tengchong, Colonel Seedlock and a local magistrate drove out to meet it and escorted it into the city. The people gave Gales and his men a tremendous welcome. On January 22, after sixteen grueling days, they delivered their eleven tons of cargo to Kunming. It was the first convoy to reach China from Burma since May 5, 1942, though it was not billed as such, since it did not take the "official" route. Despite the reception in Tengchong, the convoy elicited little fanfare in Kunming. It did prove that the Tengchong Cutoff was passable, though it remained an emergency route far too hazardous for most of the convoys bound for China. Only sixty-five vehicles made use of the cutoff before the end of the war.[3]

On January 21, 1945, Cliff Long, William Mitchell, Perry Endelman, and William Smith took off from Baoshan to cover the flag raising ceremony at Wanding. It was Long's ninety-sixth combat mission. The 25th stationed two flights of P-40s at Baoshan's grass airfield in mid-December to keep the fighters close to the front as

P-40s from the 25th Fighter Squadron at Baoshan in late-1944 or early-1945. Cliff Long, William Mitchell, Perry Endelman, and William Smith took off from Baoshan on January 21, 1945, to cover the flag raising ceremony at Wanding. ***Courtesy of Clifford Long***

the Chinese engaged in the last battles of the campaign. The squadron's P-51s remained at Yunnanyi. After circling Wanding for thirty minutes, the four pilots began to notice puffs of smoke around the town. As a small brass band labored through an unrecognizable tune, artillery shells suddenly crashed down from the surrounding hills. Dignitaries and generals dove for cover. A liaison plane radioed that the shells were coming from a gun position on a ridge south of the town. Chinese artillery marked the target with smoke shells and the P-40s dropped their external fuel tanks and rolled in for a series of strafing runs. They silenced the position within ten minutes of it opening fire. The generals and politicians dusted themselves off and the band members picked up their instruments and resumed their noise-making. The ceremony continued on.[4] Things had come a long way from May 1942, when American airplanes had no communication with Chinese troops as both fought independently to stop the Japanese at the Salween River. Thanks to the practices pioneered by the Chindits and Air Commandos, as well as efforts by YFOS tactical air control parties and of men like John Habecker and Raymond Arimond, coordination and cooperation steadily improved. By the end of the campaign, information traveled smoothly and quickly from the troops on the ground to the fighters in the air. The 14th Air Force contributed 4,677 fighter sorties and 960 medium bomber sorties to support the Salween Campaign. The 27th Troop Carrier Squadron flew 4,952 sorties and delivered over ten thousand tons of supplies.

On January 28, the road from Namhkam to Wanding was deemed safe for travel and the inaugural convoy continued to Kunming. Sixty percent of the American troops that worked on the Ledo Road were African-Americans, including fifty-two of the fifty-eight truck companies. Pick wanted them to be fairly represented in the inaugural convoy, but Chiang Kai-shek expressly prohibited any of them from entering Kunming. Pick reluctantly agreed to a compromise. The African-Americans drove most of the way; on the morning of February 4, Chinese drivers took over for the final leg. After a drive of 1,074 miles from Ledo, India, the long line of trucks rumbled into the provincial capital decorated with small Chinese and American flags. Brigadier General Pick led the convoy standing in his jeep, waving at the cheering crowds. Governor Long Yun held a banquet in honor of the open road. Chiang suggested it be named after General Stilwell. It remains a mystery as to whether he meant to be sincere or ironic.

In all, the Stilwell Road delivered 38,062 tons of cargo between February

Soldiers of the X and Y forces form up near Wanding to celebrate the end of the blockade of China. *National Archives*

Chinese and American military leaders and politicians meet at Wanding on January 28, 1944, as the inaugural convoy enters China. From left to right: Marshal Wei Lihuang, Brigadier General Lewis Pick, Major General Claire Chennault, Lieutenant General Dan Sultan, T.V. Song, and Major General Sun Liren. *National Archives*

Brigadier General Lewis Pick leads the official inaugural convoy across the China-Burma border. Pick had to make a number of compromises to finish the road on time, but it was an impressive accomplishment nevertheless. ***National Archives***

and October 1945.[5] General William Tunner, commander of the airlift, thought it was a wasted effort. In July 1945, his transports delivered 71,042 tons with an accident rate of only .239 incidents per thousand flying hours.[6] Every day, an average of 650 planes flew between India and China. Tunner argued that the campaign in Burma should have stopped at Myitkyina. Once the airfield there was in friendly hands, his transports could fly the safer route further south. Proponents of the road pointed out that given the modest beginnings and difficult conditions of the airlift, few thought of it as anything more than an emergency measure until well into 1944. Besides, even with the airlift serving as the primary means of delivering aid to China, the road could accommodate heavy equipment that could not fit on airplanes. They argued that a long-term solution still depended on retaking Rangoon or capturing a port on China's east coast.

But the Salween Campaign was about more than just a road to China. During the course of the campaign, the Chinese Expeditionary Force fought over the highest and most difficult battlefield terrain of World War II to liberate Tengchong, Longling, Mangshi, Wanding, and four hundred smaller towns and villages occupied for more than two years by the Japanese—a total of twenty-four thousand square miles. It was the first time a Chinese army defeated the Japanese and successfully removed them from occupied territory. The campaign proved that properly trained, supplied, and led, Chinese soldiers were capable of defeating a modern enemy. The CEF lost 28,384 soldiers to battle and disease, compared to an estimated 10,620 dead Japanese.[7]

It was a high price, but compared to operations elsewhere in China, it represented a dramatic improvement. During the first phase of Ichi-go, for example, the Chinese lost 21,643 killed, while the victorious Japanese lost only 1,061. At first, the Chinese required an overwhelming numerical advantage to attack their well-entrenched foe. As they learned and improved, they became more capable and efficient.[8] Though often frustrated by their poor leadership and lack of technical ability, American liaison teams were impressed by the bravery and fortitude of the common Chinese soldier. For their part, the Chinese were grateful for the Americans that fought and died with them. Throughout the course of the campaign, at least twelve Americans attached to YFOS and eighteen from the 69th Composite Wing died supporting the CEF. They did not die in vain. The campaign proved that supporting foreign armies with American airpower, equipment, training, and advice allowed the United States to successfully wage a major offensive for a relatively modest investment. It was an example on a small scale of what *could* have been accomplished had there been cooperation, instead of conflict, between Chiang, Chennault, and Stilwell.

For his part, Stilwell went on to command the U.S. 10th Army in Okinawa until the end of the war. Dorn eventually joined him and then took a job with the 11th

Chinese and American troops load horses and mules from the X Force aboard a 319th Troop Carrier Squadron (Commando) C-47 as part of Operation Grubworm, General Wedemeyer's airlift of five Chinese divisions to stop the Japanese offensive on the Guizhou Plateau. *National Archives*

Airborne Division in the occupation of Japan. While accepting the Japanese surrender at Sendai, he met Yuzo Matsuyama, commander of the 56th Division. The general presented his sword to Dorn. "Yuzo Matsuyama, I am the American general on whose head you placed a bounty when I was with the Chinese fighting your division in the Salween Campaign," Dorn told him. "Your officers and men fought stubbornly and suffered great hardships as well as many thousands of casualties. For that I respect them as soldiers. We came very close to destroying your 56th Division. Now, as its commander, you are presenting your sword in surrender to me." He paused thoughtfully for a moment. "You may keep your sword in memory of the dead who fought so valiantly. The loss of your division was enough. I will not take the sword from you." Matsuyama was stunned; he bowed respectfully and walked away. For Dorn, it was a moment of closure after being dismissed before the end of the campaign. Stilwell's closure came as he watched the surrender ceremony aboard the USS *Missouri* in Tokyo Bay. Thereafter, he returned to the United States and his health deteriorated rapidly. He died of stomach cancer on October 12, 1946. His last note to Dorn was an autographed photo which read: "To Frank Dorn: Enemy of stuffed shirts and a loyal friend in time of need. Joseph W. Stilwell, General, USA." Like his rivals, Chennault did not have the satisfaction of seeing the war in China to the end. Having made too many enemies in the War Department, he resigned in August 1945 after General Arnold moved the 10th Air Force to China and drove him to irrelevancy. Marshal Wei Lihuang continued to serve the Nationalists in the Chinese Civil War following the defeat of Japan. Chiang gave him the impossible job of stopping the Communists in Manchuria. He failed and was stripped of his rank and put under house arrest. He escaped to Hong Kong in 1949 and eventually moved to Beijing in 1955, defecting to the People's Republic. He died in obscurity in 1960.[9]

Though the Salween Campaign was ultimately successful, elsewhere in China, the Ichi-go offensive carried all the way to the Guizhou Plateau and threatened to cut the road between Kunming and Chongqing. General Wedemeyer began Operation Grubworm on December 5, 1944, to airlift over twenty-five thousand troops from the X Force in Burma to stop the Japanese in China.[10] He eventually moved all five divisions fighting in Burma to the Guizhou Plateau and moved the Y Force forward to defend Kunming. The well-trained and seasoned Chinese troops finally turned back the Japanese and pursued them as they retreated toward the coast. They were within twenty miles of Fort Bayard—where they intended to open a seaport on the south China coast—when the atomic bombs brought the war to a sudden end.

After resisting for most of the war, the effectiveness of the X and Y Forces in combat prompted Chiang Kai-shek to finally agree to a more widespread reorganization of the Chinese Army. He even announced liberal political reforms for the Nationalist government. It was too little too late. Chiang's regime did not do enough to protect the Chinese people from the Japanese invaders or to put an end to the feudal oppression of the peasantry. While most of the nation suffered, the government seemed corrupt and self-centered. China was leached dry by more than eight years of war. Out-of-control inflation reduced most of the population to poverty. Infrastructure was in a shambles. The Communists occupied six times as much territory as they had at the beginning of the war.[11] Mao Zedong played on the disillusionment with Chiang's regime. By 1949, he controlled mainland China and effectively exiled the Nationalists to Taiwan.

The Communists did their best to erase the contributions of the Nationalist Army from the historical record. For people like Liu Cheng-hua—the infantry officer from Hubei injured at Tengchong—it was particularly bitter. "I think the Chinese military under the command of Generalissimo Chiang Kai-shek contributed much to both China and the world," he said. "For us Chinese soldiers, we knew it was our job to follow the national flag wherever it went." After the war, he and a group of other Chinese veterans toured battlefields in Europe, including Normandy. "When people there knew we were veterans of the Chinese Nationalist Army, they treated us like heroes," he remembered. As a member of the Chinese Commandos late in the war, Liu was sent with a team to accept the Japanese surrender at Nanjing. Members of the Communist New 4th Army harassed and shot at his party as soon as they landed on the runway. "I will never forgive them," he said.[12] Yang Chien-chiu felt the same: "I survived the toughest battles of World War II," he said. "Most young people in Taiwan and even mainland China can't imagine it." Of the eighteen men from his class that became platoon leaders in the 36th Division, only four survived the war. "One was later captured and executed by the Communists during the Civil War," Yang remembered. "The other three made it to Taiwan. I am the only one who is still alive today to tell the story."[13] Shao Ying-jen, the orphan from Tengchong who joined the 2nd Divison, retired to his hometown as a schoolteacher. When the Communists took over in 1949, he had to flee once more. He joined a guerrilla unit operating in western Yunnan, but after a six-day battle in November 1950, the People's Liberation Army and local Communist militia drove them into Burma. The Burmese government detained them in concentration camps. Shao spent six and a half years there as a political prisoner before he and nine others from his unit were repatriated to Taiwan in 1957. Once again, he became a teacher and finally retired in 1999.[14] Shen You-chih, the conscript from Henan, acknowledged the corruption of the Nationalist government and the terrible consequences of the broken conscription system. When he returned home after the war, he could not find his family. They might have been killed by famine or the Japanese, or they might have evacuated as refugees. He never found out. "I had a younger brother and sister back then. I never had a chance to meet them again," he recalled sadly. "I did not know where to find them." Still, he was proud to have served as a common soldier under the flag of the Chinese Republic. "To me, it is the prettiest flag in the world," he said. "It symbolized the blood of us Chinese soldiers."[15]

Yang Chien-chiu and his three classmates who survived their service in the 36th Division during the war. They are, from left to right: Yang, Chen Wen-rui, Wang Chuan-fang, and Wang Pin. ***Courtesy of Samuel Hui***

The people of Yunnan remember the joint Chinese-American campaign that liberated them in World War II: "The reason we won the Battle of Tengchong," said

Bi Shixian, "was because of our American ally's support." The people of Tengchong "owe the American people a debt of gratitude which we will never forget."[16] Lu Caiwan felt very grateful for the American support in liberating his hometown: "If we wanted to beat the Japanese, the occupiers, based on our military power at the time," he said, "the gap between our weapons and theirs was really big." China had a lot of manpower, but that alone could not win battles. The weapons and training the Americans gave them proved invaluable.

Despite all the difficulties training and equipping the Chinese troops, the greatest obstacle to operations in CBI was poor leadership. Whether it was political appointees making bad decisions at the front or disagreements at the top between Chiang, Chennault, and Stilwell, a lack of strong leadership and unified vision kept China from reaching its full potential. Chiang's fear of military or political reforms loosening his grip on power certainly made things difficult. Stilwell focused on Burma to the exclusion of events in China. His blatant and public disrespect toward Chiang not only imperiled operations, but also emboldened the generalissimo's political opponents. Neither Stilwell nor Roosevelt gave Chiang credit for the impossibility of his situation. They fundamentally did not understand the precarious state of the Nationalist government or the fractured nature of the coalition of warlords and provinces. For his part, Chennault circumvented the chain of command and overstated the case of airpower. His operations, in part, precipitated a disaster of epic proportions in East China. Many historians have attempted to assign blame to any one of these men while exonerating others. I believe it would be wrong to label Chiang, Chennault, or Stilwell as simply "good" or "bad," "guilty" or "innocent." All had their strengths and weaknesses. All had their adherents and detractors. It would be far better to acknowledge all of them as "flawed," as all humans are, and to say that in the circumstances, they allowed their collective flaws to overwhelm them. They could have learned much from the collaborative spirit of Dorn, Wei, and Xiao, who built a relationship based on mutual respect and understanding to prosecute a successful campaign. They created a bright spot in an otherwise bleak picture. It was a glimpse of what could have been.

Ironically, even though Chiang thought an American air campaign would best fit his needs, he probably would have been better served had he focused on the Chinese Army. A strengthened army could have done more to oppose the Japanese in East China, or liberated more territory before the atomic bombs ended the war. In either case, it would have raised the stock of Chiang's government in the hearts and minds of the people and countered the rising Communist influence. Even just consolidating his divisions would have reduced the burden of manning and supplying such a large standing army on the starving and destitute populace. The immediate payoff of using a technologically-superior Western force—particularly airpower—has been a common temptation throughout history. Often, the short-term gains exact a long-term penalty. When he was working with the Arabs of the Hejaz during the First World War, T.E. Lawrence warned his fellow British advisors: "Do not try to do too much with your own hands. Better the Arabs do it tolerably than that you do it perfectly. It is their war, and you are to help them, not to win it for them."[17] Americans have often had the attitude that they can get it done better and get it done faster doing it themselves. But a people fighting for their own freedom, led to victory by their own leaders, creates a national feeling that foreign troops cannot replicate. It sets up the country to win the peace after winning the war. My anecdotal evidence for this is the reverence people still hold for the Nationalist Army that came to liberate them at Tengchong. It is one of the few places in China where one can see monuments boldly displaying the twelve-pointed star of the Chinese Republic. It is a point of fact that pockets of Nationalist resistance held out in Yunnan long after the rest of China fell to the Communists. Unfortunately, to the majority of the Chinese people, Chiang's overreliance on American airplanes gave the impression he was allowing his people to suffer while he hid safely behind a wall of American wings. Chennault was a tactical genius, but he may have overlooked the sociopolitical effects of this perspective. Stilwell had the right ideas about how to train Chinese troops and lead them in battle, but his emphasis on Burma put his right ideas in the wrong place. Unfortunately, the rivalry between Chiang, Chennault, and Stilwell prevented cooperation that, given the outstanding success of American aircraft and advisors working with Chinese ground troops on the Salween Front, could have changed the course of history.

A monument emblazoned with the twelve-pointed star of the Chinese Republic towers over the Graveyard of the National Heroes at Tengchong. Yunnan Province is one of the few places in the People's Republic of China where one sees the Nationalist emblem prominently displayed. *Author's Photo*

Of course, none of this is meant to suggest the Chinese were not grateful for American air support. Nor is it to suggest the United States should have withheld that support from China. Rather, in the proper context, such as in the campaign on the Salween Front, the combination of Chinese troops and American planes proved to be the right mixture of ingredients. Lu Caiwen highly praised the efforts of the 14th Air Force: "Whenever we talk about the war, we always mention American help," he said. "We can never forget their help." Prior to the arrival of American airplanes, the Japanese controlled the skies. "They were extremely arrogant," said Lu. "They occupied the entire sky. The sky was entirely their territory. After the Flying Tigers came, the sky was *our* territory."[18] When American airplanes first appeared over the Salween Front, the occupiers told the peasants they were Japanese. But those airplanes, flown by brave and skilled airmen, supplied twelve divisions by air, provided some of the best coordinated and well-executed close air support of the war, cut Japanese supply lines, and broke through the fortress walls of Tengchong. The key difference between air support on the Salween Front and Chennault's operations in East China were the Chinese armies that worked in conjunction with, and followed through on, the successes of the American planes.

Despite its success, the history of the Salween Campaign has largely been lost on the vast stage of World War II. Few know about the Chinese and Americans that fought together and died together, side-by-side, for the common cause of freedom. Though I was not involved, or even alive during the campaign, researching it has been a remarkable experience. Sometimes history seems to me as much like an unexplored frontier as the New World was to Columbus. I found myself fascinated by the anachronistic medieval siege at Tengchong in the midst of the twentieth century's greatest conflict. My trips to China, archival research, and interviews became an adventure in their own right. The men I met and became friends with throughout the course of this project are my heroes. They are the men who fought and flew over the most rugged terrain of World War II to storm the walls of Tengchong and open the Burma Road. Their story is one of Chinese and Americans together braving famine, sword, and fire to liberate southwest China.

A stone relief of a P-40 Warhawk on a World War II memorial in Tengchong. The Chinese people were grateful for the American fighters that came and took back the skies from the Japanese. ***Author's Photo***

Appendices
Timeline

1937

May 31—Chennault arrives in China

July 7—Marco Polo Bridge Incident ignites war between Japan and China

November 26—Japanese win Battle of Shanghai

December 13—Japanese capture Nanjing

1938

December—Burma Road opens

1939

May—Japanese begin terror bombing of Chongqing

October 6—Japanese advance stopped at First Battle of Changsha

1940

August—Japanese A6M "Zero" achieves air dominance over China

September 5—Japanese invade Indochina

November 25—Roosevelt authorizes one hundred planes and pilots to China

1941

July 28—First contingent of the AVG arrives in Rangoon

October 8—Chinese win Second Battle of Changsha

December 7—Japanese attack Pearl Harbor, U.S. enters the war

December—AVG meets the JAAF in combat over China and Burma

1942

January 15—Chinese win Third Battle of Changsha

February 24—Stilwell arrives in CBI

March 30—Japanese take Taungoo

April 16—Japanese attack 1st Burma Division at Yenangyaung

April 18—Sun Liren's 38th Division rescues the British at Yenangyaung; Doolittle Raid on Japan

April 29—Japanese take Lashio

May 1—AVG evacuates Loi Wing; Stilwell begins his famous walkout from Burma

May 7—"Tex" Hill leads AVG to bomb the Burma Road in the Salween River Gorge

May 8—Japanese take Myitkyina

May 10—Japanese take Tengchong

May 20—Stilwell's party arrives at Imphal, India

June 23—U.S. War Department orders most of the 10th Air Force to the Middle East

July 4—AVG disbanded; Chennault becomes commander of the China Air Task Force

August 26—Ramgarh Training Center opened in India

1943

January 14-24—Casablanca Conference

February 8—Wingate's Chindits cross the Chindwin River into central Burma

March 5—14th Air Force established in China, Major General Chennault commanding

April 4—Infantry Training Center opens in Kunming

April 13—First class arrives for training at the Field Artillery Training Center

April 30—Stilwell and Chennault meet with Roosevelt in Washington D.C.

June 18—Y Force Operations Staff officially established in Kunming, Frank Dorn Chief of Staff

August 17-24—Quadrant Conference reorganizes CBI Theater, establishes SEAC under Lord Mountbatten

October 5—Stilwell orders Sun Liren to move his troops into the Hukawng Valley

October 30—Chinese meet unexpected resistance from Japanese 18th Division at Yupbang Ga

October 31—5307th Composite Unit (Galahad) begins arriving in Bombay

November—Cochran arrives in India to establish the 1st Air Commando Group

1944

January 8—Galahad transferred From Wingate to Stilwell's command

February 4—Japanese 55th Division attacks British in the Arakan

February 19—Galahad arrives at the front in North Burma

March 7—X Force takes Walawbum

March 8—Japanese advance toward Imphal and Kohima

March 5-11—1st Air Commando Group lands nine thousand Chindits behind enemy lines in Burma

March 24—Wingate dies in plane crash

March 24-26—Battle for the road block at Inkangahtawng

March 30-April 9—Galahad 2nd Battalion under siege at Nhpum Ga

April 14—Chiang approves Salween Offensive

April 17—Japanese launch Ichi-go Offensive in East China

April 21—Stilwell creates End Run Task Force to take Myitkyina

May 1—Dorn moves YFOS Headquarters to Baoshan

May 2—69th Composite Wing Forward Echelon begins operating at Beiting Field, near Yunnanyi

May 11—Forty thousand troops of the Chinese Expeditionary Force cross the Salween River

May 15—Chinese XIth Army Group captures Pingda

May 17—H Force takes the Pamati Airfield west of Myitkyina

May 23—Japanese recapture Pingda

May 28—27th Troop Carrier Squadron begins air dropping supplies to CEF; Chinese troops capture Hopang and Panglong, securing the southern flank of the Salween Front

June 4—Chinese New 28th Division captures Lameng

June 8—Chinese 71st Army breaks through the Japanese defenses at Longling

June 12—Chinese 115th Regiment secures Hemushu

June 15—Chinese 198th Division takes North Zhaigongfan Pass

June 16—General Song abandons Longling to Japanese counterattack

June 17—New 28th and New 39th divisions take Yingdun Mountain

June 22—Japanese abandon the Shweli Valley to the XXth Army Group

June 27—Chinese 8th Army takes over siege of Songshan

June 28—Japanese aircraft arrive over the Salween Front for the first time to resupply besieged troops at Songshan

July 26—Chinese troops capture Laifengshan in best coordinated attack of the campaign

August 2—American aircraft breach the walls of Tengchong; Chinese troops enter the city

August 3—Chinese 8th Army takes Gunlongpo Mountain; X Force secures Myitkyina

August 18—64th Sentai makes two unsuccessful attacks on the Huitong Bridge

August 20—Forty-two Japanese defenders buried alive when American engineers detonate mines under Songshan

August 27—Reinforced infantry company led by Major Benjamin F. Thrailkill makes contact with CEF in the Kambaiti Pass between Tengchong and Myitkyina on the China-Burma border

September 3—64th Sentai drops supplies, raids American airfield at Tengchong

September 5—Japanese begin counteroffensive at Longling

September 7—8th Army destroys remnants of Japanese at Songshan

September 8—64th Senai attacks Baoshan, intervention by four P-38s keeps losses to only two Chinese killed and three C-47s destroyed

September 9—64th Sentai raids Tengchong airfield

September 10—American fighters thwart Japanese aerial resupply of Tengchong; JAAF withdraws from the Salween Front

September 14—Chinese capture Tengchong; Japanese order end to counteroffensive at Longling

September 24—G Flight, 35th Photo Reconnaissance Squadron, flies its first mission from Yunnanyi

September 25—Chiang demands Stilwell be recalled

October 18—Stilwell recalled; Major General Dan Sultan takes command of American forces in India and Burma; Major General Albert Wedemeyer takes command in China

October 22—Stilwell departs China

November 3—Chinese capture Longling

November 11—Five Thai fighters shot down in dogfight over Lampang, Thailand

November 20—Chinese take Mangshi

November 28—Japanese night bombing raid on Yunnanyi hits fuel dump, no casualties

December 1—Chinese take Zhefang

December 5—Wedemeyer begins Operation Grubworm to airlift Chinese troops from Burma to stop the Japanese on the Guizhou Plateau

December 15—X Force captures Bhamo

December 18—B-29s firebomb Hankou in Central China

1945

January 3—Chinese 2nd Army attacks Wanding, fails to take the city

January 4—Chinese 53rd Army occupies Mengmao

January 6—Major General Robert McClure replaces Frank Dorn in charge of Chinese Combat Command

January 9—Patrols from the 53rd Army make contact with advanced elements of the 38th Division in Burma

January 16—X Force occupies Namhkam

January 17—Mars Task Force cuts the road between Lashio and Wanding

January 19—Chinese advance into Wanding with coordinated air, artillery, and infantry assault

January 20—Chinese patrols discover Japanese abandoned Wanding

January 21—Flag raising ceremony in Wanding

January 22—First convoy over the Tengchong Cutoff arrives in Kunming

January 27—X Force meets Y Force on China-Burma border; Salween Campaign completed

February 4—First "official" convoy over the Ledo-Burma Road arrives in Kunming

August 14—Japanese surrender after B-29s drop atomic bombs on Hiroshima and Nagasaki; Chinese troops within twenty miles of Fort Bayard, on the China coast

Chinese Expeditionary Force Organization

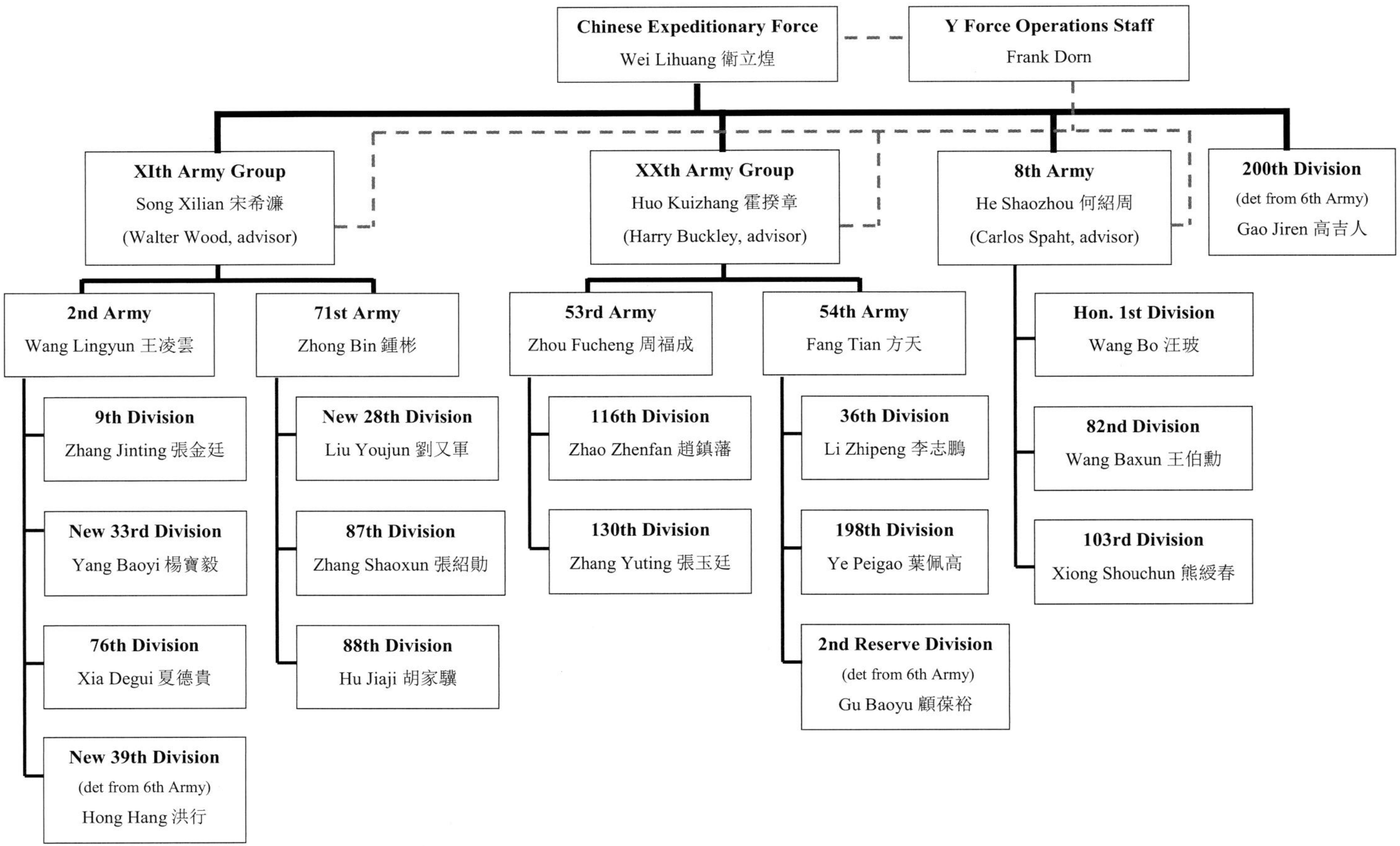

69th Composite Wing Organization

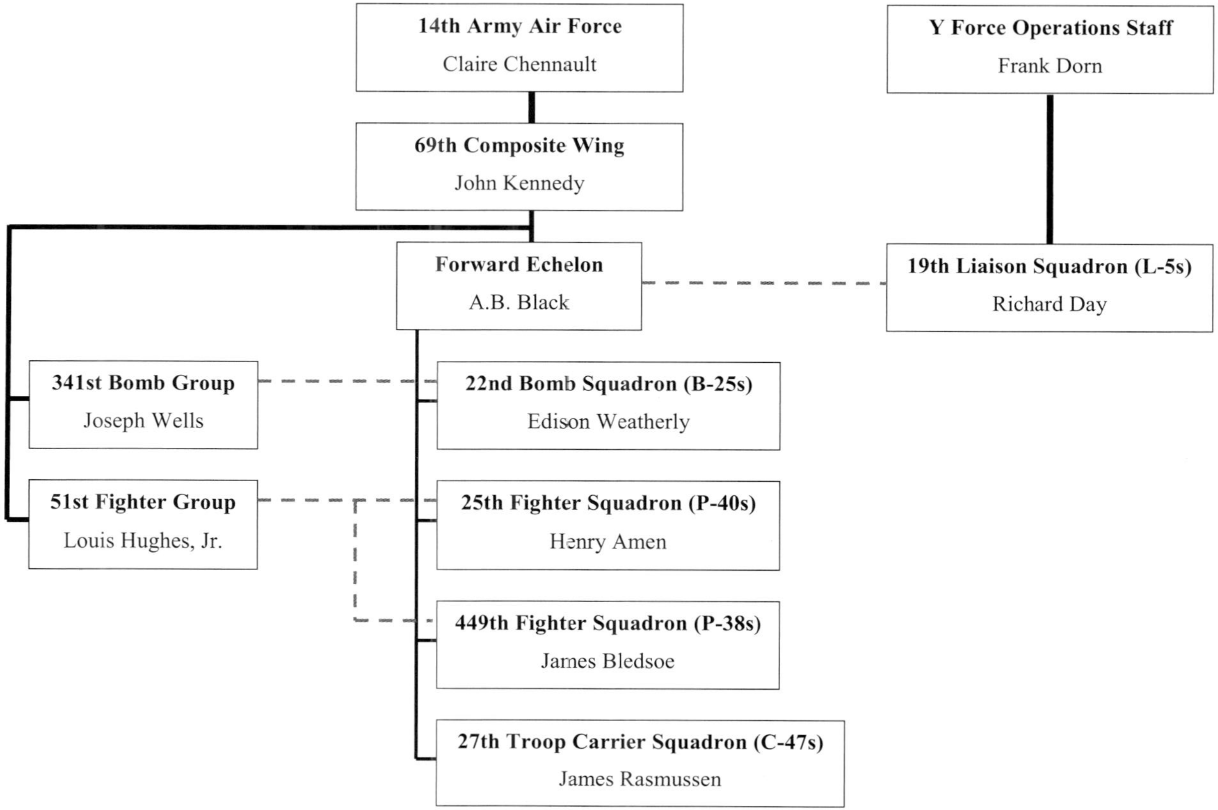

American Casualties

Date	Name	Unit
May 14, 1944	1Lt Kirk G. Schaible	YFOS
May 18, 1944	1Lt Lewis S. Earnest	25FS
May 21, 1944	Maj William C. McMurrey	YFOS
July 27, 1944	TSgt James F. Woodcock	19LS
August 18, 1944	Capt Ripley Buckingham	YFOS
August 18, 1944	Capt William B. Williamson, Jr.	27TCS
August 18, 1944	1Lt Charles B. Bierbaum	27TCS
August 18, 1944	TSgt Harold P. Holmes	27TCS
August 18, 1944	SSgt Joe T. Mann, Jr.	27TCS
August 18, 1944	Pfc Joseph Kowalick	YFOS
August 18, 1944	Pvt John J. Clark	YFOS
August 18, 1944	Pvt Robert Lawson	YFOS
August 20, 1944	2Lt William I. Loomis	14AF
September 12, 1944	Capt John W. Herstine	YFOS
September 12, 1944	T4 John Welsch	YFOS
September 17, 1944	Sgt Kenneth M. Iiames	19LS
September 17, 1944	SSgt Raymond R. Francisco	19LS
September 23, 1944	Pvt Robert H. Minnis	YFOS
September 23, 1944	Capt Gordon C. Brooks	27TCS
September 23, 1944	FO Kenneth H. Jensen	27TCS
September 23, 1944	MSgt Daniel L. Mengel	27TCS
September 23, 1944	Cpl David L. Lancaster	27TCS
September 23, 1944	Sgt Chester W. Pearce	YFOS
September 23, 1944	Sgt Leonard V. Volpe	YFOS
September 26, 1944	1Lt Benjamin L. Parker	25FS
October 15, 1944	Pvt Jerald Beitel	YFOS
August 12, 1944	SSgt Hugh F. O'Neil, Jr.	19LS
November 5, 1944	1Lt Franklin H. McKinney	35PRS
November 11, 1944	2Lt Henry F. Minco	25FS
December 18, 1944	FO Lincoln G. Seguin	25FS

Location	Cause of Death
North Zhaigongfan	Enemy fire
Tengchong	Shot down by enemy ground fire
South Zhaigongfan	Enemy mortar fire
Baoshan	Plane crash
Songshan	Enemy fire
Near Songshan	C-47 shot down by enemy fighters
Near Songshan	C-47 shot down by enemy fighters
Near Songshan	C-47 shot down by enemy fighters
Near Songshan	C-47 shot down by enemy fighters
Near Songshan	C-47 shot down by enemy fighters
Near Songshan	C-47 shot down by enemy fighters
Near Songshan	C-47 shot down by enemy fighters
Baoshan	Plane crash
Tengchong	Artillery fire
Tengchong	Artillery fire
Tengchong	Strafing by enemy fighters
Baoshan	Plane crash
Yunnanyi	Plane crash
Salween Front	C-47 crashed into a mountain in bad weather
Salween Front	C-47 crashed into a mountain in bad weather
Salween Front	C-47 crashed into a mountain in bad weather
Salween Front	C-47 crashed into a mountain in bad weather
Salween Front	C-47 crashed into a mountain in bad weather
Salween Front	C-47 crashed into a mountain in bad weather
Mangshi	Shot down by enemy ground fire, captured and executed
Lameng	Land mine
Kunming	Plane crash
Near Lampang, Thailand	Crashed in bad weather
Near Lampang, Thailand	Shot down by enemy fighters
Near Kunlong Ferry	Missing during strafing attack

Notes

Prologue

[1]Polo, Travels, bk. 2
[2]Chinese Combat Command 1945
[3]Shakespeare, *Henry V*, 3.1.1
[4]Lu 2009
[5]Chinese Combat Command 1945

Chapter 1

[1]Chennault 1949, 161
[2]Romanus and Sunderland 1953, 143; 146
[3]Byrd 1987, 12
[4]Byrd 1987, 21; 61
[5]Chennault 1935, 22; Kelley 1993, 22
[6]Byrd 1987, 76; Chennault 1949, 57-58
[7]Xu 2001, 148; Kelley 1993, 7; Luo 2013
[8]Tuchman 1970, 174; Harmsen 2013, 181
[9]Chennault 1949, 112
[10]Alison 2007
[11]Shores, Cull and Izawa 1992, 247; 250-251
[12]Bond 1984, 161
[13]Shilling 1993, 160-161; Chennault 1949, 157
[14]Bond 1984, 163; Shores, Cull, and Izawa 1993, 373
[15]Bond 1984, 164; Shores, Cull, and Izawa 1993, 373
[16]Bond 1984, 164; 166; Shilling 1993, 161
[17]Shilling 1993, 161-162
[18]Tow 2009
[19]Wambold, Jr. n.d.
[20]Chennault 1949, 162; Ford 2007, 290
[21]Ford 2007, 290
[22]Hill and Schaupp 2003, 156-157; Shores, Cull, and Izawa 1993, 373-374
[23]Chennault 1949, 161; Chinese Combat Command 1945
[24]Chennault 1949, 163-164
[25]Ford 2007, 293; Chennault 1949, 166
[26]Hill and Schaupp 2003, 158
[27]Chennault 1949, 164
[28]Smith 1986, 305
[29]Hill and Schaupp 2003, 160
[30]Smith 1986, 305; 307
[31]Chennault 1949, 166

Chapter 2

[1]Frank Dorn Papers, Box 5, 502
[2]Romanus and Sunderland 1953, 63; 66-67; 69-70; 73
[3]Romanus and Sunderland 1956, 29
[4]Romanus and Sunderland 1953, 62; 73
[5]Frank Dorn Papers, Box 5, 485
[6]Stilwell 1948, 49
[7]Romanus and Sunderland 1953, 94; 100
[8]Romanus and Sunderland 1953, 81-82; Stilwell 1948, 58
[9]Stilwell 1948, 68-69; Romanus and Sunderland 1953, 103
[10]Yang Chi-kuo 2013; CCTV 2012
[11]Dorn 1971, 67
[12]Romanus and Sunderland 1953, 109
[13]Dorn 1971, 59; 67; 83; Romanus and Sunderland 1953, 121
[14]Stilwell 1948, 87-89; Dorn 1971, 86
[15]Yang Chi-kuo 2013
[16]Dorn 1971, 85
[17]Romanus and Sunderland 1953, 86
[18]Dorn 1971, 99
[19]Dorn 1971, 104; Tuchman 1970, 293-295
[20]Stilwell 1948, 97
[21]Dorn 1971, 104-105
[22]Dorn 1971, 105; 121; 126; Stilwell 1948, 98
[23]Stilwell 1948, 98
[24]Dorn 1971, 130; 132; Stilwell 1948, 98
[25]Romanus and Sunderland 1953, 138
[26]Dorn 1971, 142; 155
[27]Tuchman 1970, 295
[28]Stilwell 1948, 99; Dorn 1971, 157
[29]Stilwell 1948, 100
[30]Frank Dorn Papers, Box 5, 560
[31]Dorn 1971, 202
[32]Stilwell 1948, 102
[33]Dorn 1971, 210; Romanus and Sunderland 1953, 140-142; Liu 2012, 106

[34]Stilwell 1948, 102; Dorn 1971, 222
[35]Dorn 1971, 213-214
[36]Dorn 1971, 234-235; 241; Stilwell 1948, 105
[37]Dorn 1971, 242; Tuchman 1970, 298
[38]Dorn 1971, 243
[39]Stilwell 1948, 105-106
[40]Tuchman 1970, 291
[41]Chennault 1949, 160

Chapter 3

[1]CCTV 2012
[2]Shao 2014
[3]Polo, *Travels*, bk. 2 ch. 52
[4]CCTV 2012
[5]Shao 2014; Li 2011, 11
[6]White and Jacoby 1947, 60; Li 2011, 12
[7]*CBI Roundup*, 22 August 1944
[8]CCTV 2012
[9]CCTV 2012; *CBI Roundup*, 22 August 1944
[10]Chang 1997, 4; 6
[11]CCTV 2012
[12]CCTV 2012; Li 2011, 13
[13]Shao 2014
[14]Yang Chien-chiu 2013
[15]Liu 2013
[16]CCTV 2012
[17]Li 2011, 13-14
[18]Romanus and Sunderland 1953, 45; 76-78; 234
[19]Plating 2011, 94

Chapter 4

[1]Chennault 1949, 161; 167
[2]White and Jacoby 1947, 148
[3]Romanus and Sunderland 1953, 135-136; 140; 213-214; 218
[4]Romanus and Sunderland 1953, 179; 225-226; 241
[5]Kelley 1993, 10; 30
[6]Romanus and Sunderland 1953, 176; 188; 190; 199
[7]Cochran 1975, 388-389
[8]Frank Dorn Papers, Box 5, 536
[9]Romanus and Sunderland 1953, 112; 162; 251; 272
[10]Tuchman 1970, 186
[11]Romanus and Sunderland 1953, 157-158; 224
[12]Song Ziwen, a Harvard graduate known even to his Chinese friends by his Americanized initials, T.V.
[13]Romanus and Sunderland 1953, 87; 375
[14]Romanus and Sunderland 1953, 227; 245; 259; 271; 273; 275; 279; 317-318; 320-324; 329-330
[15]Romanus and Sunderland 1953, 319-320; Plating 2011, 125
[16]White and Jacoby 1947, 48; 50; 68; 72; 97; 104; 126; 273
[17]Romanus and Sunderland 1953, 323, 325; 345-346
[18]Tuchman 1970, 53
[19]Romanus and Sunderland 1953, 318
[20]Tuchman 1970, 320
[21]Romanus and Sunderland 1953, 378
[22]Romanus and Sunderland 1953, 377-378

Chapter 5

[1]Romanus and Sunderland 1953, 32-33; Stilwell 1948; Tu 2013
[2]Frank Dorn Papers, Box 5, 126-131; 584
[3]Frank Dorn Papers, Box 5, 275; 283
[4]Frank Dorn Papers, Box 1 Folder 55; Romanus and Sunderland 1953, 350
[5]Chin 1948, 7; Frank Dorn Papers, Box 1 Folder 55; Romanus and Sunderland 1953, 293
[6]Frank Dorn Papers, Box 1 Folder 55
[7]Romanus and Sunderland 1959, 369-370; 370-371
[8]Shen 2013
[9]Frank Dorn Papers, Box 1 Folder 45
[10]Romanus and Sunderland 1953, 298; 293
[11]Frank Dorn Papers, Box 5, 544

[12]Frank Dorn Papers, Box 5, 600
[13]Romanus and Sunderland 1953, 294
[14]Frank Dorn Papers, Box 1 Folder 55
[15]Frank Dorn Papers, Box 5, 599
[16]Chin 1948, 7; Romanus and Sunderland 1953, 295
[17]Romanus and Sunderland 1953, 292; 296
[18]Frank Dorn Papers, Box 1 Folder 55; Box 5, 553
[19]Romanus and Sunderland 1953, 296; 298-299; 324; 351
[20]White and Jacoby 1947, 73; 101; 104; 106
[21]Romanus and Sunderland 1953, 352; Xu 2001, 180-183
[22]Romanus and Sunderland 1956, 56; Romanus and Sunderland 1953, 384

Chapter 6

[1]Romanus and Sunderland 1953, 302-303; Cochran 1975, 149; 153
[2]Cochran 1975, 153
[3]Romanus and Sunderland 1953, 304; Romanus and Sunderland 1956, 309; Department of the Army 1952; Taylor 1957, 15; Van Wagner 1998, 18-19
[4]Cochran 1975, 12; 69; 73; 146; 149-151
[5]Katz 2005
[6]Piazza 2009
[7]War Department Historical Division 1945, 8
[8]Romanus and Sunderland 1956, 34-35
[9]Luo 2013
[10]Romanus and Sunderland 1953, 348
[11]Frank Dorn Papers, Box 5, 551
[12]Harmsen 2013, 168-169; 214
[13]Romanus and Sunderland 1956, 14; 32-33; 38
[14]Taylor 1957, 18
[15]White and Jacoby 1947, 151
[16]CCTV 2012; Luo 2013
[17]Chen 1947, 3
[18]Chen 1947, 5; Romanus and Sunderland 1956, 125
[19]Romanus and Sunderland 1956, 36; 130-131; Habecker 1995, 3-1
[20]Gaither 1975, 13; 60-61; Romanus and Sunderland 1956, 146
[21]War Department Historical Division 1945, 11

Chapter 7

[1]Romanus and Sunderland 1956, 353
[2]Piazza 2009
[3]Piazza 2009
[4]Romanus and Sunderland 1956, 145; 150
[5]Katz 2005; Quaid 2005
[6]Clofine 2005; Quaid 2005
[7]Luo 2013; Farley 2008
[8]War Department Historical Division 1945, 43; 47-48; 56
[9]Piazza 2005
[10]Passanisi 2013
[11]Romanus and Sunderland 1956, 179; 181; War Department Historical Division 1945, 66; Piazza 2009
[12]Romanus and Sunderland 1956, 156; 165-167; 174; 183; 188; 196; War Department Historical Division 1945, 71-72
[13]Binzer 2008
[14]Smith 2000, 17-18
[15]Snow 2009
[16]Habecker 1995, 2-6
[17]Austin 2009
[18]Smith 2000, 20
[19]Creech 2005, 46
[20]Habecker 1995, 3-1-2; 3-3
[21]Piazza 2009
[22]Creech 2005, 51
[23]Habecker 1995, 3-2
[24]Piazza 2005
[25]Romanus and Sunderland 1956, 189-190
[26]Sacquety 2013, 119
[27]Quaid 2005
[28]War Department Historical Division 1945, 86-87; 89; 91
[29]Gaither 1975, 34
[30]Romanus and Sunderland 1956, 191
[31]Hunter 1993
[32]Habecker 1995, 5-1
[33]Romanus and Sunderland 1956, 36; 39

[34]Habecker 1995, 5-2

Chapter 8

[1]Frank Dorn Papers, Box 6 Folder 4
[2]Romanus and Sunderland 1956, 298; 301; 305; 308
[3]Frank Dorn Papers, Box 1 Folder 55
[4]Romanus and Sunderland 1956, 309; 312-314; 322; 325; 329; 369-370
[5]Chin 1948, 24-25
[6]Frank Dorn Papers, Box 5, 609-612
[7]Romanus and Sunderland 1953, 301
[8]Liu 2013
[9]Romanus and Sunderland 1953, 234; Romanus and Sunderland 1956, 93-94; 234; 329; 332-333; Chinese Combat Command 1945
[10]Tregear 1965, 230
[11]Frank Dorn Papers, Box 1 Folder 55
[12]Romanus and Sunderland 1956, 313
[13]Chinese Combat Command 1945; Chin 1948, 8
[14]Frank Dorn Papers, Box 1 Folder 55
[15]Romanus and Sunderland 1956, 337
[16]*Yank Magazine*, 29 December 1944
[17]Lai 1947, 3
[18]Judson 1947, 1
[19]Romanus and Sunderland 1956, 335; Chinese Combat Command 1945
[20]Romanus and Sunderland 1956, 341
[21]Frank Dorn Papers, Box 1 Folder 55

Chapter 9

[1]Tunner 1964, 75
[2]Romanus and Sunderland 1956, 9
[3]van de Ven 2003, 46
[4]Romanus and Sunderland 1956, 223
[5]Sargent
[6]Romanus and Sunderland 1956, 225; Hunter 1993
[7]Clofine 2005
[8]*CBI Roundup*, 25 May 1944; Romanus and Sunderland 1956, 223, 226
[9]Sargent
[10]Romanus and Sunderland 1956, 226; *CBI Roundup*, 25 May 1944; Hunter 1993
[11]Gaither 1975, 42
[12]Hunter 1993
[13]Habecker 1995, 4-1; 4-2-3; 4-5; 5-3
[14]Snow 2009
[15]*CBI Roundup*, 25 May 1944
[16]Hunter 1993
[17]*CBI Roundup*, 25 May 1944
[18]Taylor 1957, 26
[19]Hunter 1993
[20]Habecker 1995, 5-4-5; Craven and Cate 1953, 209-210
[21]Hunter 1993
[22]*CBI Roundup*, 25 May 1944
[23]Habecker 1995, 5-6-7
[24]*CBI Roundup*, 25 May 1944
[25]Romanus and Sunderland 1956, 236
[26]Piazza 2009
[27]Habecker 1995, 5-5-6
[28]Gaither 1975, 55
[29]Romanus and Sunderland 1956, 237; 240
[30]Piazza 2009
[31]Romanus and Sunderland 1956, 240
[32]Snow 2009
[33]Joseph Warren Stilwell Papers
[34]Hunter 1993
[35]Romanus and Sunderland 1956, 249
[36]Habecker 1995, 5-7
[37]Reeves 2009
[38]Craven and Cate 1953, 211
[39]Habecker 1995, 5-8
[40]Sargent
[41]*CBI Roundup*, 25 May 1944
[42]Romanus and Sunderland 1956, 254

Chapter 10

1Chinese Combat Command 1945
[2]Lai 1947, 2
[3]Romanus and Sunderland 1956, 335-336; Chinese Combat Command 1945
[4]Tregear 1965, 82
[5]Chinese Combat Command 1945
[6]*CBI Roundup*, 3 August 1944
[7]Chinese Combat Command 1945
[8]*CBI Roundup*, 3 August 1944

[9]Frank Dorn Papers, Box 1 Folder 55; Chennault 1949, 276; Romanus and Sunderland 1953, 340
[10]Frank Dorn Papers, Box 5, 630
[11]*CBI Roundup*, 3 August 1944
[12]Binzer 2008
[13]Welch 2008
[14]Romanus and Sunderland 1956, 345; 347-348
[15]69th Composite Wing
[16]Binzer 2008
[17]Disharoon 2008
[18]Simmons 2008
[19]Binzer 2007
[20]Jones 2007
[21]Romanus and Sunderland 1956, 99-100
[22]Disharoon 2008; Missing Air Crew Report 15255
[23]Judson 1947, 5
[24]Binzer 2008
[25]Romanus and Sunderland 1956, 108; Lees 2008
[26]Mitchell 2007
[27]Disharoon 2008
[28]Batchelor 2007; Lees 2008
[29]Coverdale 1947, 8
[30]Romanus and Sunderland 1956, 345
[31]*CBI Roundup*, 3 August 1944
[32]19th Liaison Squadron; Romanus and Sunderland 1956, 343-344
[33]Chinese Combat Command 1945; 19th Liaison Squadron; Binzer 2007; Cochran 1975, 270
[34]Chinese Combat Command 1945; Romanus and Sunderland 1956, 345
[35]Yang Chien-chiu 2013
[36]Chinese Combat Command 1945
[37]Chinese Combat Command 1945; Frank Dorn Papers, Box 1 Folder 55; Romanus and Sunderland 1956, 343
[38]CCTV 2011; Romanus and Sunderland 1956, 343
[39]Lai 1947, 5
[40]Chinese Combat Command 1945
[41]Chinese Combat Command 1945; Romanus and Sunderland 1956, 345
[42]Frank Dorn Papers, Box 1 Folder 55
[43]Frank Dorn Papers, Box 1 Folder 45
[44]Romanus and Sunderland 1956, 341; 346-347; 364
[45]Romanus and Sunderland 1956, 346-347; 352; Chinese Combat Command 1945; Frank Dorn Papers, Box 1 Folder 55
[46]CCTV 2011; CCTV 2012
[47]Shen 2013
[48]Romanus and Sunderland 1956, 352
[49]Romanus and Sunderland 1956, 349; *CBI Roundup*, 29 June 1944

Chapter 11

[1]Romanus and Sunderland 1956, 357
[2]Frank Dorn Papers, Box 1 Folder 45
[3]Chinese Combat Command 1945; Romanus and Sunderland 1956, 332
[4]Chinese Combat Command 1945; Romanus and Sunderland 1956, 332; 336; 343; 352; 354-355; 357; 69th Composite Wing
[5]Frank Dorn Papers, Box 5, 535; 595
[6]Claire Lee Chennault Papers, Box 9, Folder 4
[7]*CBI Roundup*, 11 January 1945
[8]Mitchell 2007
[9]Molesworth 1994, 80
[10]*Altoona Mirror, 26* January 1945
[11]Simmons 2008; *Jing Bao Journal*, February 1943
[12]Simmons 2008
[13]Mitchell 2007
[14] *CBI Roundup*, 3 August 1944
[15]69th Composite Wing
[16]*22nd Bomb Squadron Association Newsletter*, 1 February 2011
[17]Hayward 2012; 22nd Bomb Squadron Association
[18]Hale 2007
[19]*22nd Bomb Squadron Association Newsletter*, 1 August 2008
[20]*22nd Bomb Squadron Association Newsletter*, 1 November 2007
[21]Romanus and Sunderland 1956, 354; 357-359

[22]Frank Dorn Papers, Box 1 Folder 42; Box 5, 613-614, 646

Chapter 12

[1]Romanus and Sunderland 1956, 391
[2]Tuan 2008, 103-104
[3]Lu 2009
[4]Romanus and Sunderland 1956, 391
[5]69th Composite Wing; Romanus and Sunderland 1956, 391-392
[6]Heitkotter 2007
[7]Doughty 2007
[8]Heitkotter 2007
[9]25th Fighter Squadron; Chinese Combat Command 1945; Romanus and Sunderland 1956, 393
[10]Hale 2007
[11]Romanus and Sunderland 1956, 393
[12]Mark 2008
[13]Long 2008
[14]*22nd Bomb Squadron Association Newsletter*, 1 August 2010
[15]Yang Chien-chiu 2013
[16]Romanus and Sunderland 1956, 393-394; Frank Dorn Papers, Box 1 Folder 55
[17]Mitchell 2007
[18]Romanus and Sunderland 1956, 394; 69th Composite Wing
[19]Liu 2013
[20]*CBI Roundup*, 21 September 1944
[21]Chinese Combat Command 1945

Chapter 13

[1]Romanus and Sunderland 1956, 356; 394-395; Chinese Combat Command 1945; Chin 1948, 17
[2]Chinese Combat Command 1945; Romanus and Sunderland 1956, 395; Frank Dorn Papers, Box 1 Folder 42
[3]Frank Dorn Papers, Box 1 Folder 42
[4]Frank Dorn Papers, Box 1 Folder 21; Judson 1947, 3
[5]Frank Dorn Papers, Box 5, 608; Box 1 Folder 45
[6]Romanus and Sunderland 1956, 395
[7]Ichimura 2008
[8]Frank Dorn Papers, Box 1 Folder 55; *CBI Roundup*, 30 Nov 1944
[9]Frank Dorn Papers, Box 1 Folder 21; Romanus and Sunderland 1956, 395-396
[10]Romanus and Sunderland 1956, 396-397; Frank Dorn Papers, Box 1 Folder 21; Ichimura 2008
[11]Ichimura 2008
[12]Frank Dorn Papers, Box 1 Folder 21
[13]Ichimura 2008 ; Shores 2005, 245
[14]Romanus and Sunderland 1956, 397
[15]69th Composite Wing
[16]Ichimura 2009
[17]Frank Dorn Papers, Box 1 Folder 21
[18]Ichimura 2009
[19]Mitchel 2007; Long 2008
[20]Jones 2007; Ichimura 2009; 69th Composite Wing
[21]Frank Dorn Papers, Box 5, 611
[22]Frank Dorn Papers, Box 1 Folder 21; Chinese Combat Command 1945; Romanus and Sunderland 1956, 398

Chapter 14

[1]*CBI Roundup*
[2]Binzer 2008
[3]19th Liaison Squadron; Ichimura 2008
[4]Disharoon 2009
[5]Binzer 2007; 2008
[6]Heitkotter 2007
[7]Binzer 2008; 27th Troop Carrier Squadron; 19th Liaison Squadron
[8]19th Liaison Squadron
[9]Bi 2009
[10]Ichimura 2008
[11]腾越文化研究会 2005
[12]Bi 2009
[13]*CBI Roundup*, 14 Sept 1944; Li 2011, 15
[14]*CBI Roundup*, 21 Sept 1944; Chinese Combat Command 1945; Shao 2014
[15]*CBI Roundup*, 21 September 1944
[16]Frank Dorn Papers, Box 5, 653
[17]CCTV 2012
[18]Shao 2014

Chapter 15

[1]Joseph Warren Stilwell Papers
[2]Office of the Chief of Military History 1946, 91-93; Romanus and Sunderland 1956, 435; *CBI Roundup*, 21 September 1944; Romanus and Sunderland 1959, 114
[3]Romanus and Sunderland 1956, 376; 424; 435
[4]Joseph Warren Stilwell Papers
[5]Romanus and Sunderland 1956, 445-446
[6]Joseph Warren Stilwell Papers
[7]Romanus and Sunderland 1956, 453; 461-462
[8]Joseph Warren Stilwell Papers
[9]Romanus and Sunderland 1956, 458
[10]Joseph Warren Stilwell Papers
[11]White and Jacoby 1947, 212
[12]Frank Dorn Papers, Box 5, 655-656
[13]Joseph Warren Stilwell Papers
[14]69th Composite Wing
[15]Frank Dorn Papers, Box 5, 657; McLaughlin 2013, Loc 2090, 2110, 2116, 2278, 2281
[16]McLaughlin 2013, Loc 2409; 2455
[17]Frank Dorn Papers, Box 5, 657-658, 660
[18]Glines 1995, 166-167; 173
[19]White and Jacoby 1947, 246
[20]Hui 2013
[21]Frank Dorn Papers, Box 1 Folder 45

Chapter 16

[1]25th Fighter Squadron
[2]Romanus and Sunderland 1956, 93-94; Taylor 1957, 2
[3]Taylor 1956, 39
[4]Slessor 1936, 122, 143
[5]Chennault 1949, 237
[6]Fodor 2007
[7]*Jing Bao Journal*
[8]Taylor 1956, 39; 50
[9]Hale 2007
[10]69th Composite Wing
[11]Barrow 2011
[12]35th Photo Reconnaissance Squadron
[13]Barrow 2008; 2011; 35th Photo Reconnaissance Squadron
[14]35th Photo Reconnaissance Squadron; Barrow 2012
[15]Barrow 2012
[16]Clark 2012
[17]Barrow 2007
[18]Clark 2012
[19]Barrow 2007; 2011
[20]Barrow 2012
[21]Long 2008
[22]Binzer 2007
[23]Heitkotter 2007
[24]Hayward 2012
[25]Doughty 2007
[26]Barrow 2011; 2012
[27]Mitchell 2007
[28]69th Composite Wing
[29]Long 2008; *Cleveland Magazine*, June 2004
[30]Sakpinit 2012
[31]Barrow 2007

Chapter 17

[1]Mitchell 2007
[2]Ford, "Meet Colonel Tsuji, genius and cannibal," www.warbirdforum.com
[3]*CBI Roundup*, 28 Dec 1944
[4]Shen 2013
[5]Chinese Combat Command 1945; 69th Composite Wing
[6]Romanus and Sunderland 1959, 131
[7]Chin 1948, 16
[8]Romanus and Sunderland 1959, 131; Judson 1947, 3
[9]Romanus and Sunderland 1959, 131; Chinese Combat Command 1945
[10]*CBI Roundup*, 30 Nov 44; Romanus and Sunderland 1956, 108
[11]Disharoon 2008
[12]Romanus and Sunderland 1959, 133; CBI Roundup, 7 December 1944
[13]Romanus and Sunderland 1959, 90; 95; 107; 116
[14]Taylor 1957, 33

[15]Romanus and Sunderland 1959, 123; 134
[16]Frank Dorn Papers, Box 5, 659
[17]Romanus and Sunderland 1959, 236
[18]Frank Dorn Papers, Box 2 Folder 12; Box 2 Folder14; Box 2 Folder 19; Box 5, 662
[19]Judson 1947, 8; Romanus and Sunderland 1959, 134
[20]Hayward 2012
[21]CCTV 2012
[22]Yang Chien-chiu 2013
[23]Romanus and Sunderland 1959, 138

Epilogue

[1]*CBI Roundup*, 18 Jan 1945
[2]Romanus and Sunderland 1959, 40; 78-79; 136; 138
[3]*CBI Roundup*
[4]Mitchell 2007
[5]Romanus and Sunderland 1959, 141; 297; 317; *14th Air Force Pictorial*, 1995
[6]Tunner 1964, 75
[7]CCTV 2012
[8]Chinese Combat Command 1945
[9]Frank Dorn Papers, Box 1 Folder 55; Box 5, 699; 772; 786
[10]Taylor 1957, 50
[11]Tsou 1963, 51
[12]Liu 2013
[13]Yang Chien-chiu 2013
[14]Shao 2014
[15]Shen 2013
[16]Bi 2009
[17]*The Arab Bulletin*, 20 August 1917
[18]Lu 2009

Bibliography

Interviews and Correspondence

Alison, John R. Interview by author, April 2007.

Austin, Robert. Interview by author, January 2009.

Barrow, Sterling. Correspondence with author, September 2007-February 2012.

Batchelor, Bruce. Correspondence with author, December 2007.

Bi Shixian. Interview by author, March 2009.

Binzer, Robert D. Correspondence with author, December 2007-January 2008.

Clark, Arthur. Correspondence with author, January 2012.

Disharoon, Jerry. Correspondence with author, March 2008-March 2009.

Doughty, Jerry. Correspondence with author, May 2007-February 2008.

Fodor, Joseph. Interview by author, June 2007.

Hale, Chapman. Interview by author, December 2007.

Hayward, David. Correspondence with author, February-April 2012.

Heitkotter, James. Correspondence with author, August-December 2007.

Ichimura, Hiroshi. Correspondence with author, November 2008-October 2009.

Jones, Robert. Correspondence with author, December 2007.

Lees, Leonard. Correspondence with author, January 2008.

Liu Cheng-hua. Interview by Samuel Hui and Pan I-jung, March 2013.

Long, Clifford. Interview by author, February 2008.

Lu Caiwen. Interview by author, March 2009.

Luo Chih-tsai. Interview by Samuel Hui and Pan I-jung, November 2013.

Mark, Edward. Correspondence with author, 2008.

Mitchell, William. Correspondence with author, December 2007.

Passanisi, Robert E. Correspondence with author, June 2009.

Piazza, Philip. Interview by author, January 2009.

Reeves, Randy. Correspondense with author, January 2009.

Sakpinit Promthep. Correspondence with author, May 2012.

Shao Ying-jen. Interview by Samuel Hui and Pan I-jung, January 2014.

Shen You-chih. Interview by Samuel Hui and Pan I-jung, August 2013.

Simmons, Cecil. Interview by author, December 2007.

Snow, Harold. Interview by author, January 2009.

Tu Chi-liang. Interview by Samuel Hui and Pan I-jung, December 2013.

Yang Chi-kuo. Interview by Samuel Hui and Pan I-jung, February 2013.

Yang Chien-chiu. Interview by Samuel Hui and Pan I-jung. November 2013.

Archival Documents

22nd Bomb Squadron Association. *Rebirth of a Squadron: World War II, 22nd Bombardment Squadron (Medium) "Bombing Eagles" 341st Group*. N.P., N.D.

Advanced Infantry Officers School. *The Operations of the Y-Force Operations Staff, U.S. Army, in the Salween Campaign, Yunnan, China, 10 May 1944-20 January 1945,* by Wah G. Chin. Fort Benning, GA: The Infantry School, 1948.

Chennault, Claire L. *The Role of Defensive Pursuit*. N.P., 1935.

CIA Historical Review Program. *Galahad: Intelligence Aspects,* by Charles N. Hunter. Langley, VA, 1993.

Claire Lee Chennault Papers. *China. Army. Y-Force. Memoranda, radiograms, and maps, 1943-1944.* Box 9, Folder 4. Stanford: Hoover Institution Archives.

Department of the Army, Office of the Chief of Military History. *Burma Air Operations: Jan. 1942-Aug. 1945.* Japanese Monograph No. 64. Tokyo, 1946.

Department of the Army, Office of the Chief of Military History. *Burma Operations Record: 15th Army Operations in Imphal Area and Withdrawal to Northern Burma.* Japanese Monograph No. 134. Tokyo, 1952.

Frank Dorn Papers. *After the Flag is Lowered: Autobiography of Frank Dorn.* Box 5. Stanford: Hoover Institution Archives.

Frank Dorn Papers. *Chinese Eighth Army, Report on the Sung-Shan Campaign.* Box 1, Folder 21. Stanford: Hoover Institution Archives.

Frank Dorn Papers. *Efficiency Report on General Officer to the Adjutant General, Washington, D.C., from Major General Albert Wedemeyer, January 25, 1945.* Box 2, Folder 14. Stanford: Hoover Institution Archives.

Frank Dorn Papers. *Historical Report of Y-Force Operations Staff.* Box 1, Folder 55. Stanford: Hoover Institution Archives.

Frank Dorn Papers. *Letter to Gen. Ho Ying-chin (two copies with letter of July 5, 1944 attached), August 4, 1944.* Box 1, Folder 42. Stanford: Hoover Institution Archives.

Frank Dorn Papers. *Memorandum to Gen. Joseph W. Stilwell on the Chinese Commanders in the Chinese Expeditionary Forces, September 22, 1944.* Box 1, Folder 45. Stanford: Hoover Institution Archives.

Frank Dorn Papers. *Letter to Brigadier General Frank Dorn from General Joseph W. Stilwell, October 20, 1944.* Box 6, Folder 4. Stanford: Hoover Institution Archives.

Frank Dorn Papers. *Letter to Brigadier General Frank Dorn from Major General Albert Wedemeyer, January 3, 1945.* Box 6, Folder 11. Stanford: Hoover Institution Archives.

Frank Dorn Papers. *Letter to Brigadier General Frank Dorn from Major General Robert McClure, "Reorganization of Chinese Training and Combat Command", December 17, 1944.* Box 6, Folder 6. Stanford: Hoover Institution Archives.

Frank Dorn Papers. *Letter to Major General Albert Wedemeyer from Brigadier General Frank Dorn, December 28, 1944.* Box 6, Folder 7. Stanford: Hoover Institution Archives.

Frank Dorn Papers. *Letter to Major General Wendell J. Coats from Frank Dorn noting contingency plans made during World War II for the assassination of Chiang Kai-shek, May 7, 1969.* Box 6, Folder 4. Stanford: Hoover Institution Archives.

Frank Dorn Papers. *Report to the Adjutant General, Washington, D.C. from Brigadier General Frank Dorn, July 16, 1945.* Box 2, Folder 19. Stanford: Hoover Institution Archives.

Frank Dorn Papers. *Report to the Adjutant General, Washington, D.C. "Historical Report of Chinese Training and Combat Command (Y-Force Operations Staff and Z-Force), period October 25, 1944 thru December 31, 1944," January 1, 1945.* Box 2, Folder 10. Stanford: Hoover Institution Archives.

Frank Dorn Papers. *Wei Li-huang. Letter to Brig. Gen. Frank Dorn, January 15, 1945.* Box 2, Folder 12. Stanford: Hoover Institution Archives.

Fourteenth Air Force, 19th Liaison Squadron. *Squadron History.* Maxwell Air Force Base, AL: Air Force Historical Research Agency.

Fourteenth Air Force, 25th Fighter Squadron. *Squadron History.* Maxwell Air Force Base, AL: Air Force Historical Research Agency.

Fourteenth Air Force, 27th Troop Carrier Squadron. *Squadron History.* Maxwell Air Force Base, AL: Air Force Historical Research Agency.

Fourteenth Air Force, 35th Photo Reconnaissance Squadron. *Squadron History.* Maxwell Air Force Base, AL: Air Force Historical Research Agency.

Fourteenth Air Force, 69th Composite Wing. *Wing History.* Maxwell Air Force Base, AL: Air Force Historical Research Agency.

Fourteenth Air Force, 528th Fighter Squadron. *Squadron History,* by James O. Sargent. Maxwell Air Force Base, AL: Air Force Historical Research Agency.

Joseph Warren Stilwell Papers. *World War II Diaries.* http://www.hoover.org/library-and-archives/collections/east-asia/featured-collections/joseph-stilwell#n3. Stanford: Hoover Institution Archives.

Office of Air Force History. *U.S. Air Force Oral History Interview: Colonel Philip G. Cochran,* by Dr. James C. Hasdorff. Maxwell Air Force Base, AL: Air Force Historical Research Agency, 1975.

U.S. Army Chinese Combat Command. *Report on the Salween Campaign.* Kunming, China, 1945.

U.S. Army Command and General Staff College. *The Battle of Salween River,* by Lai Cheng-liang. Fort Leavenworth, KS, 1947.

U.S. Army Command and General Staff College. *China's Role in the Recapture of Burma,* by Chen Ju-Hwa. Fort Leavenworth, KS, 1947.

U.S. Army Command and General Staff College. *Galahad Redux: An Assessment of the Disintegration of Merrill's Marauders,* by John B. Gaither. Fort Leavenworth, KS, 1975.

U.S. Army Command and General Staff College. *The Operations of the Fifty-third Army, CEF, culminating in the Battle for Muse and Tachingshan 3 Dec 44—27 Jan 45,* by P.M. Judson. Fort Leavenworth, KS, 1947.

U.S. Army Command and General Staff College. *The Salween Campaign, China May 1944—Jan 1945,* by G.B. Coverdale. Fort Leavenworth, KS, 1947.

USAF Historical Division. *Air Interdiction in China in World War II,* by Dr. Joe G. Taylor. Maxwell Air Force Base, AL: Air University, 1956.

USAF Historical Division. *Air Supply in the Burma Campaign,* by Dr. Joe G. Taylor. Maxwell Air Force Base, AL: Air University, 1957.

Veterans History Project. *Interview with Herbert Clofine,* by Christy Chason. Washington, D.C.: Library of Congress, 2005.

Veterans History Project. *Interview with Philip Piazza,* by Christy Chason. Washington, D.C.: Library of Congress, 2005.

Veterans History Project. *Interview with Warner Katz,* by Sheila Dyer. Washington, D.C.: Library of Congress, 2005.

Veterans History Project. *Merrill's Marauders Interviews,* by David L. Quaid. Washington, D.C.: Library of Congress, 2005.

War Department Historical Division. *Merrill's Marauders.* Washington, D.C.: Government Printing Office, 1945.

Published Sources

Bond, Charles R., Jr. and Terry H. Anderson. *A Flying Tiger's Diary.* College Station: Texas A&M University Press, 1984.

Byrd, Martha. *Chennault: Giving Wings to the Tiger.* Tuscaloosa: University of Alabama Press, 1987.

CCTV. "Battle of Tengchong." CCTV English Website. http://english.cntv.cn/program/documentary/20110223/115123.shtml (published 23 February 2011).

CCTV. "Journeys in Time: The Chinese Expeditionary Force." CCTV English Website. http://english.cntv.cn/program/journeysintime/20121101/106987.shtml (published 1 November 2012).

Chang, Iris. *The Rape of Nanking: The Forgotten Holocaust of World War II.* New York: Penguin Books, 1997.

Chennault, Claire L. *Way of a Fighter: The Memoirs of Claire Lee Chennault.* Edited by Robert Hotz. New York: G.P. Putnam's Sons, 1949.

Craven, Wesley Frank and James Lea Cate, *The Pacific: Matterhorn to Nagasaki June 1944 to August* 1945. Volume 5 of *The Army Air Force in World War II.* 1953. Reprint. Washington, D.C.: U.S. Government Printing Office, 1983.

Creech, William T. *The 3rd Greatest Fighter Pilot.* Bloomington, IN: AuthorHouse, 2005.

Dorn, Frank. *Walkout: With Stilwell in Burma.* New York: Thomas Y. Crowell Company, 1971.

Farley, Paul C. "1st Provisional Tank Group: China-Burma-India Theater of World War II." Adapted for the Internet by Carl Warren Weidenburner. China-Burma-India: Remembering the Forgotten Theater of World War II. http://cbi-theater-6.home.comcast.net/~cbi-theater-6/1ptg/1ptg.html (published February 2008).

Ford, Daniel. *Flying Tigers: Claire Chennault and his American Volunteers, 1941-1942.* Revised Edition. New York: Harper Collins, 2007.

Glines, Carroll V. *Chennault's Forgotten Warriors: The Saga of the 308th Bomb Group in China.* Atglen, PA: Schiffer Publishing, 1995.

Habecker, John C. *The "Dragon Flys" 528th Fighter Sqdn.* Not Published, 1995.

Harmsen, Peter. *Shanghai 1937: Stalingrad on the Yangtze.* Oxford: Casemate Publishers, 2013.

Hill, David Lee and Reagan Schaupp. *"Tex" Hill: Flying Tiger.* 2003. Reprint. San Antonio: Universal Bookbindery, 2004.

Kelley, John M. "Claire Lee Chennault: Theorist and Campaign Planner." Master's Thesis, School of Advanced Military Studies, 1993.

Li Yongxiang. "The Ethnic Minorities in Tengchong County and the Anti-Japanese War." Annual Review of the Institute for Advanced Social Research (October 2011): 6: 1-17.

Liu Chung-yung. *Dinghow: Chinese Commandos and the OGs of the American OSS.* Taipei: Eternal Economy Press, 2012.

McLaughlin, John J. *General Albert C. Wedemeyer: America's Unsung Strategist in World War II.* Philadelphia: Casemate Publishers, 2013.

Molesworth, Carl. *Sharks Over China: The 23rd Fighter Group in World War II.* 1994. Reprint. Edison: Castle Books, 2001.

Plating, John D. *The Hump: America's Strategy for Keeping China in World War II.* College Station: Texas A&M University Press, 2011.

Polo, Marco. The Travels of Marco Polo. Edited by Morris Rossabi. Translated by Henry Yule. New York: Sterling Publishing, 2012.

Romanus, Charles F. and Riley Sunderland. *United States Army in World War II, China-Burma-India Theater: Stilwell's Mission to China.* Washington, D.C.: Government Printing Office, 1953.

Romanus, Charles F. and Riley Sunderland. *United States Army in World War II, China-Burma-India Theater: Stilwell's Command Problems.* Washington, D.C.: Government Printing Office, 1956.

Romanus, Charles F. and Riley Sunderland. *United States Army in World War II, China-Burma-India Theater: Time Runs Out in CBI.* Washington, D.C.: Government Printing Office, 1959.

Sacquety, Troy J. *The OSS in Burma: Jungle War against the Japanese.* Lawrence, KS: University of Kansas Press, 2013.

Shakespeare, William. *The Life of King Henry the Fifth.* The Pelican Shakespeare. Edited by Claire McEachern. New York: Penguin Books, 1999.

Shilling, Erik. *Destiny: A Flying Tiger's Rendezvous with Fate.* Published by the Author, 1993.

Shores, Christopher. *Air War for Burma.* Vol. 3 of *Bloody Shambles.* London: Grub Street, 2005.

Shores, Christopher, Brian Cull, and Yasuho Izawa. *The Defense of Sumatra to the Fall of Burma.* Vol. 2 of *Bloody Shambles.* London: Grub Street, 1993.

Shores, Christopher, Brian Cull, and Yasuho Izawa. *The Drift to War to the Fall of Singapore.* Vol. 1 of *Bloody Shambles.* London: Grub Street, 1992.

Slessor, John C. *Air Power and Armies.* London: Oxford University Press, 1936.

Smith, Peter C. *Straight Down: The North American A-36 Dive-Bomber in Action.* Manchester: Crecy Publishing Limited, 2000.

Smith, R.T. *Tale of a Tiger: The Adventure-packed Daily Diary or one of the Flying Tigers' Top Aces.* Van Nuys, CA: Tiger Originals, 1986.

Stilwell, Joseph W. *The Stilwell Papers.* Edited by Theodore H. White. 1948. Reprint. Cambridge, MA: Da Capo Press, 1975.

Taylor, Jay. *The Generalissimo: Chiang Kai-shek and the Struggle for Modern China.* Cambridge, MA: Harvard University Press, 2009.

Tow, Don. "Heroic and Critical Battles in Yunnan During WWII." Don Tow's Website. http://www.dontow.com/2009/08/heroic-and-critical-battles-in-yunnan-during-wwii (published August 2009).

Tregear, T.R. *A Geography of China.* 1965. Reprint. London: Aldine Transaction, 2008.

Tsou, Tang. *America's Failure in China: 1941-50.* Chicago: University of Chicago Press, 1963.

Tuan, Yi-Fu. *A Historical Geography of China.* London: Aldine Transaction, 2008.

Tunner, William H. *Over the Hump.* 1964. Reprint. Washington, D.C.: Government Printing Office, 1998.

van de Ven, Hans J. *War and Nationalism in China: 1925-1945*. New York: RoutledgeCurzon, 2003.

Van Wagner, R.D. *Any Place, Any Time, Any Where: The 1st Air Commandos in World War II*. Atglen, PA: Schiffer Publishing, 1998.

腾越文化研究会，东方诺曼底之战：滇西缅北战役 . Beijing: 燕山出版社，2005.

Wambold, Donald A. Jr. "Flying Tiger." World War II Veterans' Stories. http://home.comcast.net/~ralph608/peterwright.htm (n.d.).

White, Theodore and Annalee Jacoby. *Thunder out of China*. London: Victor Gollangz Ltd., 1947.

Xu, Guangqiu. *War Wings: The United States and Chinese Military Aviation, 1929-1949*. London: Greenwood Press, 2001.

Index

Persons

Units/Organizations

Places

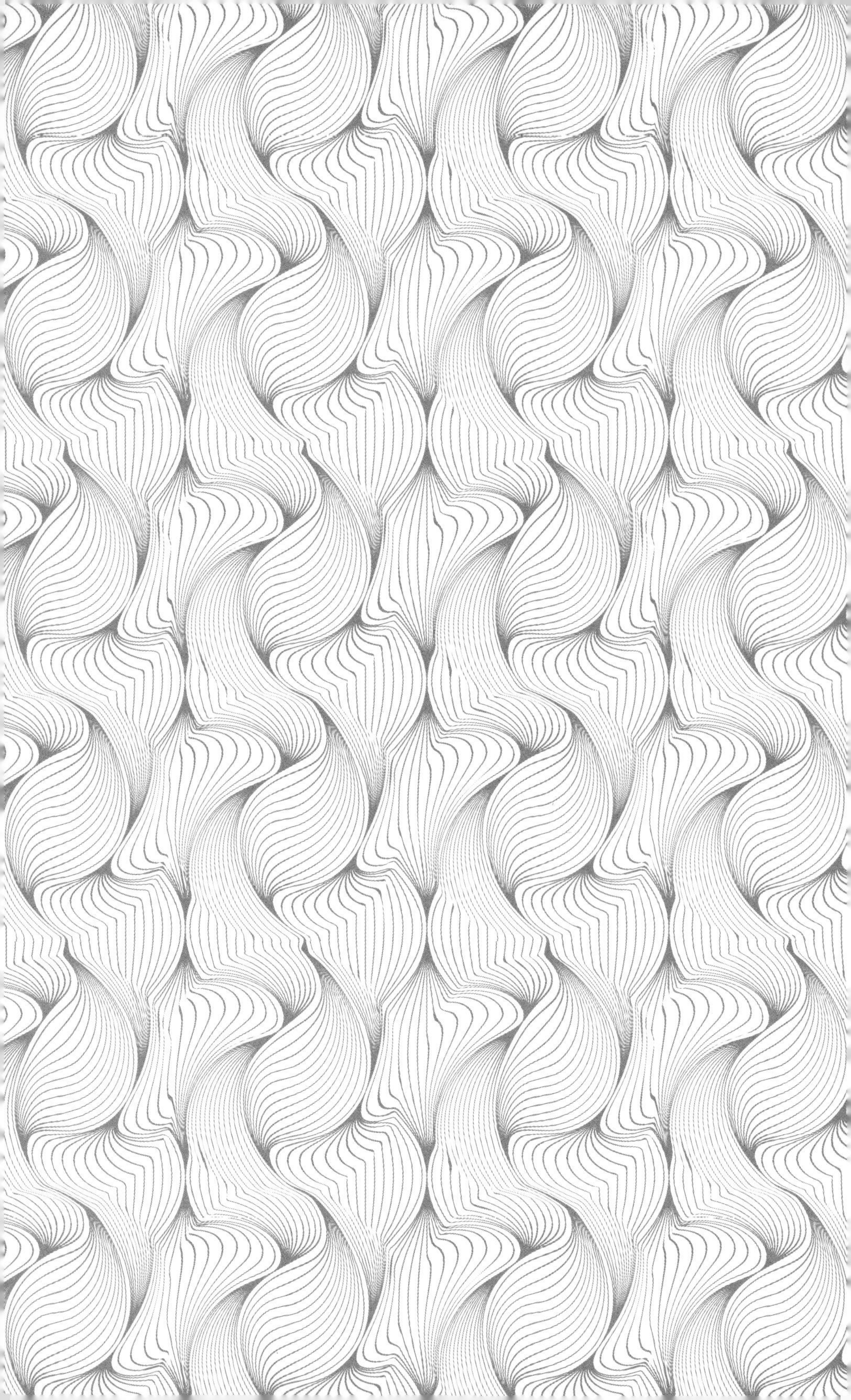